ADVANCE PRAISE FOR

# *A Postmodern Literacy Policy Analysis*

"This book provides a very insightful and useful analysis of four major literacy discourses of our times. Drawing deftly on Foucault's methodological conception of archeological geneology, Mary Frances Agnello reveals with care and detail how the discourses of human capital literacy, cultural literacy, critical literacy, and feminist literacy proliferated and were transformed between 1968 and 2000. Educators will learn much from reading Agnello's work thoughtfully."

*Colin Lankshear, Universidad Nacional Autónoma de México*

"This is an innovative study that looks at literacy through the lens of postmodern theory, particularly that of Michel Foucault, Paulo Freire, and a number of recent feminist critics. Mary Frances Agnello demonstrates how teachers can make a difference in classrooms with the manner in which they allow students to develop their literacy. Her book is an eloquent appeal to develop literacy strategies independent of dominant discourses of cultural literacy."

*Robert Boenig, Professor of English, Texas A&M University*

# A Postmodern Literacy
# Policy Analysis

# Studies in the
# Postmodern Theory of Education

Joe L. Kincheloe and Shirley R. Steinberg
*General Editors*

Vol. 125

PETER LANG
New York • Washington, D.C./Baltimore • Bern
Frankfurt am Main • Berlin • Brussels • Vienna • Oxford

Mary Frances Agnello

# A Postmodern Literacy Policy Analysis

PETER LANG
New York • Washington, D.C./Baltimore • Bern
Frankfurt am Main • Berlin • Brussels • Vienna • Oxford

**Library of Congress Cataloging-in-Publication Data**

Agnello, Mary Frances.
A postmodern literacy policy analysis / Mary Frances Agnello.
p. cm. — (Counterpoints; vol. 125)
Includes bibliographical references and index.
1. Literacy—Social aspects—United States. 2. Postmodernism and education—
United States. I. Title. II. Counterpoints (New York, N.Y.); vol. 125.
LC151 .A56    302.2'244—dc21    00-023859
ISBN 0-8204-4561-4
ISSN 1058-1634


**Die Deutsche Bibliothek-CIP-Einheitsaufnahme**

Agnello, Mary Frances:
A postmodern literacy policy analysis / Mary Frances Agnello.
–New York; Washington, D.C./Baltimore; Bern;
Frankfurt am Main; Berlin; Brussels; Vienna; Oxford: Lang.
(Counterpoints; Vol. 125)
ISBN 0-8204-4561-4

Cover art by Bernice Dudley
Cover design by Lisa Dillon


The paper in this book meets the guidelines for permanence and durability
of the Committee on Production Guidelines for Book Longevity
of the Council of Library Resources.

© 2001 Peter Lang Publishing, Inc., New York

Printed in the United States of America

To my daughter, Caitlin;
my parents, Mary and LeBon;
Paulo Freire, Grant Cooper, and Robert Slater.

# ACKNOWLEDGMENTS

First, I am grateful to a supportive administration and staff at the University of Texas at San Antonio. Foremost, I must thank Emily Gaston Maxwell profusely from the bottom of my heart. Her editorial and typesetting efforts made this book possible. Thanks also to Rebeca Kelly for her work in indexing the book. To my family and student-graders whose eternal persistence allowed me a little bit of flexibility, I am very thankful indeed. Muchas gracias to Joe Kincheloe and Shirley Steinberg who believed in my project and helped me stay on the path to its completion. Three friends, without whom I would not have thought of such an endeavor, are Paulo Freire, Grant Cooper, Robert Slater, all philosophers of education. Finally, with all my love and hopes for a realized critical literary for my daughter and students around the world, I thank my students who have continued to influence my growth and encourage my pedagogy.

American Association of University Women, *How schools shortchange girls*. New York: Marlow & Co., Copyright © 1995. Reprinted by permission of the publisher. All rights reserved.

Becker, G. S., *Human capital*. Chicago: University of Chicago Press, Copyright © 1964, 1975, 1993 by The National Bureau of Economic Research. All rights reserved.

Bernstein, B., *The structuring of pedagogic discourse*. Copyright © 1990 by Basil Bernstein. Reprinted by permission of the author. All rights reserved.

# CONTENTS

# INTRODUCTION

Teacher education, like all education and knowledge, has evolved from social discourse, all of which is political. Within a modernistic educational environment, discourses of worker literacy affect teachers' literacy development as well as the literacy that teachers in turn allow to develop in classrooms. Such modern education focuses on developing skills and content knowledge to the exclusion of postmodern considerations of how knowledge and power relations are formulated, who they serve, and who is exploited by them.

In the United States, since *A Nation at Risk* was articulated in 1983, human capital and cultural literacy policy statements have predominated educational discussions. Counterviews exist within less well known discourses of literacy, views such as critical and feminist literacy, referred to in this document as postmodern literacy.

Utilizing a method I developed that combines the theoretical orientations of critical inquiry as proposed by Michel Foucault (1972, 1978), Paulo Freire (1970), and feminist theorists (Grumet, 1988; Stone, 1994; Fraser, 1989), I analyze discourses of literacy as sociopolitically and economically motivated. I am proposing that educators employ the archaeological genealogy that I am modeling in this document to analyze official pedagogical discourses about literacy and to understand how knowledge and power relations form literacy prescriptions for society. I discuss herein how the knowledge and power relations of literacy discourses are constructed and how they become transformed into technologies of political and socioeconomic control. By participating in such study, educators question the control of literacy discourses contained within literacy policy texts and the ways that these discourses position teachers to accept designated forms of literacy; they also question the manner in which teachers are directed to develop their students' literacies.

# CHAPTER I

## THE SOCIAL ARENA OF LITERACY DISCOURSES

### Introduction

This policy discourse analysis explores how public school teachers contribute to the formation of "the body literate" according to the precepts set forth by the discourses of human capital and cultural literacy. These literacy discourses exist within a larger body of regulatory texts with foundations in scientific research. Looking at selected texts produced over the last two decades by government bureaus, corporate foundations, and legislatures, I will analyze how statements about literacy in various discourses of literacy construct the truth of literacy. Truth, in this sense, is a combination of knowledge and power relations as they exist in this historical moment (Foucault, 1972). Such knowledge and power relations of truth formulate the curriculum and, in turn, literacy practices.

### Beginning the Study

This study had its origins in the examination of my own literacy teaching and classroom practices in Houston and surrounding area public schools. Through self-examination and reflection, I found an element of control in the way that I taught reading and writing, an element that did not feel comfortable. After several years of research investigation, I found that my role within a modern system compromised my values of developing literacy. Locating within the modernist social environment present practices (including tracking, testing, textbook dependency, patriarchal curriculum, literacy for workers, and literacy for socialization and enculturation), I attempted to understand and explain policies that normalized these practices. Unlike Kaestle's (1991) history of literacy in the United States which discusses the smooth patterns of literacy history by examining racial, class, gender, and geographical aspects of literacy enhanced by media expansion, a Foucaultian archaeology looks to practices and "truths" established by discourses and expounds on what led to the formation of those truths (Foucault, 1972; Egea-Kuehne, 1995). Based on Michel Foucault's effective histories that explain present policies and practices by exploring the history of discourse, I developed a method of literacy policy analysis for educators because of what I see as a problem with teachers as well as education students not being exposed to a critical language describing literacy practices (Foucault, 1972, 1977, 1978).

## Statement of the Problem

According to the postmodern paradigmatic representation of literacy, educators can understand how individuals are formed within socioeconomic contexts; and, accordingly, they are able to envision sociopolitical transformation through democratic literacy practices. Given the propensity of institutions to remain entrenched and the facility of all individuals to transform themselves through a process of becoming, if they desire, I built this project on the concept that teachers can make a difference in literacy practice through classroom exercise of democratic literacy. However, teacher education focused on skills education and development of competencies—this is often typical of teacher education programs today— may not address the relationship between democracy and literacy. Teachers need analytical skills to enable serious self- and social critique in order to become effective agents of change. Knowledge of literacy as a democratic practice is not typically the focus of any disciplinary subject or course that teachers study during their preparation. In modernistic preparation programs, educators rarely question their formations as literate subjects and, consequently, are unaware of the sociopolitical and economical implications of the literacy skills they teach to their students.

## Statement of the Question

Three assumptions led to the development of this critical literacy policy analysis model. First, I believe that through explication of mainstream literacy pedagogy from philosophical, sociopolitical, and economic perspectives, rather than from a methodological perspective, educators can better understand their role as agents of the state. Second, by focusing on the emphasis of official literacy policy on human capital and cultural literacy, teachers can place official literacy statements into a dominant literacy framework. Third, through demonstration of critical policy discourse analysis, educators can better comprehend the links between the dominant discourses of literacy and their classroom practices.

The overall question driving this research project was, How can a model of critical policy discourse analysis for educators explicate, demonstrate, and render problematic the mainstream dynamics of modern, scientific literacy to reveal the importance of teachers' shifting to more democratic literacy practices within a postmodern paradigm? In order to answer this broad inquiry, three questions directed this discussion: What broad theories underlie mainstream literacy pedagogy? What is problematic about the dominant discourses of literacy? How can educators use critical policy discourse analysis to transform dominant literacy discourses and practices?

Social, language, and pedagogical theories formulated my development of a critical method to engage teachers in critical and feminist analyses of some landmark literacy and teacher education policies that have influenced the most recent educational reform over the last fourteen years. The educational policies and practices discussed and interpreted herein contributed to my current thinking about literacy. Having been influenced by Paulo Freire, Michel Foucault, and feminist thought, I defined oppressive aspects of modern literacy practices, found scholarship that has dealt with such oppressions, and looked to the transformative potential of genealogical study of literacy policies. But, before going further into this discussion, I will now define five principal concepts that are critical to understanding this project. The following terms originate within the areas of literature that will be reviewed in chapter 2.

## Key Definitions

*Archaeological genealogy* is the study of the existence of discourses and their relationships to each other within a totality of sociopolitical circumstances, a method developed by Michel Foucault's scholarship (1972, 1977, 1978).

*Discourses* are the rhetorical representations that develop and mediate disciplinary technologies of the self, the set of social and cultural practices associated with codes of meaning. Discourses themselves are textual because they also have been constructed by producers, contain encoded messages, and are interpreted by receivers. They can be identified as systems of thought which aim, tacitly or overtly, to produce and regulate knowledge (Foucault, 1972; Butler, 1995).

*Effective histories* are analytical attempts to understand the historical within the present by considering how social, political, economic, cultural, educational, and institutional discourses form the human subject (Foucault, 1972, 1978, 1980).

*Genealogy* is a term Foucault borrowed from Frederich Nietzsche. Through genealogical study, Foucault examines how discourses and social practices manifest the limitations of traditional historical study; the process discloses the human power plays of domination, imposition of order, subjugation, and struggle through resistance.

*Literacy*, viewed from a Foucaultian perspective, is one among many technologies of the self and is developed through an objectification process that orders bodies in time and space in order to induce conformity among those subjected to various educational mechanisms that produce knowledge of language systems. Those socialized to be literate become literate subjects; literacy standards are determined by the most powerful in the society, who define knowledge as what has descended from the historically powerful.

With these definitions, the reader can consider how official literacy policies are constituted officially through governmental procedures to control the knowledge and power relations that help define the relationship of the citizen-worker to the state. A Foucaultian archaeological genealogy attempts to explore how the knowledge and power relations that came to comprise official educational policies resulted from many nonlinear complexities of social, cultural, and economic interaction within the nation-state. Discourses of educational policy, including discourses of literacy, are technologies of the self that are utilized by individuals to exert self-control. The technologies of the self that are learned in schools are products of discourses that are consciously constructed by power-wielders to affect the identity formations of those who internalize the mechanisms of literate self-control. Literacy instruction, as will be discussed in subsequent chapters, is a combination of many language discourses and practices that are perpetuated through tradition, culture, economics, and politics. This document will illustrate many facets of literacy construction of individuals in the nation-state through discourses and contextualize them in a sociocultural, historical, and political framework.

The relationship of the individual to the many in a democracy has been an ongoing source of debate in political thought. One area of political language theory that developed around the tensions of citizenship between democratic pluralism and universalism is communicative ethics. Weisburd says, "Among other endeavors, communicative ethics includes exploring procedures and conditions for civic conversations predicated on non-dominance, communicative virtues, and openness" (1994, p. 32). Because talk and language are necessary to communicative ethics, speech is regarded "as a means and actualization of social legitimization" (Weisburd, 1994, p. 32). The speech act is conceptually related to Paulo Freire's (1970) notion of praxis. *Praxis* constitutes the practical usage or practice of power through communication in action. Communicative competence for Habermas (1984) contributed to the intersubjective constitution of the self. Habermas developed the notion of a communicative competence through the "ideal speech situation," which must meet the following three conditions: First, all potential participants in discourse must have the same opportunity to initiate discourses and to perpetuate them through asking and answering, making and replying to objections, giving arguments and justification. Second, all participants in interaction must have the same chance to express their feelings, intentions, attitudes, and needs. Third, all participants must have the same chance to demand, to permit, to forbid, and to give and receive promises, all of which ultimately lead to action through speech (Habermas, 1984, pp. 273–338).

Such communication requires contextual understanding and involves context making (Gutierrez, 1994). Also, the participants in speech acts understand themselves as players within public spaces. What is perhaps not so obvious about the speech act or its speaker is that the political self and community are formed through language. This project focuses on how language through discourse formulates which literacy is promoted to undermine and emphasize certain aspects of the formation of the literate self. This book undertakes to describe how the literate self is formed through the knowledge and power relations established among policymakers, educators, and students. By tracing the recent historical developments of literacy policy, educators can begin to follow the discourses of literacy to better comprehend the nature of unequal hierarchical power relations determined through the demands of literacy policy by educational policymakers.

Supplementary definitions that provide informative guidance to this study elaborate poststructural terminology and are also provided in this chapter. Key terms that will be utilized in the overview of recent developments in literacy discourses are presented. In brief reiteration, the problems and the questions guiding my research assume both little exposure of teachers to powerful (secondary or critical) literacy by teacher education programs and little or no literacy policy analysis by teachers. Such endeavors by educators can reveal the power and knowledge relations that exist in deploying any discourse of literacy.

Additionally, in the next section of this chapter, I will define poststructuralism and its relationship to postmodernist, critical, and feminist theories. I will rely on Gee's (1991a) linguistic expertise to define discourses extensively. The political frameworks within which various discourses originate will also be discussed briefly. Some introduction to Foucault's theories will provide foundation for the concept of effective histories. Inasmuch as it is possible to do so, I will attempt to illustrate what effective histories are by employing them in the discussion that follows their introduction. For example, when I discuss effective history of literacies, I define the various discourses of literacy and establish their dialectical connections to each other. An overview is provided to explain the organization of the book.

## Background

Since the educational statement made in *A Nation at Risk* (U.S. Department of Education, 1983), over eight hundred texts have been issued, produced, and commissioned—books, reports, and statements about educational, national, cultural, economical, and schooling crises (Popkewitz & Brennan, 1994). Through passionate calls for basic skills and worker preparation promoting far right policies of socialization and enculturation, these educational texts look to schools and teacher credentialing to solve social problems. Since the 1940s, the reconstitution of state bureaucracy has attempted to make the school more responsive to economic and cultural priorities.

During the post–World War II period until 1983, informal mechanisms worked within urban and rural locales enabling coalitions of interest toward centralization, yet these maintained an appearance of a stateless state in the educational sector (Popkewitz & Brennen, 1994). From the perspective of policymakers, however, informal controls have not steered schools in the direction deemed necessary for national economic strength to carry the political economy into the next century. Evidence of this is that President Clinton recently promoted literacy at large and encouraged governors to promote national testing, which state educational bureaucracies have been slow to support (Hoholik, 1997; "Clinton Urges," 1997).

Increased regulation and administration of teacher education occurring in the late 1950s through the National Defense Education Act and continuing through the present is correlated with national strength. The metaphor of educational disarmament strikes us within the first pages of *A Nation at Risk*. Metaphorical connections between national defense and education connect aggressive monitoring of teachers' work through student achievement to reveal state-by-state comparisons of school output and production (U.S. Department of Education, 1984b). Monies are mobilized to target research agendas through a national network in more than thirty research laboratories and technical assistance centers (Popkewitz & Brennan, 1994, p. 38). The goals are economic recovery, cultural redefinition, and leadership through scientific management. Before going further into this discussion, I will now turn to define concepts which will enable better understanding of this project. The following terms originate within the areas of literature elaborated in chapter 2.

## Supplementary Definitions

*Cultural literacy* is a cognitive acquaintance and working relationship within a system of language and culture that is dependent on history and heritage; in the United States, since the 1980s, cultural literacy has been defined as the knowledge and foundations of Western society from a Eurocentric perspective, correlational to the English language and the Anglo-centric formations of sociopolitical, religious, and economic institutions. In the 1970s, cultural literacy referred to intercultural understanding.

*Critical literacy* is a consciousness that recognizes oppression in power exerted within the institutions of knowledge, language, and social organizations; reading the world in addition to the word enables actions to change oppressive social relations (Freire, 1970).

*Critical theory* is social theory emanating from Marxism, neo-Marxism, the Frankfurt School, European social theorists, and scholars in the United States who study social structures and institutions to determine how social inequalities are perpetuated.

*Desire* directs the will to knowledge.

*Disciplinary technology* is a discourse or instrument used as a surveillance technique by the state or other disciplinary organizations; subjects become conditioned to discipline themselves.

*Discontinuity* is a nonlinear explanation of human events; what Foucault refers to as breaks or ruptures within which traditional views of history have been explained as linear and progressive.

*Exclusivity* is what is claimed by those who are authorized to speak with authority about a given subject.

*Exteriority* is Foucault's term used to describe the impossible stance to achieve in research where one is able to totally detach from that of which one is a part (Foucault, 1978).

*Feminism* is a reformulation of reality from a female perspective, formally, a study of women's lives. Theoretically, feminisms from various perspectives rewrite Western knowledge founded on patriarchal knowledge and conditions.

*Feminist pedagogy* is a conscious, caring effort to overcome some of the problems with rational and scientific education; it is also an effort to educate for and about women or in the manner of one who questions the existing knowledge and power relations of patriarchy.

*Feminist literacy* is a facility with language that enables critical textual analysis leading one to read and write from a female perspective.

*Feminist standpoint theory* comes from several feminist theorists constructing knowledge from females' perspectives and noting the differences between women's and men's situations and the manner in which scientific advantage is afforded to those who can make use of the differences (Butler, 1995).

*Human capital literacy* is literacy that allows functioning in the job market; it also connotes worker skills and dispositions. Human capital theory denotes investment in worker education, thus, it follows that human capital literacy is investment in worker literacy.

*The Other* is the object and subject of study, one who is controlled through domination. De Beauvoir (1949/1993) employed this term to describe women. Foucault used it to refer to subalterns.

*Paradigm* is a view of the world; i.e., a scientific perspective of a fixed view of reality versus an assessment of reality as dynamic.

*Patriarchy* is control of societies through male power and structures, the domination of individual males over females. In Western society, a minority of white males formulate social, economic, and political power.

*Postmodernism* is a form of society emerging after the classical, modern, capitalist society; this emergence is still incomplete, indeterminate, and problematic (Bauman, cited in Crook, Pakulski, & Waters, 1992). What is most promising about this new form of society is its democratic attempt to respond to cultural differences and move beyond modernism's inequities and rational man's overdependence on scientific applications over nature and human interaction.

*Poststructuralism* offers a naming system to disclose the relativity of truth by asserting that the logic of any system is dependent upon the systems that rationalize it and that the power of discourses over human activity is dependent on the disciplinary authorities and structures that legitimate discourses and their practices; poststructuralism is a shift from viewing the small text (novel, poem, film, etc.) as a closed entity "to seeing it as irreducibly plural, an endless play of signifiers which can never be finally nailed down to a single center, essence or meaning" (Eagleton, 1983, p. 138).

*Reversal* means that for every positive statement made within a routine statement there also exists a negative statement; by emphasizing a point or issue, others are excluded (Foucault, 1972)

*Rhetoric* is communication structure, figures of speech, symbols, arguments developed; particular language utilized; methods of substantiation (Butler, 1995).

*The signified* is the object of study or the idea represented by signs of language in poststructural terminology. In this study, the interpretation of literary policies (signifiers) will uncover the policies' signified meanings.

*Specificity* is a system of meaning-making that contextualizes signification within certain time frames of an era or period.

*Structuralism* is embodied in the scholarship of those who study humans, language systems, social institutions, and their interactions relying on precepts that explain their structures as naturally occurring rather than socially constructed.

*Subject* is the socialized self or individual whose identity is constructed within a network of social relations comprised of texts and discourses; subjects, in turn, reproduce texts and discourses (Foucault, 1972; Fiske, 1993; Butler, 1995).

*Truth* is that which is legitimated by grids of social regularity; truth is connected to power and knowledge; more powerful knowledge is regarded as truth; the most powerful truth is regarded as science.

With this working vocabulary, it becomes possible to discuss literacy as a social construction of knowledge and power relations. A postmodern framework assumes understanding of some political positions that ground the academic theories to analyze educational policy in general and literacy policy specifically. This framework will be discussed in chapter 2. Within an era of reform and restructuring, this research will look to policies (three mainstream landmarks and a minor one) that have attempted to reform education beginning with *A Nation at Risk* in 1983. A critical search for the nature of proposed changes in literacy policies will assume knowledge of discourses of literacy and literacies (McKay & Hornberger, 1995).

## Recognizing Problems With Modern Schooling

The problems of modernistic schools are now being addressed through reconceptualization of science, knowledge, and literacy. Within the postmodern educational framework, democratic literacy practice and awareness become recognizably related to the knowledge and power formations of truth (Green, 1993; Edelsky, 1991a; Egea-Kuehne, 1995). The once accepted truth that the Western canon constituted the foundation of American education and literacy has come to criticism in several domains of the academy (Stone, 1994; Martin, 1994; Willinsky, 1990; Lankshear & McLaren, 1993). Postmodernist educators have turned to the problems of women, ethnic groups, and minorities to formulate new sociocultural and political frameworks of education, often referred to as the politics of difference.

According to the precepts of the politics of difference, postmodernists render problematic the exclusion of women, minorities, ethnic groups, and the poor by powerful elites who decide what comprises knowledge, curricula, literacy, and other important social policy decisions (Sleeter & McLaren, 1995; Banks, 1994; Young, 1990; Ellsworth, Hedley, & Baratta, 1994). The politics of difference exposes the tensions between social control and individual freedom within a poststructural examination of language (Foucault, 1972). The postmodern era includes poststructural and feminist thought questioning the regimes of power or ideological framework that socializes the masses and questions the relationship of literacy to the state. In sum, the problems with modern schooling are related to bureaucratic efficiency, commodification of knowledge, and the manner in which elite power and knowledge relations exclude a majority of people from deciding which knowledge and language most appropriately represent and address public education.

**Literacy and Power**

All linguistic interactions have communicative potential as well as power potential. In Fairclough's *Language and Power* (1989), he posits the connections between language, power, and ideology. He named this approach to linguistics *critical language study*. In his view, all linguistic interactions reflect the social order; however, this social order is dynamic because it can be changed or remain the same. In Fairclough's view, assignment of social roles by texts allows or disallows change, as well as the assumption of social roles by literate subjects. He maintained that

> [L]inguistic phenomena are social in the sense that whenever people speak or listen or write or read, they do so in ways which are determined socially and have social effects. Even when people are most conscious of their own individuality [and uninfluenced by their environment] . . . they still use language in ways which are subject to social conventions. And the ways in which people use language in their most intimate and private encounters are not only socially determined by the social relationships of the family, they also have social effects in the sense of helping to maintain (or indeed, change) those relationships. (p. 23)

Paulo Freire (1970) was a major proponent of using literacy to change the modern social order. His work and influence maintained that the roles of the oppressor and the oppressed are unhealthy, inhumane, and unethical. Freire's literacy instruction helped Brazilian peasants to articulate their life occurrences and needs. Through Freire's critical pedagogy, poor workers came to understand their role in making history. Transforming their consciousness enabled the act of transforming their lives through literacy. Freire's *Pedagogy of the Oppressed* (1970) was the seminal work that helped me articulate the malaise I felt about modern literacy instruction.

## Moving Toward Postmodern Literacy

A postmodern way of thinking about literacy, called critical literacy, as inspired by Freire, proposed literacy as reading and writing the world. His work has influenced criticalists and feminists alike in the United States, its problems not withstanding (Luke & Gore, 1992). For Freire, questioning literacy policy involved looking at cultural and social history, asking who pays for literacy policy implementation, and determining who is acted upon and benefits by the policy (McLaren & Lankshear, 1994; Escobar, Fernandez, Guevara-Niebla, & Freire, 1994). Freire's *Pedagogy of the Oppressed* led me to question the manner in which the authority embodied in the classroom teacher, the textbook, and standard language set the stage for teachers' contributions to literacy success and failure in the classroom. Freire's initial and continuing work has been emulated by United States scholars (Giroux, 1988b; Lankshear & McLaren, 1993; Shor, 1986a,b; Kincheloe, 1993).

A postmodern manner of thinking about literacy seeks to enhance educators' critical thinking as well as reading and writing skills. This methodological approach to discursive analysis looks beyond literacy as reading and writing skills to the knowledge and power relations that determine literacy discourses within the larger social contexts and within individual classrooms. Foucault (1972) warned that practices at the micro-level are not necessarily a miniature version of the macro-level and that such assumptions are not empirically borne out. Rather, he looked to locations of discursive practices as centers or nexuses of their own peculiar power relations. His works sought to explicate *époques* or periods through discursive formations that merit discussion for the light that they shed on understanding the development of human intellectual thought as well as entrenched institutional practices, such as reading instruction (Shannon, 1989; Luke, 1992). Assuming the school and the classroom are microcosms of the macrocosmic society or world is a structural approach to studying learning. Structuralism for Foucault has led to misunderstanding and misrepresentation of patterns in history.

Although classroom power relations are not necessarily the microcosm of the macrocosmic society in which they exist, the power relations formulated by classroom literacy practices nonetheless demonstrate some likenesses to governed technologies which are present across society. Such technologies exist in educational and social policies as governmental systems set their goals to care for their constituencies (Gordon, 1991; Shutkin, 1994). In the case of literacy, the technologies of literacy include the institutions, methods, materials, scholarship, policies, and practices that relate to the dissemination of the skills and attitudes associated with literacy as both attainable and measurable.

## Political and Academic Context

One of the most salient features of postmodern developments is the politics of difference (Hoeveler, 1996; Crook, Pakulski, & Waters, 1992; Sleeter & McLaren, 1995; Giroux, 1991). Over the last thirty years, the center of national and educational politics has not managed to account for the many in the margins of political decision making—women, the poor, and people of non-European descent (Hoeveler, 1996; Sleeter & McLaren, 1995). As the limitations of Newtonian-Cartesian science to explain human experiences became more apparent, two research innovations occurred: (1) social theorists from many fields realized the importance of researching discourses to explain social phenomena and (2) the impediments caused by structuralism (structural presumptions of social phenomena) were called into question through poststructural social theories. Such questioning of structuralism does not discount the whole of structuralism's explanation of human experience. To a large degree, poststructuralism builds on structuralism. European and American scholars who questioned the assumptions of structuralist impositions on reality, usually from an academic or political position, are referred to as poststructuralists and feminists. For the purposes of this discussion, the umbrella term "postmodernists" embraces poststructural, feminist, critical, constructivist, and multicultural education researchers. The broad scope of their work is known as postmodernism. Two commonalities of these academic positions involve informed interpretation of the manners in which metanarratives and/or social myths (1) overgeneralize human experience and (2) oppress or control individuals through ideology and taken-for-granted social practices.

The crux of this project involves utilization of postmodern philosophy, theories, and methods to help teachers develop social conscientization that questions contemporary literacy practices (Freire, 1970, 1973). Explanation of the problematic nature of present literacy practices requires looking at scientific and efficient educational discourses and contrasting their myths and realities with their net effects (Mitchell & Weiler, 1991; Edelsky, 1991b). When the disparities of undemocratic and controlling literacy practices are contrasted with rhetoric of democratic education, teachers may better decide their roles as part of the problem of undemocratic literacy practices or part of the solution to create a more democratic society through literacy empowerment.

## Literacy as Multifaceted

Several connotations of literacy have historically developed through knowledge and power relationships that resulted from knowing and utilizing a common code of written and/or spoken communication. Functional literacy represents the lowest level of knowledge, signifying a simple mastery of reading and writing skills. "Literate" also has a connotation of literacy that focuses on developing the mind, explicit tastes, art appreciation, social graces, morality, and other trappings of elite culture (Cook-Gumperz, 1986).

The social construction of literacy has been discussed by many linguists, anthropologists, and educational philosophers (Cook-Gumperz, 1986; Heath, 1983; Hudson, 1980). Paulo Freire locates literacy within the language and culture of learners as they experience a conscientization process (Freire, 1970; Freire & Faundez, 1989; Macedo, 1994a). Literacy, as developed by workers, women, and the lower classes over the last two centuries in England, South America, and to a degree in the United States, represents a struggle for voice, empowerment, and humanity and differs from the literacy that became the focus of compulsory education during the

Industrial Revolution or literacy as measured by competency testing (Mitchell & Weiler, 1991; Luke, 1995; Donald, 1983; Macedo, 1994a).

Historically, the power to decide what counts as literacy resides within the elite ruling class who establishes the standards which measure literacy of individuals whose backgrounds do not necessarily conform to elite language and social mores (Green, 1993; Mitchell & Weiler, 1991). Thus the knowledge of a small elite is given legitimacy as "official." Such practice is problematic in a postmodern society where democracy is a priority (Knoblauch & Brannon, 1993; Martin, 1994). Macedo (1994a), citing Freire, explains how this undemocratic practice becomes reified:

> From this viewpoint the dominant class, which has the power to define, profile, and describe the world, begins to pronounce that the speech habits of the subordinate groups are a corruption, a bastardization of dominant discourse. It is in this sense that sociolinguists are making an enormous contribution to the demystification of these notions. What they show is that, scientifically, all languages are valid, systematic, rule-governed systems, and that the inferiority/superiority distinction is a social phenomenon. (p. 101)

Those who had mastery of the printed word in Western societies traditionally maintained social and usually economic power that accompanied such knowledge, particularly in the execution of government, economy, law, medicine, and many liberal arts disciplines (Foucault, 1972). In our contemporary society, literacy as basic worker skills and technical know-how has come to the forefront of educational policy concerns (U.S. Department of Education, 1983; Hoholik, 1997).

**Literacy and Political Relations**

The word "literacy" has a relatively short history. Referring to basic reading and writing skills, literacy entered the English lexicon around the end of the nineteenth century (Donald, 1983; Willinsky, 1990). That particular era in United States history marked a moment of political, economic, and social unrest. Such a context of great social change, according to social theorists, represents a time when power holders increase measures by which the citizenry conform to the needs of the state (Foucault, 1990; Green, 1993; Giroux, 1988a). Gramsci (cited in Giroux, 1988a), the Italian hegemony theorist, asserted that when state policies promote literacy, the goal, regardless of the rhetoric, is cultural hegemony (promotion of one dominant, oppressive culture as the optimal in a society).

Present-day literacy theorists find it no coincidence, at this time when great technological and social changes are displacing many workers, that we see many literacy policy reforms (U.S. Department of Education, 1983; Green, 1993; Lankshear & McLaren, 1993; Giroux, 1983). Knoblauch and Brannon (1993) discuss the representation of literacy within any era as dependent on the power structure's decision about literacy's definition. Literacy policies that potentially marginalize citizens' democratic literacy development operate within a field of discourses about the curriculum and the kinds of literacy that result from such a curriculum. Such decisions are reached by an elite hierarchy of educational policymakers. On this topic, Macedo (1994a) says that knowledge is created by a minority ruling class to be learned and accepted by the majority. He captures the class distinctions created by knowledge and power relations:

> Only those who have power, for example, can define what is correct or incorrect. Only those who have power can decide what constitutes intellectualism. Once the intellectual perimeters are set, those who want to be considered intellectuals must meet requirements of the profile dictated by the elite class. To be intellectual, one must do exactly what those with the power to define intellectualism do. The intellectual activity of those without power is always characterized as nonintellectual. (Macedo, 1994a, p. 102)

It is within this field of struggle over what constitutes literacy as knowledge and power relations that we can now begin to distinguish between prevailing discourses of literacy.

## Critical Policy Analysis of Literacy Discourse

In a manner described by Michel Foucault (1972), I approached critical policy discourse analysis of two dominant discourses of literacy in schools and society at large: human capital literacy and cultural literacy. Counter-discourses of literacy emanating from feminist and critical discourses have made significant statements about sociocultural, political, and economical control exerted by the dominant discourses (Giroux, 1981; Luke & Gore, 1992; Luke, 1996; Grumet, 1989). Rewriting literacy as understanding the world of lived experience beyond the word locates the tensions of social control in the dominant discourses of literacy. These tensions are dialectical. In the dialectic relationship, the tensions comprise both the bases of cultural wars and the conditions of imminent change with encouragement of next-generation intellectuals (Aronowitz & Giroux, 1985, 1993; Bloom, 1987; Hirsch, 1987; Bennett, 1992a,b; Giroux, 1983, 1988a,b, 1991, 1993; Kincheloe, 1993; Stone, 1994; Luke & Gore, 1992; Gore, 1993). Within the discourses of literacy lie views of the world that formulate ideology emanating from the politics of social organization. Understanding those politics helps promote reflection about the teacher's role in literacy instruction.

### Literacy Discourses and Ideology Defined

James Gee's definitions of discourses are helpful for entering into a discussion about literacy or the discourses of literacy. Gee (1991a) defines discourse as

> a socially acceptable association among ways of using language, of thinking, and of acting that can be used to identify oneself as a member of a socially meaningful group or "social network" [social circumstances often determine discourse communities]. (p. 3)

Some points about discourse, few of which Americans embrace readily, follow.

> 1. Discourses are inherently "ideological." They crucially involve a set of values and viewpoints in terms of which one must speak and act, at least while being in the discourse; otherwise one doesn't count as being in it.

> 2. Discourses are resistant to internal criticism and self-scrutiny since uttering viewpoints that seriously undermine them defines one as being outside them. The discourse itself defines what counts as acceptable criticism. Of course, one can criticize a particular discourse from the viewpoint of another one (e.g. psychology criticizing linguistics). But what one cannot do is stand outside all discourse and criticize any one or all of them . . . [Foucault called this phenomenon exteriority; simply put, this means that we all are objects and subjects of what we have learned and it is therefore impossible to totally detach from that of which we are a part. With relevance to this work, the ideas that I have about literacy are formulated based on the discourses which have been influential in my formation.]

3. Discourse-defined positions from which to speak and behave are not, however, just defined internal to a discourse, but also as standpoints taken up by the discourse in its relation to other, ultimately opposing, discourses. [The discourses which are formulated in opposition to other discourses would be different if the discourses in power would change or disappear.]

4. Any discourse concerns itself with certain objects and puts forward so it will marginalize viewpoints and values central to other discourses (from Macdonnell, 1986, pp. 1–7). [Because some discourses of literacy get more attention in the media, in social and educational policy, and in school curricula, it is important to become familiar with discourses that question who benefits by the dominance of certain kinds of literacy in a populace.]

5. Finally, discourses are intimately related to the distribution of social power and hierarchical structure in society. Control over certain discourses can lead to the acquisition of social goods (money, power, status) in a society. . . . Let us call discourses that lead to social goods in a society "dominant discourses" and let us refer to those groups that have the fewest conflicts when using them as "dominant groups." [These dominant discourses are relative and change in different contexts.] (Gee, 1991a, pp. 4–5)

Gee explains that the ways in which we master discourses are through *acquisition* and *learning*. *Language acquisition* occurs in natural settings through the process of trial and error, without formal teaching. On the other hand, *learning* occurs through explanation and analysis, and sometimes through attainment of some meta-language about a matter. It helps to distinguish between the two by pointing out that most people acquire their first language, and, in Gee's words, "[l]earning to read is always learning some aspect of some discourse" (1991a, p. 6). The oral mode of communication that all people, barring those with serious debilitations, learn is a primary discourse used in the immediate family or living environment.

Unlike the primary discourse, secondary discourses are learned through exposure in "secondary institutions" (for example, schools, workplaces, stores, government offices, businesses, or churches) and they usually entail a written code. Gee proposes that the secondary discourses build on the primary discourse, and they are more or less compatible with the primary discourses of different social groups. The discourse analysis that becomes a vehicle of analyzing other discourses is a learned literacy and therefore secondary. Because such secondary literacy involves looking critically at language's effects on various groups in society, it is meta-analytical. Meta-analysis of four discourses of literacy involves discussing their origins. Because the discourses exist in their proponents' and opponents' conversations, they respond to each other. The tensions among four discourses of literacy have evolved from political, economical, social, and cultural differences and from the interactions of the four discourses.

## Four Discourses of Literacy

*Human capital literacy* refers to producing basic literacy skills in workers. *Cultural literacy* entails the promotion of the primacy of Eurocentric male culture and English, as well as cultural socialization into the American way of life. My position on these two fields of literacy development is that they serve to preserve the present power and knowledge relations that marginalize most citizens (Pinar, 1995; Grumet, 1995).

*Critical* and *feminist literacies* contrast with these social and educational measures of producing literate workers who identify with the traditions of power and knowledge as they have been established traditionally in this country by powerful Euro-American males. The scholarship of Paulo Freire and many of his followers, including feminists from various political persuasions, promotes such critical literacy (Freire, 1970, 1973; Giroux, 1988b; Lankshear & McLaren, 1993; hooks, 1994; Tozer, Violas, & Senese, 1998). In their training, teachers learn human capital and cultural literacy grounded in positivist modernism, as do most serious students of mainstream disciplinary studies. However, teachers do not necessarily encounter critical and feminist literacy in their training.

The discourses of critical and feminist literacy are poststructural. Poststructuralism developed as intellectuals recognized in their scholarship that the practices of the social sciences were not objective, but rather they were grounded in the vocabulary of the social sciences that purported to be objective (Foucault, 1971/1993, 1972). Poststructural theories are utilized in the study of literature; however, critical social theory and feminism receive little attention within Enlightenment-based and utilitarian schools of education. Poststructuralism within the broad scope of postmodernism characterizes or describes the philosophical orientation of the intellectual seeking new ways of exploring knowledge, ways of knowing, and ways of explaining power. For the purposes of this work, postmodernism serves as a perspective from which to question existing modern frameworks. In education, the postmodern scholar is concerned with many contradictions of present-day institutional life. In particular, the postmodern teacher questions class, race, and gender constructions by reading traditional teaching and learning practices through critical social theories.

## Effective Histories

Michel Foucault (1972, 1977) and others, including Jacques Derrida (1976), are continental philosophers who applied forms of linguistic analysis to explore what Foucault called effective histories. Effective histories were analytical attempts to understand the historical within the present as determined by the social, political, economic, cultural, educational, and institutional forces. Foucault felt that in order to understand humans, one must look to the discourses originating in the social sciences that form human subjects (1972, 1978). Foucault developed his concepts of academic knowledge and truth as discursive formations and then traced how discourses since the sixteenth century constructed individuals through institutional practices of medicine, psychology, law, and education. He expanded his views of the politics of power from that which is concentrated through governmental agency of the monarch to dispel power to many locations where it exists to control and be resisted in several facets of life (1980, 1984).

Foucault focused on social, historical power and knowledge relationships which defined networks organized around social institutions and within their discursive practices, now known as the academic disciplines (Foucault, 1972). Grids of regularity are influenced by pervasive policies and practices. The state, popular cultures, higher education, local school districts, information technology, industry, and business, among other social institutions and forces, have formulated the present-day discourses of literacy.

The deployment of literate subjects, as developed by Foucault (1972, 1980, 1984), is related to communication in the home and in the local, state, interstate, and international economy, as well as in classroom practices and other forms of community life (Shutkin, 1994; Goins, 1997). Literacy itself as viewed from a Foucaultian perspective is one among many technologies of the self that is developed through an objectification process. This process orders bodies in time and space to induce conformity among those subjected to various educational mechanisms producing knowledge of language systems and ways of being (Luke, 1992).

**Effective History of Literacies**

Ongoing debate about literacy and a proliferation of meanings associated with literacy determine how we come to think about literacy. Some of the meanings of literacy follow from scientific views of literacy as a measurable skill. These include literacy prescribed by competencies as outlined by state agencies—usually emphasizing reading comprehension and writing as prescribed by narrowly defined parameters. These literacies also include critical or powerful discourses of literacy, discourses that occur at the university and within university networks but that are not widely acknowledged within teacher education or in schools.

Such powerful literacies, grounded within critical and feminist theories, question the epistemological foundations of traditional knowledge and tend to question various social and academic policies. Because such powerful literacies follow in a postmodern mode of articulation, they question the taken-for-granted as a valid intellectual undertaking. Powerful literacies also deviate from the truths upon which the structures of modern schools, modern literacy, and testing practices are founded (Macedo, 1994a; Gore, 1993).

In response to these new democratic practices that hinge on political engagement through conscientization of the learner, educational conservatives formulate policies that continue to raise standards, delimit the meaning of literacy, and that, in general, do not promote open participation in democratic institutions across society. Through channels of literacy control, experts define various domains and inform social and economic policies that subjectify and objectify humans, usually in aligning the curriculum with societal needs (Scheurich, 1994; Kincheloe, 1993, 1995; Tozer, Violas, & Senese, 1998). Although there is little agreement about the definition of literacy and its relationship to the state, the state nonetheless formulates policies to educate a literate populace (Harper, 1990).

Consistent with modernist and controlling practices that keep power and knowledge relations intact is the focus on technological literacy. Through deployment of the child as subject and information technology, an educational revolution is occurring—an expensive one that may change the media of knowledge relations but does not necessarily alter their power relations (Shutkin, 1994). Below the surface, computer literacy is additional human capital literacy that has been deemed a required skill expected of future workers. The discourses of school literacy follow rhetorical assumptions of industrial traditions and historical preparation of workers and citizens (Luke, 1995; Tozer, Violas, & Senese, 1998).

Traditionally, there are two principal tracks of school literacy development. Basic literacy, in the view of many educators, is usually thought of as a transmittable skill to less able students. Literacy for highly capable students enables exploration within the Western canon (Kincheloe, 1993; Hiebert, 1991). According to new standards of technological literacy, all students will learn some computer literacy (U.S. Department of Education, 1983). In the implementation of all of these literacies, scientific methods have been developed and reified through such technologies as the textbook (Shannon, 1989; Goodman, Shannon, Freeman, & Murphy, 1988). Through institutional deployment of technologies, scientific literacies are produced in schools, reified by the examination, and normalized through internalized self-monitoring techniques. Through management of media, including schools, such dominant literacies of work and cultural socialization are reproduced (Foucault, 1972; Spring, 1996; Shutkin, 1994).

No claims can be made about the extent to which human capital and cultural literacies are effective at precluding the development of other kinds of literacies. However, we can deduce that, because the system persists and because these discourses of literacy are described and prescribed within the official pedagogical discourse (Bernstein, 1990), some influence is exerted on the student population by human capital and cultural literacies. The extensive efforts of schools to join the ranks of the technologically equipped attests to the perceived import of technological literacy and the role of technology in education. These dominant discourses of literacy proliferate from the state level through educational policy and initiatives and through educational practices. They describe the kinds of literacy that students should develop in utilitarian and rights-based educational models (Kahne, 1996). The kinds of literacy on which this discussion will elaborate are the kinds that emerge in a more democratic communitarian society within those who possess a transformative vision of education (Kahne, 1996; Giroux & McLaren, 1988, 1989; Martin, 1994; Grumet, 1988).

Transforming social structures and classrooms is expressed in a language describing hope, struggle, and a vision of social justice. Neither changing social structures nor reforming teacher education will necessarily produce more democracy in schools or society. Such profound changes occur within community work, whereby participants define and strive for and achieve democratic input into schools and working environments (Kincheloe, 1995). Often more democratic approaches to education are foiled by structural, bureaucratic, and utilitarian efficiency.

## Political Framework

Utilitarian principles that inform mainstream educational policy associate education with worker preparation and national security, whereas the rights-based education promotes education on the basis of civil rights and differentiated education for those with varying abilities, catering particularly to choice, charter, and college preparation (Kahne, 1996; Shor, 1986a,b). The democratic communitarianists and humanist psychologists, on the other hand, promote education for democracy and individual-driven learning (Kahne, 1996; Kincheloe, 1991, 1993; Block, 1995). Needless to say, the utilitarianists and rights-based proponents tend to dominate educational policy, more frequently than not tying basic skills literacy to the international and technological economy (Tozer, Violas, & Senese, 1998; U.S. Department of Education, 1983).

In a nutshell, advocates of utilitarianism and rights-based education rely on "scientific" ways of viewing objective knowledge and operate within the liberal democratic paradigm which has always advocated elitism of the few and paid lip service to democracy of the many. On the contrary, the democratic communitarians and humanist psychologists promote a Deweyan view of education as preparation for social democracy by developing individual talents (Dewey, 1916). The latter is an ideal proposing a different paradigm from which to view education. Rather than being founded on science, the communitarian view is based on the belief in human experience and more intuitive ways of knowing—often considered by the scientists to be arbitrary and therefore irrelevant to the business of educating a nation's young.

These paradigmatic references (ways of thinking about reality) of knowledge continue to be debated and contested political terrain, even as the traditional curriculum continues to guide the development of students' literacies with emphasis on preparation for work in the international economy and maintenance of Euro-American culture as it is embodied by powerful individuals and groups within social and political structures (Spring, 1996, 1997). Critical discourses of literacy question these modern scientific literacies in their reliance on undemocratic knowledge and power relations that have accomplished an effect of cultural hegemony.

Hegemony denotes the propensity of culture to be dominated in the special interests of elitist groups so insidiously that those controlled by the power-wielders often participate in their own oppression (Tozer, Violas, & Senese, 1998). Education in the United States has been hegemonic in that for many years the assets and knowledge of conquered groups and colonized people were excluded and devalued to the exaltation of white, Anglo-Eurocentric and patriarchal knowledge (Spring, 1996, 1997; Kincheloe, 1993).

Postmodern literacy reinvents literacy as located within the reader and writer as defined by social, cultural, and economic circumstances (Freire, 1970; hooks, 1992). This critical literacy brings to the forefront various aspects of oppression accompanying traditional reading and writing practices, aspects that go unrecognized unless we examine the meanings found within discourses of literacy. The discourses of critical theory and feminist theory not only challenge the existing power and knowledge relations of educational institutions and science but are also considered powerful literacy (Macedo, 1994a).

In accord with powerful literacy, the non-mainstream critical and feminist ways of knowing constitute the postmodern literacy that I am advocating for educators. Through such postmodern literacy, reading and writing become enhanced methods for exploring the democratic self and its formation through ideological exposure to knowledge and power relations formulated by educational policy texts. Through such exploration, literacy becomes a tool for self-, student, and social advocacy rather than a commodity to determine whether one measures up satisfactorily on test scores.

## Conclusion

In this chapter, the concepts of scientific, modernistic literacy and democratic, postmodern literacy have been contrasted. Modern literacy carried over from an emphasis on literacy for religious participation to the modern industrial era when Horace Mann promoted education for the accumulation of wealth and investment in workers (Tozer, Violas, & Senese, 1998) and endured until the rise of the Information Age. Literacy policies, as they have been articulated within statements of reform, support state concentration of power occurring since World War II. Part of that state-building process has included teacher education reform wherein increased regulation and administration have ensued since the late 1950s.

Two discourses of literacy, human capital and cultural literacy, predominate in state education. As teachers are formed to be workers of the state, they do not necessarily develop critical and feminist literacies, which are dialectical to human capital and cultural literacy discourses. The vehicle which will be utilized to discuss four discourses of literacy in this presentation is an archaeological genealogy, or effective history, as inspired by Foucault. Implicit in the archaeological genealogy is social critique; influences of Paulo Freire and several feminists enhance this literacy genealogy.

To reiterate what this project entails, an effective history looks at present practices to understand the histories that generated those practices. Implicit in this discussion is a view that educators are beginning to question literacy policies from multicultural perspectives (Nieto, 1996; Ellsworth, Hedley, & Baratta, 1994). Critical and feminist literacies, although part of the multicultural education domain, often become overpowered by cultural sampling of various majority minorities, including Hispanic American, Asian American, African American, and Native American histories and cultures.

The problem and questions guiding my research assume both little exposure to powerful literacy by teacher education programs and little or no literacy policy analysis by educators. Such exposure can reveal to teachers the power and knowledge relations that exist in any discourse of literacy. A political framework for utilitarian and rights-based education foregrounds human capital and cultural literacies, whereas democratic communitarianism and humanistic psychology are enhanced and developed through critical and feminist literacies (Kahne, 1996; Block, 1995). Educators can become more critical of utilitarian-based education with powerful discourses.

In review, structuralism refers to a school or group of scholars who study human phenomena by looking at existing structures rather than the social construction of those structures (Jackson, 1994; Foucault, 1972; Weedon, 1987; Dreyfus, Rabinow, & Foucault, 1982). Poststructuralism developed because researchers were too limited by structuralism's parameters to question the taken-for-granted. Distinctions have been made between poststructuralism as an approach to analysis and postmodernism as an umbrella term which includes poststructuralism. In chapter 2, postmodernism will be elaborated as the time frame in which cultural transformation is occurring.

The distinctions between a modern versus a postmodern state also follow in chapter 2. Embedded within the discussion of postmodernism is a review of poststructuralism, which provides the foundation for my methodology. After the poststructural section, some history of teacher education and teacher education reform will ensue, followed by insight into the potential for successful reform through change. Chapter 4 will analyze literacy policies employing the method described in chapter 3. Chapter 5 will analyze teacher education reform policies following the same format as that presented in chapter 3. Finally chapter 6 will look to classroom applications of the theories advanced in this policy archaeology. Prospects and implications for future transformation of literacy practice are deliberated therein.

# CHAPTER II

## MOVING TEACHER EDUCATION FROM
## MODERNISM TO POSTMODERNISM

### Introduction

Educational restructuring and reform have been widespread within the United States for the last two decades (Cuban, 1990). As the nation approaches the twenty-first-century Information Age, this historical moment characterizes one of the three major waves of educational reform. The first wave of reform addressed the country's rural-based society; the second wave responded to industrialism (Goodman, 1995a). The third wave is marked by a concerted effort of officials at all levels to keep the United States competitive in an international, informational economy (U.S. Department of Education, 1983).

Policymakers have given new attention to education as a way to keep the nation in the forefront of economic stability and growth. They have emphasized literacy, math, science, and technology within the discourses of prescriptive, ameliorative reform policies formulated in various bureaucratic domains of decision making (Spring, 1996; Tozer, Violas, & Senese, 1998; U.S. Department of Education, 1983). Reform extends from the efforts of many within the hierarchy of policy formulation, administrations, public school and university teaching faculty and within communities across the country.

A postmodern look at these policies involves an analysis of educational policy in general and literacy policy specifically. It assumes understanding of the academic and political positions that ground the academic theories in order to analyze policy. This historical treatment will direct specific attention to literacy and teacher education policy prescriptions found in official pedagogical discourses (U.S. Department of Education, 1983; U.S. Department of Education, 1991; Murray & Fallon, 1989; Holmes Group, 1990).

## Policy Textual Analysis

The study of meanings associated with policy texts requires textual analysis of signifiers (the policy texts) and their resultant signified meanings and practices. A semiotic analysis of policy requires an identification of the paradigms, the codes, and the contexts within which the denotative meanings of the codes may be interpreted (Manning, 1989; Sontag, 1982). The policy analyst seeks to discover the code that articulates the political and social concerns embodied in policy text. Manning describes the process succinctly: "Discourse analysis must place discourse within the context of political interests and values, and note the selective vision that perspectives provide on the world" (1989, p. 216).

As discussed in chapter 1, an effective history of the discourses of literacy will be the means to achieve the objective of this research, which proposes a method of critical literacy policy analysis. In order to grapple with the idea of paradigm shifting from a modern to a postmodern paradigm of literacy, it is necessary for the policy analyst to have a command of three domains of information. This literature review will attempt to place the discourses around these topics into the contexts of their political values and their articulations.

## Chapter Objectives

In this chapter, I will discuss three broad areas. First, as determined by sociopolitical and economic theories, I will distinguish between modern and postmodern systems and define modern literacy and postmodern literacy within those systems. Second, I will establish the theoretical foundations of my method as they emanate from critical, postmodern scholarship. Third, I will discuss teacher education from reform and change perspectives. The overall objective is to examine the broad theories underlying mainstream literacy pedagogy and the potential for transforming this tradition of literacy practice to more holistic and democratic practices.

# Modernism

## The Modern Society

Modernization theory was developed by U.S. sociologists during the 1950s and 1960s, building on earlier work by the German sociologist Max Weber. The theory holds that various processes were necessary to the development of modern industrial society. The rationale was generalized from the experience of the Western world and utilized to explain the evolution required for other non-Western societies and nations to attain a similar degree of development (Stearns & Hinshaw, 1996). Although modernization theory has been largely dismissed most recently for its Western ethnocentricity and unilinear view of historical development, understanding what modernization is from this model is helpful for differentiating between modern and postmodern polities.

Characteristics of a modern society include industrialization accompanied by technological change resulting in several social and political phenomena. Modernization consisted of new and more efficient bureaucratic functions for the state, with popular support of the masses (Smart, 1993). Education has played a large part in modernization, and modernizing states have developed educational systems (Maynes, 1985; Smart, 1993). The modernizing process to a large degree has coupled itself with education, literacy movements, and efforts to standardize knowledge dissemination (Maynes, 1985). Other aspects of modernization include population control, development of democracy, greater belief in science, and more rights and freedoms for women (Hoeveler, 1996; Burchell, Gordon, & Miller, 1991). A "modern" personality refers to a personality type; a modern person possesses attributes such as being "open to change, eager for progress, individualized" (Stearns & Hinshaw, 1996, p. 173).

Shifting from modern to postmodern ways of thinking about knowledge, education, and literacy and passing those cultural artifacts to next generations institutionally through teacher education involves change. But surface change or change for the sake of change has been the case for much of educational reform (Gibboney, 1991; Borman & Greenman, 1994; Cuban, 1990; Goodman, 1995a). Shifting from a modern to a postmodern paradigm is difficult because administrative logic and the nature of top-down bureaucracy make surface changes without the structural alterations necessary to achieve real change.

This look at literacy discourses is concerned with developing postmodern teachers who will adapt literacy practices to their classroom communities' needs. Accordingly, understanding the difference between a modern and a postmodern system is necessary. This discussion will focus on the United States as a modern state, as opposed to European or other industrialized modern states. Three distinguishing features of the United States as a modern state stem from political and economical arrangements that have resulted in massification, commodification, and rationalization (Smart, 1993; Spring, 1996). Through scientific rationalization, originating in Enlightenment thought, the nation is founded on interest politics (Smart, 1993). These politics were based on tenets of equality as interpreted through ideology of Protestant Christendom and aristocratic values of classical and progressive liberalism. However, the American democracy has ostensibly promoted equality for all, unlike aristocracies.

Modernism includes characteristics of Enlightenment thought exaggerated by industrialization. With the particular sort of political arrangements established in representative democracy, the nation-state is authoritative under the guidance of oligarchical government, government of the masses by the few (Crook, Pakulski, & Waters, 1992; Tozer et al., 1998; Spring, 1996). Tensions between the authority of the state and that of the nation-state give U.S. politics a particular character that often involves questions of the law and jurisdiction of the state versus the federal government. Nonetheless, the state or the nation-state is authoritative over manners concerning the citizenry (Spring, 1996). From the mid-nineteenth century through the 1960s, industrialization rationalized and commodified mass American society. Since that time, through technological mass media, the dissemination of art forms and services functions to reproduce people, goods, and services as commodities of production and consumption (Crook et al., 1992; Kincheloe, 1993, 1995). Social, cultural, political, and economic structures have contributed to segmentation, centralization, capitalism, and bureaucracy in the progressive, liberal, democratic state.

Industrial capital and corporate management drive production in this complex society, whereas workers perform the labor to accomplish production. Capital and labor are two sectors comprising integral parts of the modern political economy, resulting in a differentiated class system. The existence of an underclass is implicit and is exacerbated by racial, ethnic, and gender discrimination within a capitalist system. Disparities between the upper, middle, and lower classes of people in urban centers of population and neglected rural areas result in great differences in wealth (Kozol, 1991; Tozer et al., 1998; Crook et al., 1992). Differentiation in this modern society is exacerbated by scientific practices which create more differentiation.

As rationalization of sociocultural activity drives leadership of the masses, differentiation requires a disconnecting effect that divides existence into many parts: knowledge, life, work, art, etc. As these aspects of culture are further differentiated, knowledge becomes diffused over many disciplines, and people are organized through differentiation. Social surveillance becomes necessary through schooling, prisons, hospitals, and examinations (Foucault, 1977; Crook et al., 1992; Jackson, 1994).

Rational activity often manifested in bureaucracy becomes tied to the economic and political forces that maintain equilibrium in the modern society. From the hierarchy of bureaucracy, decision making about education is also rationalized. Such rationalization of education and literacy instruction requires that specific knowledge bases be mastered and examined (Kliebard, 1995). Because the politics of power and the finance holders are more easily maneuvered through the bureaucratic hierarchy of government, elite culture, politics, and economic interests drive the business, political, and scientific communities (Gubrium & Silverman, 1989; Crook et al., 1992; Kincheloe, 1995). Avid belief in Enlightenment expertise of scientists required to manage such amorphous social systems and in the Greco-Roman foundations of Western culture leads to reverence of science and scientific activity in this culture (Foucault, 1972, 1977). "Big science" has been responsible for technological advancement, the space program, and military arms production "and offers the paradigm case of development through differentiation" (Crook et al., 1992, p. 25). Habermas observed that "modern science and technology have become, in combination, a leading productive force" (1971, cited in Crook et al., 1992, p. 26). Looking to the connections between science, commerce, and the state, we obtain a clearer view of the origins of modern education policy.

The role of modern education as accomplished by the corporate-state's role in education—to prepare students as future workers—becomes one of differentiation, through mass education and the commodification of knowledge and workers. Marx based his structural interpretation of society on the differentiation between workers and aristocracy engaged in struggle, defining history as the result of that struggle. Postmodern and neo-Marxist critics have moved beyond these structural interpretations of society, calling them grand narratives. However, critical theorists have held onto Marx's view (1848/1993) of class struggle and have developed his idea of critical theory, which he defined as clarification for oneself of the struggles and wishes of the age. The use of critical theory and analysis will come later in the analysis of literacy policy interpretation. For the purposes of this discussion, I will now turn to effects of rationalized, commodified, and mass-produced modern literacy education beginning with economic theory that regards education as a capital investment rather than an issue of human development.

**Human Capital Theory**

Within a modern industrial environment, the education of the worker-citizen overshadows the education of the citizen-worker (Tozer et al., 1998; Spring, 1972, 1980). Economist Gary Becker prefaces his analysis of education and economics with a description of his analysis that began in 1957 and continued until the third edition of his book was published in 1993. During this time, Becker's premise, originating in Robert Schultz's work, which looked at the development of human capital concepts since post–Civil War industrialization, involved an attempt to look at census reports on the incomes of persons with various educational backgrounds and to explain the returns of education as Office of Education expenditures. He reasoned that "if education were economically important, . . . money rates of return on education ought to be significant" (Becker, 1993, p. xxi). Between the time he initiated his study of economics of education and the present, there has been a proliferation of research and policy proposals: a bibliography of the economics of education ballooned from 50 entries in 1957 to 450 entries in 1964 and to over 1,300 entries in 1970 (Becker, 1993, p. 3).

A Foucaultian discussion of human capital education responds to the questions, What enabled such an emphasis on the economics of education? and How do the discourses of economics regulate society? Education for humans as economic beings describes the social conditions created by a recent network of complexity, described succinctly by Becker. He submits that before the presidential campaigns of former President Bush and President Clinton, and even fifteen years ago, using the terminology to invest in education for "human capital" to improve the quality of the labor force was unthinkable (Becker, 1993, p. xix). However, since that time the existing conditions allowed the discussion of national investment in human capital. Becker defines human capital investment as those "activities that influence future monetary and psychic income by increasing the resources in people" (p. 11).

Although Becker's research is more relevant to those interested in economics, it is nonetheless important to this discussion because it speaks about literacy of workers. What is important in this analysis is reconstructing how a Foucaultian vantage point of understanding depicts the history of educational practices by looking at their present practices. The grid of regularities of discourses that lead to more regulation and testing is consistent with modern Industrial Age and postindustrial discourses (Foucault, 1972). In approaching the millennium, as more multicultural forces are growing in the United States, and as more jobs are being displaced by technocratic forces, disillusionment in the populace runs high. For the current power holders and molders of society to remain in control, more social control over workers becomes necessary. *Thus human capital literacy, a knowledge developed for workers, rather than by workers, becomes imminently important.* A formulaic knowledge of literacy described by policymakers is handily addressed in education policy as attainable (Bennett, 1984; U.S. Dept. of Education, 1983; U.S. Dept. of Education, 1993a).

Although new insights into language, literacy, and culture emphasize the contested terrain of both knowledge and literacy as they have been promoted in factory-model schools, literacy spokespeople from various locations in society formulate what literacy is and how it should be improved. Measurement of literacy through testing, textbooks, and differentiated curriculum remains the mainstay of literacy in school (Edelsky, 1991a; Mitchell & Weiler, 1991; Livdahl et al., 1995; Shannon, 1989). The return to vocational education and the promotion of computer technological skills for all students are prescribed as necessary for worker knowledge.

**What Knowledge Do Modern Workers Need?**

In any society, one's stance on what comprises knowledge determines the knowledge that is needed. For Foucault, knowledge in a modern society was differentiated information over a range of subjects, topics, disciplines, and fields that serve ultimately to regulate and monitor human behavior (Foucault, 1972). Social constructivists hold that knowledge is constructed information that becomes the connection between social phenomena and the learner (Vygotsky, 1962; Dewey, 1916). Traditional, classical liberals hold that knowledge is a canon of information—letters, literature, and structures representing the values and morals for which society needs to ethically reconstitute itself (Bloom, 1987; Hirsch, 1987; Bennett, 1992a,b). Feminists, criticalists, and multiculturalists assert that accepted knowledge consists of patriarchal history, literature, and sciences that have descended from a long line of rationalist and, therefore, sexist, racist, and classist social and cultural practices (Stone, 1994; Martin, 1994; Giroux, 1983; Gatens 1991). These groups are rewriting culture within academic disciplines from their various perspectives.

Despite the contentions of what exactly comprises knowledge that future generations should know, efficient education has differentiated knowledge into many subjects, levels, and disciplines (Foucault, 1977; Ball, 1995). The knowledge within those subjects is differentiated on a scale of difficulty (Shannon, 1989). What is taught in schools becomes tied to a host of social practices including the curriculum and the hidden curriculum (Sowell, 1996; Tozer et al., 1998; Martin, 1994).

The curriculum as defined by Sowell defines what is taught to students. Thus, the curriculum includes

> 1) the cumulative tradition of organized knowledge; 2) modes of thought; 3) race experience; 4) guided experience; 5) planned learning environment; 6) cognitive/affective content and process; 7) an instructional plan; 8) instructional ends or outcomes; and 9) a technological system of production. (Sowell, 1996, p. 5)

The hidden curriculum, according to Tozer, Violas, and Senese (1998), consists of all the unplanned teaching and learning that goes on in school usually as a result of the social and structural arrangements of school. The hidden curriculum, according to Darder, is "informed by ideological views that silence students and structurally reproduce the dominant society's assumptions and practices" (1995, p. 331). McLaren (1998) describes curriculum from a critical perspective as the initiation into a particular form of life that prepares students for dominating or subordinated positions in society.

Looking to the differentiated organization of schools, to a brief Foucaultian analysis of how the curriculum becomes the vehicle of knowledge delivery between the state and the student, I will illustrate the dynamic of literacy as a function of knowledge. If workers are expected to develop worker literacy, there are two strands of literacy taught in schools: one for professionals, future leaders, and administrators and another for vocational workers who do not fit into one of these categories (Kincheloe, 1995).

The state, along with corporate and special interest groups, decides what knowledge is legitimate and required of workers in either capacity (Calderon & Ramos, 1997, February 6; Ramos, 1997, April 14; Denton, 1997, May 19; Ramos, 1997, June 10; Ramos, 1997, June 13; Ramos, 1997, July 11; Ramos, 1997, July 12). Superintendents, principals, teachers, and students become objects of scientific study to determine what kinds of education have optimal effects for national productivity. As President Clinton continues to support the national testing movement, he has called on governors, who will join the hierarchical train of surveillance. The governors will oversee the states' educational hierarchy to assure that the states comply with the rigors of national standards ("Bush Lends Support," 1997). In such a manner, officials become the objects of policy as well as the subjects who enact those policies through various discourses (Foucault, 1972). To be sure that everyone is on task, surveillance is perpetrated so that superintendents observe school districts, principals observe teachers, teachers oversee students, and competency examinations determine compliance and certify legitimacy of knowledge attained as directed (Foucault, 1977; Jackson, 1994; Calderon & Ramos, 1997, February 6).

Official literacy instruction, as specified by general educational policies and specific literacy policies, is accomplished when testing differentiates between the skilled and unskilled (Kunen, 1997; Foucault, 1977). Those whose skills are commensurate with an arbitrary, numerical assignment are successful and may enter the gate to more social and economic opportunities; those who do not possess such skills have limited possibilities for scholastic and professional development. Over time, the standards are raised by the state to oversee more compliance and performance (U.S. Dept. of Education, 1983; "Clinton Urges Governors," 1997).

As standards are routinized and become taken for granted, literacy practices become reified as scientific. The scientific measure of literacy is assumed with competency testing. Passing the exam indicates, as scientifically verifiable with the quantifiable test score, that literacy has been attained. As scientific practices such as testing become reified, the scientific discourses around literacy produce notions of truth. In this fashion, the truth of literacy, its importance, and its measurement come to exert control over individuals (Foucault, 1972).

In the United States, the history of testing is tied to social values, morals, and beliefs about the worth of people from various genetic backgrounds (Tozer et al., 1998; Tyack, 1966). Although literacy is not the only skill tested in IQ testing, literacy testing has been carefully deconstructed to tie it to the same values as those associated with the growth of middle-class Euro-American attitudes that led to the social emphasis put on literacy. Literacy for national strength was already present in Thomas Jefferson's plans for early American education (Tozer et al., 1998). The founding fathers' belief in a system whereby those whose abilities and talents merited more responsibility and reward could excel aligned with a capitalist, competitive economy. The forceful myths of individualism, fair competition, and commensurate rewards promoted the growth of a system that was efficient at mass production, differentiation, and commodification, first in the business corporate sector, and later in education. Testing and meritocracy forged a powerful relationship in the field of psychology, which has been applied in reading instruction and testing (Block, 1995; Shannon, 1989; Tozer et al., 1998).

## Curricular Tradition Versus Innovation—Literacy Controversy

Testing and meritocracy are tied to human capital and cultural literacy traditions. An ongoing debate about a traditional versus a more contemporary, inclusive curriculum continues. *Cultural literacy* as advocated by E. D. Hirsch (1987), Alan Bloom (1987), and William Bennett (1984) proposes to pass on to the next generation social morals, cultural values, and traditions through a body of literature referred to as the Western canon. Critics of such literacy through language, education, and unquestioned power and knowledge relations declare such an educational focus too limited in its Anglo-European, male-dominated scope. In contrast to an exclusively "American" cultural literacy, proponents of an alternative (sometimes referred to as multiculturalists, criticalists, or feminists) seek to include in the curriculum more historical and literary studies by and about "other" groups formerly excluded from the classical Western canon. Some of the formerly excluded groups include women, indigenous peoples, and African Americans, among others, like those with disabilities. Despite the ongoing attempts to reconceptualize the histories and present-day struggles of various groups within the United States, the curriculum has focused on mostly white males of Western European and English origins, as well as U.S. white male writers, as the mainstay of "literary" literacy. Upon analysis, we note that with the exception of more technology in schools— which also serves to deploy the child in a technological consumer society— the restructuring and reformation of the 1980s and 1990s has done little more than make cosmetic changes to the curriculum, leaving the Western canon in place.

Additionally, more than ever, the preparation of workers within the frameworks of capitalistic technological consumerism represents the contemporary focus on *human capital literacy* formerly tied to the Industrial Age. The present-day argument for human capital literacy centers on notions (some more mythical than others) of laissez-faire economics, private enterprise, careerism, and work traditions adopted from Industrial Age practices, as well as social relations dictated by power and management. Also important to the discussion of human capital literacy are the notions of social and economic success within a meritocracy—the mythical idea that anyone can succeed, that those who work hard in both school and the work world will reap economic and social success. Policymakers and educational administrators justify their requirement for literacy skills in a highly technical work world with the argument that such skills will enhance the individual's chances for success.

My argument does not seek to de-emphasize literacy development or skills refinement within students; rather, it promotes learning such skills and going beyond such literacy to master a secondary literacy that enables critique of dominant discourses which do not work in the best democratic interests of the many, including most schoolteachers and their students (see also McLaren, 1998).

## History of Testing and Meritocracy

The ethic of literacy testing necessitates reference to the testing movement developed by corporations for social "betterment" or eugenics (Tyack, 1966). Through corporate foundations, scientific testing and the state joined hands to promote the discourses of psychological testing. During the late nineteenth and early twentieth centuries, the social and scientific constructions of literacy merged with testing and a notion of social improvement and racial purity. Specifically, schooling became closely tied to the progressive notion of the state, which was aligned with corporate interests and a eugenics movement. Karier's perspective is helpful for understanding how literacy testing came to "fashion the peculiar meritocracy within th[e] state":

> Although the testing movement began with Thorndyke's mass testing of 1.7 million men for classification in the armed forces in World War I, the roots of the American testing movement run deeper than sorting of manpower during the national crisis of the Great War. Imbedded in the American progressive temper lies a belief in progress, racial attitudes, and faith in the scientific expert. This expertise works through state authority to ameliorate and control the evolutionary progress of the race. Whereas America has had a long history of eugenics advocates, some of the key leaders of the testing movement were the strongest advocates for eugenics control. In the twentieth century, the two movements often came together under the direction of the same people under the name of "scientific" testing with [corporate] foundation support. (Karier, 1972, p. 163)

In keeping with the belief in the racial superiority of the white race, Jeffersonian thought associated talent and virtue. In accord with founding fathers' values, the testing movement during the nineteenth-century Progressive Era was based on elements of the classical liberal tradition. As mentioned earlier, virtue was also tied to the social construction of literacy. Consistent with Thorndyke's expectations, his research showed a higher morality among those with more intelligence. Lewis B. Terman's work mirrored Edward Thorndyke's to find lesser intelligence and lower morality at the opposite end of the spectrum (Karier, 1972, p. 163).

Terman argued that "the feebleminded were incapable of moral judgments and, therefore, could only be viewed as potential criminals" (Karier, 1972, p. 163). His involvement with the testing movement was aimed at discerning the "potential criminals," who, of course, came from the lower sectors of society and whose performance on the intelligence test indicated as much. In keeping with postmodern Foucaultian insight, the objectives of testing were fulfilled by the expectations implicit in its foundations.

As history has shown, the eugenics movement served many purposes. Other social problems besides excluding those of "lesser intellect" from the armed service were addressed with this social sorting mechanism. Similar testing was used to limit immigration of Southern Europeans from around the turn of the century until about 1920, as well as to exclude people of racial and ethnic backgrounds unlike Anglo and European Americans from schooling, jobs, public places, and full participation in the democratic process.

A look at psychology and corporate foundations for social sorting by means of testing highlights some modern aspects of the formation of literate subjects. When it adopted the belief in objectivity and the efficiency of tests to determine aptitude, the state, under the guidance of the experts, became tied to the idea of psychological testing. Although the concept of testing originated under Binet in France and German cognitive psychologists, American educational policymakers developed the concept further and put more faith in the science of testing than Binet had. James Conant, president of Harvard during the 1930s, moved the United States closer to the meritocratic society through the development of the Educational Testing Service, which would help sort and classify students by their aptitudes as measured by tests (Tozer et al., 1998). The discourses of the state and scientific method became linked in the effort to improve society scientifically through examinations, and progress attainment was monitored (Foucault, 1977; Jackson, 1994).

**Other Modern Educational Practices**

Other practices within the modern political economy developed alongside testing. Citing organizational theorists, Shannon (1989) maintains that schools are " 'loosely coupled' " institutions ". . . based on public confidence in the certification of teachers, students, and curricula" (p. 56). "Education is a certified teacher teaching a standardized curricular topic to a registered student in an accredited school" (Meyer & Rowan, cited in Shannon, 1989, p. 56). The adoption of Frederick Taylor's scientific management system introduced standardization of labor and practices into the schools at the turn of the twentieth century (Tozer et al., 1998; Shannon, 1989; Luke, 1992).

Shannon explicates that the adaptation of scientific management to reading instruction had profound effects on reading programs:

> First, it reduces the goals of reading instruction from the development of students who love literature and can use literacy effectively in their daily lives to a standard identifiable level of reading competence. . . . Second, the process of reading is segmented into discrete skills so that increments of progress can be identified across grades. . . . Third, objective tests replace teachers' judgment concerning whether or not a student is to be considered literate because teachers' judgment is unpredictable. . . . (1989, p. 57)

The growth of the textbook industry and other commercial materials to accomplish verifiable literacy is the norm within school practices across the spectrum. Literacy is commodified through production and sales of textbooks and other media. Students' reading levels are differentiated by grade levels and levels within classes. Teachers' work in literacy instruction is rationalized and made scientifically dependent on manufactured measures and resources. With modifications, some programs utilize basals and textbooks as supplementary materials; however, Shannon surmises that

> basal reading materials met the expectations of a public and educational community enthralled with business, science, and psychology as they tried to find a remedy for the apparent crisis in reading instruction in schools at the turn of the century in order to prepare students for the rapid changes of an industrialized America. (1989, p. 27)

However efficient such a factory model was and remains today, the schools that de-skill also alienate teachers through reified assembly-line teaching and learning models. Teachers are de-skilled by commercial reading materials in at least three ways: personally, through one-to-one interaction with other teachers; bureaucratically, through school structures such as hierarchical management, merit pay, control of pacing and time spent on certain topics; and technically, through the controls of packaged materials, evaluations, and the tasks deemed natural to the job of teaching reading

(Shannon, 1989, p. 80). Apple (1989) discusses the de-skilling of teaching as a gendered and classed activity. Female teachers, many from the lower classes, are predominantly charged with passing the knowledge of the upper class to their students. Although there are some guarantees of employment benefits in teaching, when the political economy is faltering, teachers are subjected to the same kinds of employment difficulties as lower-wage laborers. In essence, teachers are caught in the class struggle, which represents the public struggle for language, knowledge, and culture, of which literacy is a great part. They are not of the upper class, yet they teach the upper-class knowledge, values, and literacy to their students, reinforcing and reproducing the system that exploits them (Cochran-Smith, 1991). The curriculum becomes the vehicle through which literacy policies are practiced.

**Plural Literacy Meanings and Practices**

 Like many of the topics discussed in this research, policies that refer to literacy are plural, just as literacy, feminism, and poststructuralism are plural. However, there are grids of regularities that manifest themselves around the discussion of these topics. The grid of regularity that formulates the discourses of literacy comes from the state, popular cultures, higher education, local school districts, information technology, industry, and business, among other social institutions and forces.

Hiebert (1991) outlines some school district and school policies that emanate initially from higher political arenas into curriculum and instruction discourses that are referred to as "literacy." They include (1) variation on policy implementation, (2) literature curricula that has not changed despite the growth of diversity in student population, (3) "special" meanings of literacy given to literacy and learning by classroom teachers, special reading teachers, and administrators, (4) standardized assessment used to measure literacy, (5) certain tracking, retention, and special education policies that penalize recipients of special programs, and (6) reductionist views of learning (pp. 215–216).

Although all of these literacy policies are important, the sixth one—the reductionist ways of learning as related to discourses of literacy—is the area that is most discussed in this project. As I will argue herein, the discourses of literacy are reductionist, narrowing the field whereby the child and adult student as well as the adult citizen/worker may define their social realities through the literacy they develop (Macedo, 1994a). Thus, modern literacy is teacher-, text-, and content-centered, rather than student-centered. Knowledge in this sense is a commodity to be deposited by teachers and consumed by students, illustrating *banking education* as referred to by Freire (1970).

## Literacy as Contextual and Purposeful

Akin to Freirean thought, Dewey's theory of subject matter knowledge is both sociohistorical and sociopsychological, two different aspects of the same process. As a sociohistorical phenomenon, knowledge is contextual within time and dependent on a place; as it becomes part of a student's experience, knowledge is relevant to the learner through the learner's engagement with it in some "purposeful action" (Dewey, 1916, pp. 181–182). Freirean literacy is engaged, purposeful action resulting from learner interaction as political empowerment through praxis. For both Freire and Dewey, the distinctions between teaching and scholarship are blurred. Scientific research is inextricably woven into pedagogy, despite the deprecating attitude of some researchers toward pedagogical function as a less worthy activity than pure scientific endeavor. This dialectic between pedagogy and scientific research is crucial to postmodern literacy within a new emerging scientific paradigm (Barker, 1992; Kuhn, 1970). Since the system is still functioning in a modern mode, modern scientific educational practices have not embraced the evolution of scientific thought to encompass more postmodern aspects of the emerging paradigm. Some of the characteristics of a postmodern scientific theory include holism, less stable rules of explaining natural phenomena, and the acceptance of theory and knowledge building as tentative and always expanding with new understanding (Kincheloe & Steinberg, 1993).

## Constructing Modern Literate Subjects

Within a modern state, the tenets of positivism establish the foundations for epistemological considerations of what constitutes truth and knowledge. In Cartesian-Newtonian adherence to separating the object to be learned or researched from the learner or the researcher, learning and/or researching are established as "objective." Such thought about learning and researching places knowledge outside of individuals to be mastered by them, despite the relevance or meaning to their lives. Marxist thought, describing the alienation of individuals from their work, helps to describe the control of teachers through the curricula they are expected to teach and of students through their learning that occurs in a modern polity (Marx, 1844/1993). They are controlled, expected to produce, and are examined to assure that the proper teaching and learning have occurred. Literacy within modern schooling is other-centered, tied to commercially packaged materials, and is informed by Enlightenment knowledge and research (Shannon, 1989; Kincheloe, 1993). Through scientific management and state administration, the conduct of literate subjects is a concern of government in all of the hierarchical levels from which it determines education of the masses.

## Movement Toward Postmodernism

### Postmodernism Defined

The roots of postmodernism are traceable to the late nineteenth century; however, the term itself was employed in the 1930s. Utilized by Federico de Onis, *postmodernismo* appeared in literary criticism to describe "a kind of exhausted and mildly conservative *modernismo*" (Smart, 1993, p. 19). In the 1950s the term connoted the denouement of the modern movement and the rise of a new sensibility. By the 1970s, the term was widely employed in relation to architecture, dance, painting, film, and music (Smart, 1993, p. 19). Still a widely contested terrain, postmodern has multiple meanings. Postmodernism, broadly explained as it is most meaningful for this discussion, is "a broad range of aesthetic, literary, and cultural responses to modernism" (Smart, 1993, p. 18).

Postmodernity as a social future has yet to be realized and is a reconstitution of utopian thought (Smart, 1993, p. 12). In response to a modern capitalist state, postmodernity includes "a post-scarcity order, multilayered democratic participation, demilitarization, and a humanization of technology" (Giddens, 1990, cited in Smart, 1993, p. 12). Jameson employed the term to describe an era in which "everything in our social life—from economic value and state power to practices and to the very structure of the psyche itself—can be said to have become 'cultural' " (cited in Smart, 1993, p. 18).

The postmodern United States is dependent on a global economy that allows international corporate expansion in search of lower wages and at the same time has more domestic competition from abroad. The politics of postmodernism have come to question the possibility of an emancipatory politics for all. Due to a number of social, religious, and economical factors, there has been a shift toward neo-conservative politics within the mainstream dialogue about politics. The trends of conservatism, globalism, and highly technical information systems and networks constitute the external contexts within which postmodern academic discussions occur. In these postmodern discussions, considerations and formulations of the importance of educating literate individuals for community and democracy in a rapidly changing, corporate-driven political economy become important to those kinds of literacy both teachers and students need to develop.

### Critical Postmodernism

As I employ the term in this document, postmodernism is an era in which deconstruction and resistance of the status quo of modernism is possible. Ludic postmodernism, as described in McLaren's *Life in Schools* (1998), is one which poses little hope for an articulation of universal problems, much less solutions to those problems. Critical postmodernism is the position of postmodernism that is worth embracing if we wish to transform school and society. Involved in the transformation of the modern polity into a postmodern one is recognizing the shortcomings of a modern system. Also extant in any postmodern or poststructural consideration of human experience is the multiplicity of voices. A plurality of postmodern concepts are defined by ideas or signifiers, including "critical theory," "feminisms," and "poststructuralisms" (Weedon, 1987). Critique of the modern society as problematic comes from critical, poststructural, and feminist theories and insights discussed in the following sections.

### Critical Theory

Critical theory extends from four traditions of critical scholarship: (1) the neo-Marxist critique of history as social progress and the problem of capital exploitation of labor; (2) the Frankfurt School, wherein sociologists questioned the possibilities of social policies such as those perpetuated in Nazi Germany, as well as critical formations of the self and society; (3)

Freirean thought about social transformation through conscientization of the problems with present and historical social relationships; and (4) Foucaultian historical, cultural, and social critique as understanding of the self and society within a complex relationship of power exercised and suppressed (Kincheloe & McLaren, 1994). The principal concern of critical theory is locating social inequity and developing power for transformation of repressive social policies

In exercise of critical analysis, language becomes the primary point of interest. The metanarratives of progress and scientific rationalism are suspect as criticalists attempt to disarm the truth/logic of Western rhetoric (Derrida, 1976; Weedon, 1987; Kristeva, 1988; Mitchell & Weiler, 1991). The poststructural educational currents associated with Derrida (Egea-Kuehne, 1995), Foucault (Popkewitz, 1991; Shutkin, 1994; Gore, 1993; Jackson, 1994), and Francois Lyotard (1979/1993) question Western rhetorical logic, power, privilege, and the oppression that accompanies them. In this respect, feminists' arguments proceed along similar lines as the postmodernists'. On the other hand, feminists find some deconstruction applications to be destructive to the efforts made by women to discount patriarchy (Stone, 1994; Luke & Gore, 1992). The feminists' rationale in this matter is that the leaders in the critical movement are still struggling for the ideal of a male-dominated liberal democratic system. Some feminists also describe the problems that Foucaultian theory imposes on females because of the manner in which his theory constructs a system hostile to women (Sawicki, 1991).

## Foucault's Work as Foundation for This Critical Policy Analysis

Foucault's theories and applications of those theories reinterpret history, power, knowledge, and truth from a poststructural, hermeneutic, and phenomenological perspective (Dreyfus, Rabinow, & Foucault, 1982). Concerned primarily with knowledge and power, Foucault (1990) explains the harnessing of "biopower" of the masses to tie the interests of the individual to those of the state (p. 140). This idea correlates with the idea of measuring education as part of the investment in the gross national product as discussed in Becker's human capital theory (Becker, 1993).

Gordon (1991) expounds on Foucault's big picture of governmental rationality as "the conduct of conduct" and "a form of activity aiming to shape, guide, or affect the conduct of some person or persons" (p. 2). A rationality of government for Foucaultian inquiry refers to "a way or system of thinking about the nature of the practice of government (who can govern; what governing is; what or who is governed), capable of making some form of that activity thinkable and practicable both to its practitioners and to those upon whom it was practiced" (Gordon, 1991, p. 3). Governmentality accomplishes both totalizing and individualizing effects on individuals within the populace. Governmentality is accomplished through the discourses of regulation that emanate from science, law, medicine, social sciences, social and regulatory institutions, as well as the practices that result from the discourses in their various milieus.

As recommended by Foucault (1972), the exploration of the serious statements within given discourses points to formations of truth. Borrowing the term *genealogy* from Frederich Nietzsche, Foucault examined how truth changes as it is constructed in various contexts over time. For Foucault, discourses represent processes of layering of civilization that deposit and redeposit texts, practices, and technologies as sociocultural relics of their origins. Thus, he employed the archaeology metaphor to describe his historical pursuits as archaeological genealogy. Particular works of Foucault that have been instrumental in this study are *The Archaeology of Knowledge* (1972), *The History of Sexuality* (1978/1990), *Discipline and Punish* (1977), *Power/Knowledge* (1980), and scholarship inspired by his governmentality concept in *The Foucault Effect* (Gordon, 1991).

Within *The Archeology of Knowledge*, Foucault sets forth rules for discourse analysis, concerning himself with looking beyond the structural limitations of traditional historical research to locate the "breaks," "ruptures," and "gaps" in discourses—the discontinuities, the reversals, and contradictory aspects of discourses and their implementation in various locations of practice (Foucault, 1972, p. 169). In *The History of Sexuality* (1978/1990), Foucault applied his method to locate the applications of sexual morality and other social practices to control the populace, linking the life forces of individuals to the welfare of the nation-state.

Social regulation par excellence is explored in *Discipline and Punish*. As revealed by Foucault, the growth of the social sciences coincided with the establishment of the hospital, prison, school, asylum, and other social agencies to regulate individuals. His insight describes how tactics and technologies are so effective at perpetrating control that individuals adapt self-surveillance to discipline themselves. Through narrative construction, Foucault locates social repression at the points where knowledge and power relations intersect to form notions of "truth" (Foucault, 1965, 1972, 1985; Fiske, 1993). The net result of the formations of truths through discourse is the formation of docile bodies. When the discourses of literacy are examined in a Foucaultian manner, they describe how control is exerted over individuals to form the "body literate" (Luke, 1992), "docile bodies and disembodied minds" (Davis, 1996b), and "deployment of the cyborg child" (Shutkin, 1994).

Recollections of the Foucaultian scholarship are reconsidered in *Power/Knowledge*. Here Foucault refines some of his theories about power and knowledge, removing them from the state and other governmental agencies to the many locations where power is exercised and resisted in society. *The Foucault Effect* applies, revisits, and reconsiders much of the discourse analysis set forth in *The Archaeology of Knowledge*. In sum, the body of Foucault's work directed attention to the harnessing of the state's power to the desire of individuals. Plays of human power were examined with three assumptions: (1) no concrete foundations for understanding exist, (2) events and chance occurrences give insight into relations of power, and (3) common forms of knowledge and existence found in the locations of understanding human experience replace the reliance on great ideas from noblest periods (Foucault, 1965; Jackson, 1994; Fiske, 1993).

## Deconstructing Science and Humanism

Foucault stated that the crux of his work was to dismantle Cartesian-Newtonian science (Dreyfus, Rabinow, & Foucault, 1982). Overall, Foucault criticized humanism, science, reason, and Western institutionalized culture since the Renaissance. His perspective was that positivism, grounded in Cartesian-Newtonian views of a fixed, mechanical, and predictable world, had founded psychology as an oppressive technology. Hence, an inextricable relationship between psychology and scientific methodological assumptions has been united to regulate human beings violently. Humanism, for Foucault, falsely advocated the individual as self-forming, whereas too much about social life and its discourses of control form individuals. Foucault's work is also a reaction to the extension of scientism into structural explanations of human behavior. Structuralism, as it is practiced by social scientists, attempts to explain human and cultural experiences with suppositions about language, culture, and social institutions as given, rather than as they are socially constructed within complex networks of social interchange of economy, government, hierarchy, and bureaucracy. Foucault criticized the social sciences and structuralism as prohibitive to understanding because they were determined and controlled by the languages to which they ascribed.

Some terms he employed to describe the power of discourse include *anonymity* and *commentary* (Foucault, 1972). Anonymity describes the consequence of discourses taking on a life of their own, irrespective of their originators, and acquiring some "truth" value. Commentary allows the use of the text of discourse to say something that is not the text but which for all intents and purposes is the text. The multiple references to *A Nation at Risk* (U.S. Dept. of Education, 1983) provide commentary in many areas of education. The conversations that refer to *A Nation at Risk* often hardly refer to the actual text of the reform statement; additionally, *A Nation at Risk* provides commentary with anonymity of the authors who contributed to its creation. Similarly, Foucault's work has acquired characteristics of commentary in references to the discussions about prisons, insane asylums, and social regulation. In many ways, Foucault mastered structuralism, not only because of his interest and desire to go beyond its borders, but because French education, in general, is potently formed along Cartesian guidelines. White (1987) said of Foucault's work that it "is extraordinarily difficult to deal with in any short account . . . because his thought comes clothed in a rhetoric apparently designed to frustrate summary, paraphrase, economical quotation for illustrative purposes, or translation into traditional critical terminology" (p. 104).

## Structuralism and Beyond

Structuralism, as previously stated, is a movement that can be traced to the disciplines of the social sciences and literary studies. Structuralism essentially was and remains a strong movement to explain human behavior, phenomena, and text in terms of innate structures. Although labeled as a structuralist, Foucault consistently denied his affiliations with structuralism. Well-known scholars who have examined various human faculties as frameworks within a structural paradigm include Sigmund Freud within the field of psychology, Claude Levi-Strauss in the area of anthropology, and Ferdinand de Saussure in the domain of linguistics. Simone de Beauvoir is also considered a structuralist in her assertion that "The category of [woman as] the *Other* is as primordial as consciousness itself" (de Beauvoir, 1949/1993, p. 368). Foucault (1972) said that structuralism avoided the description of realistic and chaotic social phenomena by studying genesis, systems, synchrony, development, relation, cause, structure, and history.

An understanding of structuralism is important to both poststructuralism and postmodernism. The elusive characteristic of language to mean what it says and say what it means is an essential component of structural and poststructural theory. The use of symbols, metaphors, and experience of the interpreter, coupled with the delicacy of the act of interpretation, render language and meaning often arbitrary, inconsistent, and just beyond expression (Ricoeur, 1974; Sontag, 1982). Defining both the signifier and the signified, the French structuralists attempted to differentiate between the sign and its many meanings. Borrowing from the French, a structural and poststructural school of literary critique later developed in American academia (White, 1978, 1987). In general, the discourses of poststructuralism critique structuralism as it is informed by positivism and scientism. Included within the camp of poststructuralists are critical theorists and feminists who advocate the construction of knowledge, gender, and identity formation as a highly subjective activity.

Deconstructing knowledge within the poststructural frameworks, Foucault and Jacques Derrida applied forms of linguistic analysis to explore what Foucault called effective histories. Whereas Derrida is known for his pioneering of the "deconstruction" of language by rhetorical analysis of Saussure's theory of language and signs, Foucault is better known for his effective history. Effective histories were his analytical efforts to understand the historical within the present as the social, political, economic, cultural, and educational institutional discourses form the human subject (Foucault, 1972, 1978). In coming to understand how human subjects were formed by discourses, he explained the formation of truth as a process that results from knowledge and power relations, but that is not static and therefore is ever changing. Looking beyond bourgeois reporting of historical narrative, Foucault felt it necessary to describe society from the position of subalterns—the subordinated, insane, criminal, marginalized—those he described as *others*. His genealogy discloses the human power plays of domination, disorder, subjugation, and struggle.

Foucault said that men govern themselves and others through the production of truth. Truth is determined by social and power relations constructed through discourses and construction of the "other" at the intersection points of discourses and practices. Foucault referred to the other as the object of study as well as the subaltern (Foucault, 1978/1990). Relying on structural terms, a Foucaultian framework aims to describe the signified, fleshing out many meanings of signifiers within the formations of discourse. His work revealed how truth as developed through discourse is variable, changes over time, and is legitimated within the social context that enforces it. Knowledge and power relations construct the truth of discourses; however, the tactical polyvalence of discourses, as set forth by Foucault, asserts that

> we must not imagine a world of discourse divided between accepted discourse and excluded discourse, or between the dominant discourse and the dominated one; but as a multiplicity of discursive elements that can come into play in various strategies. It is this distribution that we must reconstruct, with the things said and those concealed, the enunciations required and those forbidden, that it comprises; with the variants and different effects—according to who is speaking, his position of power, the institutional context in which he happens to be situated. . . . Discourses are not once and for all subservient to power or raised up against it, any more than silences are. We must make allowance for the complex and unstable process whereby discourse can be both an instrument and an effect of power, but also a hindrance, a stumbling-block, a point of resistance and a starting point for an opposing strategy. (1978/1990, p. 101)

Foucault holds that "power produces things, it induces pleasure, forms knowledge, produces discourse. It needs to be considered as a productive network which runs through the whole social body" (1980, p. 119). Power and knowledge relations that produce literacy as interrelated parts of the deployment of literacies are both produced through and productive of those power relations in the field of education. As forms of power, the actions and reactions around the deployment of literacies modify the actions of others. The others, over whom power is exercised, are recognized and maintained as actors (Foucault, 1980, p. 189).

Foucault held that as the identity of the other is naturalized or normalized, the ideological process of subject construction is less apparent, rendering analysis of such construction less likely. Vanguard in the essence of Foucault's work is the problematization of the formations of the self in relation to truth and knowledge (Fiske, 1993). The postmodern penchant for problematizing the taken-for-granted requires that the discourses that encourage such sorting of individuals be a forefront consideration, especially in the contemplation of more humane and democratic educational practices.

Probing discourses that imprisoned humans was Foucault's intention. Within the constraints of discourse, the researcher's task is to find the discontinuity, disorder, and violence that exists in the power exercised through control of discourse and individuals. Foucault undertook his discourse analysis utilizing precepts explained below.

Reversal: Foucault held that for every positive statement made within routine statements, there also exists a negative statement. He located the use of power to objectify and subjectify persons by asking, "What is the negative side to the growth of the human sciences?" By looking at the mainstream and bourgeois values that called for development of prisons, schools, and insane asylums, he asked, "Who are the others who are separated from the rest of 'productive' society?"

Discontinuity: The traditional view of history as linear and progressive was called into question by the Foucaultian perspective that described it as discontinuous. Although he opposed the concept that the present develops from the past in a continuous process, he did not see the new as totally separate from the old. This idea is demonstrated by Foucault's understanding the conditions of classical, modern, and poststructural man. From the Enlightenment view, individuals construct themselves. Within the more current insights that Foucault shed on power, a new perspective on this concept is that individuals are constructed through the disciplines and social interrelationships between and among human players within institutions.

Exteriority, expanded from the chapter 1 reference to it, holds that the technologies, discourses, and subjects of power-knowledge are inextricable from the external conditions of existence for which events and discourses emerged during a given period of time. Analyzing the exterior of discourse seeks to explain the chance series of events that fix the limits about the development of discourse.

Ultimately, in Foucaultian archaeological genealogical studies, the researcher attempts to explain how power and knowledge direct each other, tying power to emotion and the motivator desire. The exercise of power through discourse and discourse analysis has become the focus of several academic positions. Foucault's influence has been extensive within the postmodern era. Within a Foucaultian framework, individuals become objects of study and power, yet Foucault's rule of reversal assumes all individuals have the capacity to exercise power and change the self and others. However, exercise of analysis to articulate social differences must be continued from many locations in the postmodern community.

## Postmodern Politics and Loss of Difference

The many theoretical positions that are included under the postmodern umbrella are often combined to locate parallels or similarities between and among theories. The meanings of postmodern, poststructural, feminist, and feminist poststructuralist have become conflated. All of these genre are not synonymous, yet possess overlapping characteristics. These lenses expand the view of a patriarchal social policy and enable critique. Understanding the contribution of literacy discourse to the construction of females largely by, about, and for white Euro-American males is important for discerning what is excluded as certain discourses are emphasized in social policymaking. Looking to feminists' arguments about social structures, welfare, and education helps to expand the landscape of social understanding from patriarchal dominance to a more inclusive realm.

## Feminist Discourse, Education, and Literacy

Feminisms' theoretical origins also go back to Europe to individuals like Simone de Beauvoir (1949/1993), considered a structuralist in her differentiation between male and female, and more contemporary feminist scholars including Julia Kristeva, Helene Cixous, and Luce Iraguaray. Feminists in education most recently have looked to the international scope in order to understand women's social and political positions (Stone, 1994; hooks, 1992, 1994; Collins, P., 1991). Both critical and feminist political theorists explain the social and cultural constructedness of cultural reality, as opposed to accepting innate characteristics of individual and social behaviors. There are some aspects of critical theory and feminisms that overlap, arising in reaction to the structures of mainstream policies and practices that often disregard the tenets of equality that are implicit in a political democracy. Both criticalists and feminists challenge the myths, grand narratives, and historical knowledge and power relations as mainstream fabrications to rationalize the political and economic status quo. A recent emphasis on excellence in education by policymakers has elicited debate in reaction to inequitable practices for the many in order to privilege the best and brightest (Shor, 1986a). Feminist and critical reactions to such debate are concerned that the assumed "best practices" in education privilege Anglo-European males and are less optimum for most females and many males of other backgrounds, particularly those from diverse backgrounds (AAUW, 1995; Shakeshaft, 1986).

## Critical Discourse Analysis

The work of poststructuralist criticalists and feminists seeks to reveal the various unquestioned practices of the liberal democratic and late capitalistic state, including those of the present educational reform movement. The manner in which these two groups achieve critical analysis of the "taken-for-granted" involves discourse analysis. Critical discourse analysis attunes itself to the ways in which language is used to describe what is unfair, problematic, or transgressive and turn it into something that is acceptable, normal, or benign (Kress & Hodge, 1979). Kress and Hodge looked at the structures and levels of language to ascertain that

> In societies characterized by conflict and contradictions, forms of double-think will be a condition of survival, and languages will show a wide variety of strategies for achieving and interpreting it. . . . A large part of the resources of language [is] designed to allow people not only to say what they mean but to mean the opposite as well, without ruffling the smooth surface of life or discourse. (p. 150)

Fraser (1989) says that "a critical social theory frames its research program and its conceptual framework with an eye to the aims and activities of those oppositional social movements with which it has a partisan, though not uncritical, identification" (p. 113). A way to assess the validity of critical theory, Fraser asserts, is to determine the answers to two questions about critical theory's relationship to feminism: "How well does it theorize the situation and prospects of the feminist movement? To what extent does it serve the self-clarification of the struggles and wishes of contemporary women?" (p. 114). Issues that speak to these questions include child rearing, the power of the father figure in the nuclear family, public and private spheres, and females' opposition to gender inequality (p. 114).

After analyzing the role of males in society versus females, Fraser points out that several characteristics of gender inequality are implicated presently and historically: Male dominance is intrinsic rather than accidental to classical capitalism realized by gendered roles, relevant concepts of workers, consumerism, and wage scales. The subordination of women is not limited to the field of economics and "gender-economic" issues, but is also linked to citizenship through "gender-political" relationships.

In assessing the postmodern state, Fraser states, "it is overwhelmingly women who are the clients of the welfare state, especially older women, poor women, single women with children" (1989, p. 132). Feminists' objections to positioning and representing women are projected as the opposite of "possessive individuals." They are not eligible for the job market or consumerism to the degree that males are, with their status often complicated by motherhood. The feminists' project accordingly becomes one of struggle

> to redistribute and democratize access to, and control over, discursive resources . . . over the means of interpretation and communication sufficient to permit us to participate on a par with men in all types of social interaction, including political deliberation and decision making. (Fraser, 1989, p. 135)

Fraser indicates that this is the predicament of women internationally. She describes the situation as traceable to women-headed households as well as to women who comprise much of the adult poverty population:

> Not just the United States but every late capitalist welfare state in Western Europe and North America is facing some version of it. And the fiscal crisis of the welfare state coincides everywhere with a second long-term, structural tendency: the feminization of poverty. (Fraser, 1989, p. 144)

Fraser encourages feminists to become part of the discourse occurring around "the politics of need interpretation" as it prevails within the dominant policy framework (1989, p. 145). By analyzing the social meanings couched within welfare programs, it is possible to shed light on structural and ideological problems within a supposed "gender-neutral" environment that legislates and formulates the "interpretation of women's needs" (p. 146). Fraser contends that not only are more women dependent on social welfare systems, but women also depend on the social welfare system as paid human-service workers. (For statistics, see Fraser, 1989, p. 148.) To put women's economic situation into context, in 1980, 17.3 million paid jobs in the human-service sector of the economy were held by women. For women of color, 37 percent of paid employment and 82.4 percent of their professional employment is recompense for human-service work (p. 148).

There are juridical, administrative, and therapeutic procedures that link political issues and the interpretation of peoples' needs (Fraser, 1989, p. 154). The system, Fraser contends, is able to work in the way that it does because of "institutionalized patterns of interpretation" that are stabilized and reproduced over time (p. 156). She explores three ways in which "needs" are discussed: (1) "expert" needs discourses of, for example, social workers and therapists, on the one hand, and welfare administrators, planners, and policymakers, on the other; (2) opposition movement needs discourses of, for example, feminists, lesbians and gays, people of color, workers, and welfare clients, and (3) "reprivatization" discourses of constituencies seeking to repatriate newly problematized needs to their former domestic or official economic enclaves (p. 157).

Fraser favors translating justified needs claims into social rights. Like many radical critics of existing social welfare programs, she is committed to opposing the forms of paternalism that arise when needs claims are extricated from rights claims (1989, p. 183). In order to probe the inequities in the existing system, Fraser recommends that we ask about the manner in which life is conducted as part of the task of social criticism. She questions needs formulation through examination of discourses to distinguish regimes normatively. She proposes that Foucault's genealogy of power does not promote the ideal analysis of the practice of power in the functioning of the state, especially in its treatment of women through social programs. She carries social critique forward to engage in micro- and macro-analysis of social programs.

If we consider that literacy policy is a determiner of social and educational practice, then we might transfer some of Fraser's questions to the realm of literacy policy examination. Limiting the discussion of what educational policy should address and the range of possibilities of that policy solution excludes changing the economical system in which the problems are occurring (Foucault, 1972; Scheurich, 1994). Adopting Fraser's view, we can ask if changes in literacy policy and practice are possible. If change is possible, we ask to what degree. Finally, upon implementing changes in literacy policy, we must determine what kinds of changes are optimal.

When the literacy problem is conceptualized as a deficit within the populace, the issues of poverty, such as equal funding of schools, equity of opportunity and access, and irrelevant curriculum, as well as the fascistic control of inner city schools, are beyond the scope of the articulated question that elicits the proposed policy solutions of a better educated teaching force and more technological know-how. Because poverty, literacy, and female issues are not formulated as problems within the existing system, they occur outside the arena of policy consideration. Foucault and Scheurich questioned not only the delimitation of the policy range, but also the field of such policy study as complicit in the problems of those affected by such policies.

Understanding the limitations of social policies and their discourses articulated around social problems requires critical discourse analysis. Defined by Fairclough's "Critical and Descriptive Goals in Discourse Analysis" (1985), critical discourse analysis requires "first and foremost, investigating verbal interactions with an eye to their determination by, and their effects on, social structures" (p. 747). Fairclough describes critical linguistics as the interpretive efforts to bring to light the manner in which language fosters "exploitive social relations" (p. 4). Fairclough describes institutions as "discourse communities" (p. 749). In what Fairclough describes as IDF (ideological discursive formations), institutions set up positions between agents (subjects), speech events, participants, settings, topics, goals, and ideological representations.

A similar process is known as critical literacy, although perhaps it is not as attuned to details as the sociolinguist's work. Proponents of critical literacy define critical literacy simply as reading the world and the word. A more complex formulation by critical scholars proposes analysis of knowledge and power relations within educational practice (Giroux, 1983; Lankshear & McLaren, 1993; Shor, 1986b; Kincheloe, 1991, 1993). The pedagogical process within which critical literacy operates is called critical pedagogy. Critical pedagogy, as formulated by Freire (1970) is dialogical, dialectical, multisourced, student-centered, heterogeneous, and cooperative-group focused (Tozer, Violas, & Senese, 1998, p. 355)

Critical pedagogy involves moving away from the fixed curriculum to an experiential view of constructing knowledge whereby the learner's experiences promote constructing meaning about the word from the world. Ideally, such learning enables more understanding through issues often glossed over in the core curriculum. For example, usually not taught is the struggle that various groups have endured for democracy, not only for the right to be educated but also for the right to employ that education for economic gain and for equal protection under the laws provided within the Constitution of the United States.

**Feminisms and Education**

The feminists' positions, although occurring in the same criticalist vein of rhetorical and political debate that questions the status quo and centrist and far-right positions within the political arena, look to the private and public sphere as the source of discrimination against women. Women who have traditionally upheld the home, child rearing, and lower-paying jobs thought of as women's work have not benefited from the public and professional life that many males have. *Feminisms* propose various policies to voice women's concerns within academic, economic, and sociocultural domains of life.

Several versions of feminisms include radical, liberal, black, and other minorities, as well as socialist feminists—who ascribe to various ideals of social improvement to be gained by political inclusion of women and economic equity for women's work (equal pay for equal work; the socialist feminists would seek compensation for women's roles in the home). More than being anti-male, feminists are anti-patriarchy. The radical feminist position proposes the revamping of the whole of social institutions which they feel are inherently sexist, exclusionary, male-dominated, and therefore anti-democratic.

Education for the feminist is important. Feminist movements have maintained impetus since the 1960s through political organization. Women's studies, sociology, feminist literature, philosophy, and foundations of education are the disciplines where feminist theories are read, discussed, and used to analyze the discourses of other political persuasions.

Other realms of feminist influence in education include pedagogy and an ethic of caring, as asserted by particular feminists (Noddings, 1984; Grumet, 1988). Many feminists in education promote more inclusion, more thought of social roles, more discussion of the "taken-for-granted" in all academic disciplines (Stone, 1994; Luke & Gore, 1992). The idea of a more humane approach to social institutional management has been embraced by the feminist economists and philosophers (Fraser, 1989; Greene, 1993a,b). Other feminists seek to rewrite women's history as different from male, particularly white male, history (Kristeva, 1988; Martin, 1994). Going beyond theory, political organization and lobbying have been present in women's movements such as the American League of Women Voters in the community and the American Association of University Women (1995) in academia.

Facility with women's discourses is important for the teaching profession, since the continued low status and inadequacies of education are constantly addressed by conservative and liberal political positions. Without knowledge of feminist theories, "efficient" and "scientific" literacy emphasis drives testing, curriculum, and classroom practices, even to the point, as indicated by Zeichner, to call that which is not reflective practice, reflective practice. By manipulation of teachers who are not savvy to all of the political implications of the literacy discourses of human capital and cultural literacies, undemocratic policies affecting teachers that are in turn mirrored in classroom practices against students will prevail unquestioned. Feminist literacy is part of a postmodern project seeking to understand and rectify some of the inequities resulting from gendered socialization. By rewriting literacy, the definitions, connotation, and limitations of standard literacy practice are reconceptualized (Stone, 1994; Mitchell & Weiler, 1991; Weedon, 1987).

**Postmodern Literacy Defined**

*Postmodern literacy* encompasses the precepts of critical and feminist theories. It enables voice to articulate the problems associated with the feminization of teaching, its de-skilling, and its continued disparagement by the business management and policymaking sectors of society (Apple, 1989). Articulation of these conditions is possible by utilizing critical literacy policy analysis.

Foucault's work is helpful for looking at discourses to discern the relationships between power, truth, and the self, to discern how individuals become the object and subject of discourses. Discourses constructed within government to legislate educational programs are powerful because they are legitimized through social practices emanating from the sovereign state. In their sovereignty, governments and social institutions produce knowledge with truth-values. When individuals interact within the social realm, the self becomes both an object and subject of discourses of truth. The truth of science and legitimized knowledge, with the imprimatur of official policy, consequently affects social actors, sorting them, judging them, and regulating them as deemed most appropriate by the "true" discourses.

The legitimation of certain discourses grants more power to some knowledge than others. These knowledge-power relations are defined and redefined as the conditions in the environment (i.e., the sociocultural political domain) create the limits of what constitutes a phenomenon like literacy. In the case of literacy, the traditions of knowledge and power serve to uphold the legitimacy of cultural and human capital literacies. The school is the location that exerts control as it acts upon students as objects. In turn, the students become subjects through internalization of the values specified by pervasive discourses and reenact the power-knowledge relations in the manner specified. Collins describes the school's relationship to literacy:

> Schools show in stark relief the association between symbolically valued literate traditions, mechanisms of social control, and the shape of what gets called "literacy" as a field wherein power is deployed in particular discursive practices. (Collins, J., 1991, p. 230)

**Shifting Paradigms: Modern to Postmodern Literacy**

Shifting the literacy teaching paradigm from one of skills practices to one of political engagement involves a paradigm shift for classroom teachers whose school literacies are formed by basic skills, textbooks, and testing competence. The problem with making the paradigm shift from modern to postmodern literacy practices is that people find change difficult and the present system is still operating in the modern mode. Looking to the history of teacher education, the limitations of literacy development are apparent in the control of the teacher subject through official discourses.

## Some History of Teacher Education

This section will explore historical discourses of teacher education, particularly within the contexts of centralization of power driving educational reform. After discussion of the reform of teacher preparation within the contexts of national reform movements, I will shift to a postmodern paradigm to interrelate how poststructural, critical, and feminist interpretations of power and knowledge relations enable critique of the taken-for-granted history of the profession of teaching. Through interpretation of linguistic and textual politics, with tools of social, anthropological, curricular, and cultural critique, educators can see undemocratic schooling practices. Such critique involves rereading our educational world.

Some of the areas pertinent to the way that we begin to make sense of the postmodern paradigm's relevance to education look to the origins of the politics of teacher education. Critical readings of official pedagogical discourses emanating from policymakers at the national and state levels enable better understanding of the perpetuation of undemocratic schooling practices.

Pertinent to comprehension of social and educational inequities is a discussion of three areas related to the professionalization of teachers. The first area of discussion is (1) the growth of the profession of teaching as it is depicted historically, (2) the concept of the reflective practitioner or public intellectual, and (3) teachers as critical researchers.

**Historical Depiction of Teacher Professionalism**

Teacher education, now grounded within the disciplines of the liberal arts, social sciences, and sciences, was an entity unto itself in the era of the normal school. Teacher education later grew alongside educational psychology and administration, usually subjugated as "practice" to the scientific theory of educational psychology and the management of educational administration.

Professional organizations, otherwise known as teacher unions, have promoted professionalization of teachers vigorously since the last century (Spring, 1996; Tozer et al., 1998). Two such organizations are the National Education Association and the American Federation of Teachers (Spring, 1996). Inasmuch as a rise in status would indicate a raise in salary, most teachers are in favor of professionalization. Institutions that seek public and governmental approval and accreditation of their professional educator programs also favor such professionalization that essentially legitimizes their programs. However, despite the rhetoric about professionalization, the efforts of teacher organizations, and the good work that many teachers do, teachers are still managed, reformed, and essentially have little decision-making power about school administration or the curriculum (Labaree, 1992; Zeichner, 1996a; Tozer et al., 1998; Spring, 1996).

Accordingly, the labor of the teacher, unlike the work of lawyers and doctors, is not thought of as professional. Despite the fact that teachers may have a calling and be committed, they lack autonomy, as well as rigorous requirements determined by peer review, training, and an esoteric knowledge base that would serve to enhance their public image (Weber, 1947, cited in Labaree, 1992, 1995). According to the criteria set forth by Etzioni (1969), teachers possess characteristics of semiprofessionals. Characteristically, teachers, like other semiprofessionals, possess five qualities: (1) they are white-collar workers; (2) they provide services; (3) they are subject to supervision; (4) they are salaried bureaucrats; and (5) they lack standards of excellence such as those of the medical and legal establishments. Although teachers perform a valuable role in society, they are not as well respected in the United States as they are elsewhere in the world (Spring, 1996), nor are they as well respected in this culture as doctors and lawyers are.

Labaree (1992, 1995) indicates that the professionalization track of most fields is neither well defined nor necessarily permanent. The modern paradigm of teacher education arose from changes centered on the rise of the science of teaching. As in other disciplines, a science of teaching relies on establishing, developing, codifying, and transmitting such specialized knowledge of professional education and clinical practice (Foucault, 1972; Labaree, 1992; Bennett, 1986b; Smith, 1980). Historians (Tyack, 1966; Cremin, 1964) have described the development of teacher education as part of the rationalization movement that also helped to formulate the disciplines of educational administration and educational psychology. Tyack's and Cremin's interpretations of the history of education in this country elaborate on Industrial Age centralization that carried over from business to education. As modernism embraced centralization, concentration, accumulation, efficiency, and speed, many small schools consolidated into larger more bureaucratic ones, leading to the development of "scientific" management or Taylorization in schools (Kincheloe, 1995). One way that management is realized is through raising standards.

**Raising Standards**

Although public school teachers have always been scrutinized to assure that they taught appropriate subject matter acceptably, management of teachers and curriculum through standards came about gradually and has increased over the years. As late as 1917, about half of the nation's elementary and secondary teachers had no more than four years of education beyond eighth grade and had no special professional preparation for their work (Haney, 1990, p. 46). As secondary school attendance became compulsory, secondary teachers were required to attend college or university in order to qualify for high school teaching positions. With the need for more training and expertise beyond the normal school came the development of teachers' colleges. In the normal school, specialized bodies of knowledge were taught, yet standards were never universal.

As initiated by Horace Mann in Massachusetts in the nineteenth century, standards and a moral code of behavior were to be learned in the normal schools as presented by the state and enforced within local districts. Many normal schools became state colleges of education and prepared teachers for a century (Tozer, Violas, & Senese, 1998; Haney, 1990). During the 1950s, over 100 institutions specialized in teacher education

(Haney, 1990, p. 48). By 1967, only 9 state teacher colleges remained along with 1,200 nationwide colleges and universities offering teacher preparation programs (p. 48).

With this growth of the bureaucracy and specialized fields and disciplines within institutions of higher learning, teacher education of the late nineteenth and early twentieth centuries entered into the university within the realm of the liberal arts and eventually social sciences (Labaree, 1992; Tozer et al., 1998; Cremin, 1964). As a part of social sciences or humanities, education courses functioned often as an add-on to programs in the sciences, mathematics, liberal arts, or the humanities. The requirements for teacher education were largely determined by university admission requirements (Haney, 1990).

However, as Tozer, Violas, and Senese discussed, within specific centers of educational expertise, such as Teachers College, Columbia, for example, rigorous programs developed with specific missions for the betterment of public life. At Columbia in the 1930s, programs advocated distinctive preparation of teachers in the history, philosophy, and sociology of education. With this background, it was argued, teachers could become "educational statesmen capable of leading the schools and their students to the forefront of democratic change in America" (Tozer et al., 1998, p. 290).

A strong populist movement around the time of the Great Depression, fueled by John Dewey and the Progressive Education Movement,[1] emphasized the philosophical purposes of education for democracy over the education of workers. However, the strength of business, capital, patriotism, and social efficiency prevailed to put educational emphasis on worker-citizen preparation, where the emphasis remains, particularly in times of great economic change (Goodman, 1995a; Spring, 1980, 1996).

The vicissitudes of the United States' political economy has had great effects on teacher education, the teaching profession, and education in general. Through a series of reforms from 1940 through 1990, we see a growing effort of national government control over the teaching profession as a "managed occupation" (Tozer et al., 1998). Without rigid and competitive admission requirements, colleges of education were perceived less capable of upholding reputations of rigor or high quality control than schools that specialized in postbaccalaureate education of lawyers, doctors, or architects, for example. Because colleges of education are not perceived to be as rigorous as other professional development schools, they have come under attack by the national and state governments and media as well as national organizations and policymaking institutions, particularly since the 1950s. In the early 1950s, Arthur Bestor's *Educational Wastelands* attacked the curricula; after the launching of Sputnik by the Russians, Bestor called for "greater academic rigor," "ability grouping," and increased emphasis on math, science, and vocational training. James B. Conant's *The Education of American Teachers* and James D. Koerner's *The Miseducation of American Teachers* advised teacher preparation in academic content areas (Tozer, Violas, & Senese, 1998)

Most recently, since *A Nation at Risk* (U.S. Dept. of Education, 1983), several general public surveys, and much media attention, the ethos in the public arena that led to *A Nation at Risk* and that also emanates from the report is affected by a general consensus that teachers should be of a higher caliber intellectually (as measured by SAT scores and assessment instruments) and policy has followed to improve educators' abilities in three ways: (1) more rigorous entrance standards, (2) more in-service teacher evaluations, and (3) more focus on science, math, literacy, and technological training for both pre-service and in-service teachers.

In teacher education programs, prospective teachers studied more education courses over the last half-century, up until the last few years (Haney, 1990, p. 51). In the late 1960s, an equivalence of 10% to 30% of required semester course hours for an undergraduate degree were done in professional education courses (Haney, p. 51). Between 15 and 36 hours of education courses were requisite for elementary teacher certification and between 12 and 29 hours for secondary certification (Haney, p. 51). With the new focus on discipline knowledge bases, students of education are required to major in their areas of expertise and take fewer education courses.

According to present requirements for successful completion of programs, students' grade evaluations in other course work are more vital to their success than their assessments in education courses. Education courses are often thought to be not serious, unacademic, or unscientific. Yet, students' performances in their areas of concentration do not necessarily correspond with their teaching abilities (Haney, 1990). Educators who develop critical and feminist insights can make some sense of the negativity toward teacher education when they understand that elites formulate educational policy and that those studying to be teachers and teacher-workers are obligated to follow those policies.

## Grids of Regularity and Teacher Education

Four issues at the heart of the debate about professionalism in teacher education as outlined by Tozer, Violas, and Senese (1998) include the following:

1) Preparation and licensure of practitioners for a mass profession that must serve the entire population, not just private clients with specific needs;
2) The consequences of public funding of the profession as compared with private funding;
3) The role and status of women in the profession;
4) The tension between public and professional control over teaching practice and what will be accepted as the specialized knowledge base of the profession. (p. 288)

## Serving the Entire Population

In regard to Tozer, Violas, and Senese's first point, licensure of teachers must run the gamut of public needs rather than focus on individual or specific clients' requirements. The "public" involvement in teacher education reform is evidenced in Prestine's description of the Wisconsin state education agency and the flagship campus university education department (1991). Prestine's work describes the conflicts and negotiations that endured over time between the state and the most powerful university educational department in the state. She explores how the give-and-take and bargain-striking aspects of political systems must help explain teacher education reform, yet may not necessarily effect needed or desired changes in educational programs.

Zeichner (1996a) explains that more professional training and hollow empowerment of teachers support undemocratic approaches to education. One critique of hypothetically empowering teachers is that they would not necessarily promote democratic education because teachers with more power can more adeptly exclude parental and other community input into the curriculum. Also, powerful teachers might not necessarily be concerned about the larger social environment which must be understood and transformed if education is meant to inspire democratic social reforms.

With respect to Tozer et al.'s second point on attention to public funding as a basic part of teacher professionalization, more basic economic concerns of sustaining schools in many parts of the country, as discussed in Kozol's *Savage Inequalities* (1991), promote expenditure on buildings, upkeep, resources, and technology, often with teachers' salaries not among the top priorities. In this sense, the public will be responsible for allowing enriched salaries for teachers. With shrinking resources, threats of legislative rollbacks of property tax revenues, and a cynical view of teachers' abilities to teach and make a difference in education as measured by test-score achievement of students, the public's interest in endowing public educators with more respect and money is not great. While public funding is waning, private funding of schools has gained more prominence as foundation money is sought for various educational projects. As ignited during the Reagan era, choice is promoted in a seemingly democratic attempt to equalize educational opportunities. Through the promotion of vouchers for choice and charter schools within the existing educational structure, students are ostensibly given the opportunity to escape poor schooling. Such a cause shifts the interpretation of how public money is to be spent and even clouds the distinction between public and private money.

Furthermore, few teachers in impoverished urban, suburban, and rural school systems across the country have the opportunities to find better schools in which to teach. In a truly democratized nation, all students and teachers deserve not only adequate but also equitable learning and working environments. Formerly and presently, the treatment of teachers and students within highly disparate spectrums of resource allocation is undemocratic. Additionally, giving magnet schools and specially funded academies within schools more funds and resources and special treatment takes funding away from other students in the same setting. A serious overhaul of educational funding to all American citizens is promoted by Kozol (1991) and postmodern proponents of democratic educational policies.

Undemocratic practices are also relevant to Tozer et al.'s third major concern about the feminization of the educational field. The discussion in this research looks at various ways that women's roles in education have led to and perpetuate low status for women and the profession (Apple, 1989; Stone, 1994). Horace Mann, the father of the common school, promoted the feminization of the teaching field ostensibly to harness the nurturing aspects of women's characters to enhance students', especially urban students', citizenship, socialization, and economic opportunities through compulsory state education (Spring, 1996; Tozer et al., 1998). He also developed the concept of the normal school that would prepare teacher candidates with the proper moral and subject matter knowledge deemed appropriate by conservative political forces including business, the ruling elite, and those intent on building and promoting nationalism in public schools. His rationale for female teachers was well accepted by the business community as female teachers earned one-third the salary of male teachers and could be easily controlled.

Since the inception of women as the primary labor force in the teaching field and the rise of male domination within the field of educational administration, female teachers have remained subject to the whims of rational, scientific, and industrial modes of school management (Cremin, 1964; "Clinton Promotes," 1997, February 11; AAUW, 1995; Sowell, 1996). Their salaries remain lower than their male counterparts, they are not consulted about educational policies, and the criteria of high-quality performance on their parts is determined by elite policymakers. Understanding the international subordination of women and the recent and ongoing impoverization of women informs critical and feminist perspectives on the necessity to promote women's economic and political welfare. In most countries, as in the United States, decisions about knowledge descend from the top of governmental hierarchy downward to teachers and students. Yet, it is at the bottom of the hierarchy where the policies are enacted and, thus, that is where they should originate (Freire, 1970; Macedo, 1994a,b).

## Postmodern Teacher Education

The next topic of discussion about teacher preparation will look to postmodern teacher preparation, including teachers as reflective practitioners and teachers as researchers. In the following sections, I will look to three discourses of teacher empowerment that have excited debate within academic discussions of teacher education. They are dialectical to the discourses of the state, representing a reaction to the power of science as it is tied to the power of the state through teacher power or empowerment (Popkewitz, 1991; Cochran-Smith, 1991; Edelsky 1991a).

## The Reflective Practitioner or Public Intellectual

Zeichner attributes an international movement developing under the banner "reflection" to a reaction against attempts by government to centralize control of schools and teacher education. As he and others have noted, the rhetoric about teacher empowerment has been hollow as discourses of reform have determined the teacher subject rather than the teacher subject determining social conscience about reproducing inequality through teaching practices (Tozer, Violas, & Senese, 1998; Spring, 1996; Carnegie Task Force on Teaching as a Profession, 1986; Labaree, 1992). Teachers as reflective practitioners must be cognizant of the politics of the greater social system in which schools function to educate future generations (Giroux, 1988b, 1991; Schon, 1983; Zeichner, 1996a). Teachers as intellectuals who practice reflective practitioning become engaged in social transformation through work in classrooms and communities, as opposed to teachers as technocrats who follow regulations, questioning policy little.

## Teachers as Critical Researchers

The concept of teachers as critical change agents in this sense does not guarantee teachers higher salaries. More importantly, postmodern literacy that engages teachers in understanding their role in social reproduction through promotion of literacy as an education in the classical curriculum or in a purely basic skill curriculum can promote social and political change. Critical and feminist literacy enhance understanding the role of teachers' work to society. With postmodern teacher education, educators can better appreciate the politics of schooling that create inequities which subjugate women and other groups economically and politically (Kincheloe, 1993, 1995; Grumet, 1989; Patterson, Stansell, & Lee, 1990; Knoblauch and Brannon, 1993). Understanding how teachers and educational practices have contributed to socialization in the past helps us to promote positive change through political interest generated by critical and feminist literacies.

The discussion about reflective teaching, its requirements, and its potential effects runs counter to what is expected of technocratic teachers. Whereas the technocratic teacher practitioner evaluates behavioristically, focuses on experience-based initiative, looks to the success of emotional intuition of rule following, follows analytical procedural processes, and becomes a self-actualized expert, the postmodern teacher with critical and feminist literacy and understanding follows a different course (Kincheloe, 1993, pp. 200–201). Reflective practitioners who are critically reflective employ what Schon has called reflective conversation with the situation (1983), what Zeichner has called reflection as a political act (1996a), what Freire called education as the practice of freedom (1973), and what Kincheloe and Steinberg refer to as postformal teaching (1993).

## Postformal Practitioners

For Kincheloe, postformal teacher thinking enables heuristic or interpretive abilities and informed decision making on the teacher's part. However, this "informed"-ness is not limited to knowledge base and professionalizing features that move to self-aggrandize the teacher. On the contrary, the teacher becomes a constructor of knowledge for social transformation through postformal ways of making sense of schooling. Kincheloe and Steinberg (1993) characterize postformal teaching in some concrete attributes that have influenced postmodern educators. The influences have come from critical, feminist, phenomenologist, humanistic, and democratic communitarian views of educational policy:

1) Inquiry oriented—The inquiry-orientation of teacher education becomes a paradigm of reference from which action research is possible. Teachers who are research-oriented teach their students to do the same kinds of questioning that becomes the basis of problem posing for everyday life experience, the larger society, and the curriculum.

2) Socially contextualized and informed about power—The postformal teacher is aware of the power and knowledge relations that have developed worker and elite education. Engaged in social awareness and its relationship to schooling, the teacher helps students to understand the ways in which thinking is guided through the educative process and how to monitor what it is that leads to social beliefs.

3) Grounded on a commitment to world making—With critical and feminist understanding, the postformal teacher or postmodern literate instructor helps students understand how knowledge is produced by experts and in contrast constructed by teachers and students.

4) Dedicated to an art of improvisation—Thinking in action is necessary to confront the many unique insights and abilities that students bring to school. Teaching artistry derives from flexibility to help students learn through experiences that provide little risk.

5) Dedicated to the cultivation of situated participation—Urging and encouraging universal participation in the culture of the classroom, the critically literate postmodern teacher engages the students in genuine dialogue. Such teaching involves setting the stage for the students' words, concerns, and experiences, rather than silencing them.

6) Concerned with critical self- and social-reflection—Such work involves understanding how we speak to each other in the classroom. For example—whose voice is preferred? ignored? sublimated? Ultimately students would question, Who benefits from seeing the world as the school reveals it to us? What do we need to know? From whose perspective am I formulating my opinions about sociopolitics? What do social politics have to do with education?

7) Concerned with democratic self-directed education—The vigilant and flexible postmodern educator helps students develop their rights to speak, to disagree, to point out teacher errors, and to be engaged in their own education.

8) Cognizant of multicultural educational perspectives—By thinking about race, class, and gender differences, teachers stay informed about the growth of student interrelationships to be sure that dominant perspectives do not marginalize those in the minority or those who are usually silenced in typical classroom routines. The majority opinions should be informed by others who may agree to disagree with majority thought.

9) Geared toward action—A postmodern educator averts the propensity of authority to determine meaning for students by inspiring them to take action. The education process begins with thought and moves to understand the implication of thought in action as determined by problems posed by students.

10) Guided by human consideration—Rather than stopping with technical and logical comprehension, the ethic of care from feminist understanding motivates the postmodern teacher. Emotional reflection is encouraged and valued. (Kincheloe, 1993, pp. 201–203)

## Teacher Professionalization and Public Issues

### Expert Knowledge

Several attributes of American ideology contribute to the deep respect that powerful and knowledgeable people hold for expert knowledge. Early American liberal ideology was highly influenced by faith in reason, natural law, and scientific knowledge. As discussed throughout this consideration of the discourses as formulations for truth at given times and places in history, a critical stance enables the deconstruction of scientific discourse, particularly as it applies to enhancing teacher qualification and professionalism as compared to other professionals.

The expert knowledge of medicine and law has been carefully protected from the public. Medical and legal expert knowledge, guarded by their respective communities and educational institutions, did not extend into the public domain. Just the opposite is true for teacher knowledge. In fact, a popular view of what qualifications are required of a teacher includes very little that the average person does not possess, except perhaps for content-specific knowledge. Labaree (1992) and Zeichner (1996a) discuss the differentiation between the expert knowledge of the higher education community and that knowledge possessed and utilized by teachers in classrooms. The former has been granted more credence and prestige than the knowledge of teachers who practice in classrooms. Such a view leads to marginalization of teacher voices in policymaking and educational research. The argument for expert knowledge is that teachers who possess this knowledge may pass it to their students. Since this knowledge is deemed most important by official policymakers, it is scientific; and since it is scientific, it may be measured through student achievement.

As discussed throughout this document, such successful education might extend knowledge of facts to students yet not avail them of their creative and analytical abilities. Critical thinking and analysis are rarely extended to include political potential through critical and feminist literacy practices. At the expense of the many average and below-average students marginalized from the "official knowledge" content areas of the curriculum, discipline or departmental or subject knowledge becomes the mainstay of education. From a curriculum reconceptualization as promoted by Pinar and Grumet (in Kincheloe & Steinberg, 1995), learning the history and culture of European androcentric ancestors de-emphasizes the majority of the students who are Asian, Hispanic, Native, and African Americans; women; and homosexuals. In the rhetoric of educational policy and reform, the minority of the population (white males) is referred to as the majority, whereas the majority of people (women and all of those nonwhite males) are referred to as minorities. The back-to-basics curriculum teaches little or nothing about the majority of the United States population.

Pinar (1995) holds that the insistence on teaching a classical curriculum that is comprised of expert knowledge serves neither European white males nor everyone else (the others) efficiently. Such knowledge is not basic to life, although educational policymakers attempt to force and control literacy development about such expert knowledge as "the basics" of the curriculum. Expert knowledge as advocated in a scientific, mathematical, and technological-focused curriculum does not teach us who we are, nor does it address the power relations that we possess in relation to each other. By not teaching about others besides Eurocentric male personalities and their accomplishments, all groups, including white males, suffer as the education system perpetuates its traditional inequities.

Yet, the dominant image of the white male reigns supreme in politics, media, business, and schools. When expert knowledge labels name others and represent them as inferior or undesirable anomalies to be studied and altered, representation becomes pernicious. Extensive studies and discourse about disinterested minority student populations, at-risk students, single-parent households, unwed teen parents, and illiterates sustain racist, sexist, and classist behavior in classrooms and in society (Scheurich, 1994). Thus, expert knowledge tends to support many negatives in schooling.

As a product of modernism, expert knowledge needed to be an effective teacher is reinforced in pre-service teachers' concentrations in subject/content areas and knowledge bases. Adhering to the limitations of rational and linear traditional science and traditions promotes measurable ways of knowing. Kliebard (1995) describes the seeds of social scientific knowledge and educational reform as part of the progressive liberal ideology of the late nineteenth century. Effective practices as promoted by social scientists in education "may be embodied in generalizations and rules of action, even though the prescribed practices may represent only some degree of probability for success or may be qualified by particular circumstances" (Kliebard, 1995, p. 297). The knowledge base, in Kliebard's deference to Deweyan thought, cannot be assumed to be transferable from the researchers' scientific domain into teacher practice in the field. Knowledge bases assume that teachers are technical production managers in this manner. Moving toward a more postmodern practice of education informs us that the scientific, modernistic metaphor of factory-model schooling is no longer appropriate.

## Rationalization Promotes Depoliticalization of Teacher Education

With the focus on a knowledge base, the learner and the social setting are omitted from the teaching dynamic. The most effective relationship formed between learners and the teacher is emotional, affective, and therefore often deemed unscientific. The belief in a knowledge base from which teachers draw and dispense their knowledge to students sidesteps social and theoretical ways of thinking about social production and reproduction in schools. Discussion of ideology moves far into the background and foregrounded is a set of competencies and skills which students must master.

In the scientific view, if the teacher is competent, he or she will attain the goals of the designated objectives. And in order to assure such success, the state and local district will hold him or her accountable to the tasks. The professional knowledge of teachers is discounted. When students and teachers attain the objectives of the assessment instrument, the criteria are readopted. (Texas state policymakers have recently approved the Texas Essential Knowledge Skills curriculum to replace the Essential Elements that preceded it.) As long as teachers' work is dictated to them, professionalism will remain elusive. Although an internship as it exists in the legal and medical professions is being discussed in education, educational training is still not regarded as something that should endure more than four to five years of study.

## Teacher Education Remains an Undergraduate Program

Despite the attempts by the Holmes Group (1990) and a national effort to establish a school of pedagogy (Smith, 1980), as well as efforts by other groups to make teacher education into a five-year advanced degree credential, those attempts have not succeeded (Haney, 1990). Smith (1980) argues that teacher education autonomy has not resurfaced since the normal school was subsumed by liberal arts colleges and that "the normal schools, however poorly staffed and financed, were devoted solely to the preparation of teachers and more nearly met other criteria of professional institutions than the pedagogical colleges today" (p. 12). His premise is that the upgrading of the normal school caused the demise of the "single-purpose, autonomous, professional school for the education of teachers" (p. 13).

Lacking autonomy and training that are considered prestigious and therefore worthy of professional status, the teacher is accountable to communities, school boards, textbook committees, and a whole array of power holders. Yet, as Smith (1980), Labaree (1992), Spring (1996), and Crowell (1989) have pointed out, it is implicit, in restructuring professional teacher education and the work roles of teachers, that formal knowledge and workplace autonomy define and legitimate the power of educators within the field of pedagogy. Nonetheless, evidence of the vulnerability of teacher professionalism can be detected in the many reforms, mandates, and policies that are formulated and implemented without decision-making input from teachers (U.S. Department of Education, 1983; U.S. Department of Education, 1993a,b).

In the case of status afforded teachers, although hardly analogous to the professional position of physicians in our society, Labaree (1992) believes that the professionalization of teachers will have some effects on school restructuring. However, the teacher as authority figure and reorganization of schools around teacher autonomy (Labaree, 1992, p. 127) are not likely outcomes of school and teacher education restructuring. On the other hand, the status of higher education professors of education has risen, particularly in those universities that are ranked as research institutions, again indicative of the power of scientific knowledge to attain and retain prestige.

In the former teacher colleges, however, the status of education professors is not as high as that of professors in other disciplines (Labaree, 1992). Yet, the benefit of extending some prestige to a few of the professors at the more well-respected universities has been helpful for gaining national attention for improving teacher preparation. Consider the effect that Goodlad's *Teachers for Our Nation's Schools* (1990), *Places Where Teachers Are Taught* (Goodlad, Soder, & Sirotnik, 1990), and various other works have prompted in colleges of education. Looking to the ethics of teaching, Goodlad's ten precepts have inspired informed conscientization about the kinds of slipshod programs that are established alongside regular programs as expedients when teachers are in demand. His cautionary message is that we would not allow a doctor to practice medicine with only an abbreviated training program. Furthermore, great disparities exist in the respect afforded professors in research versus teacher-training institutions. And as Tozer, Violas, and Senese (1998) indicate, teacher status can divorce teachers from the ethical nature of their work.

## Moving Educators Toward Activism

Some postmodern theorists have encouraged ethical behavior in educators, particularly that which allows teachers to be activists as well as educators. Cochran-Smith (1991) proposed that pre-service teachers who aspired to be social transformationalists should look to experienced teachers who are struggling to reform their own classrooms, schools, and communities. Citing Antonio Gramsci, Cochran-Smith calls on all teachers as responsible individuals to be accountable for the role they play in a larger (or smaller) political struggle (p. 279).

> [Teachers] must be asked to account for the manner in which [they have] fulfilled the task that life has set [them] and continues to set [them] day by day; [they] must be asked to account for what [they have] done, but especially for what [they have not done]. . . . It is time that events should be seen to be the intelligent work of [teachers] and not the products of chance or fatality. And so it is time to have done with the indifferent among us, the skeptics, the people who profit from the small good procured by the activity of a few, but who refuse to take responsibility for the great evil that is allowed to develop and come to pass because of their absence from the struggle. (Gramsci, 1916, in Cochran-Smith, 1991, p. 279)

My first understanding of a political struggle involved in my own education was the luxury I had as compared to my parents, who did not possess finances and time to be educated. They had to work. My second understanding of that political struggle became particularly clear when I taught in an inner-city high school my first year out of university. I was equipped with neither social theory nor the skills needed to tap my students' backgrounds, upon which literacy could be built. I taught them textbook literacy as I had been taught, but they had more difficulty with it and less interest in such literacy. This was the beginning of my understanding of the need to transform literacy to the political struggles of the learners, although they may not be aware of it in such terms until some later point.

**Articulating Oppression—Women and Teaching**

The following discussion responds to the third attribute of the educational environment that Tozer et al. (1998) discussed as the feminization of teaching. A largely ignored political struggle of teaching and its respective lack of professional esteem is explained by the fact that teachers are predominantly women (Spring, 1996; Tozer et al., 1998; Grumet, 1988). As the educational bureaucracy became inextricable from state bureaucracy, educational administrators with the knowledge of business management and educational psychologists with the credence of science became more respected. Teacher educators and public school teachers who educate the majority of students in the nation never gained status. In all of the educational documents that propose raising literacy standards, that seek to make teachers more qualified, and that propose to professionalize the vocation of teaching, the issue of women's political power is not raised. The knowledge and power relations of teachers to the official pedagogical discourses are excluded. Teachers' influence on educational policy is restricted. Blue-ribbon commissions have been traditionally comprised of men (AAUW, 1995; Shakeshaft, 1986; Grumet, 1989). Awareness of gendered difference and the inequities that result from it in social practices can come about with a process of reflection and reflexivity. A reflective view helps us better understand the reproductive role of women. The reproduction of social life in schools through the work of women teachers is not only based on a factory model; it is also part of the feminine project to nurture new generations through nature. It is

> [an] art that women who teach must bring to our work, studying the relations in which we came to form, reflecting on those relations and creating new forms in the curricula that express our appreciation, our critique and transformation of the processes that constituted our subjectivity (our identities) and objectivity (the world we share). (Grumet, 1988, p. 190)

For Grumet, it is most important in the reconceptualization of the curriculum to furnish the empty house of education with feminist theory. The connectedness of life experiences with community, family, and institutions, as understood in feminist theory, would not allow a woman to say, "I made myself." Feminists including Grumet say that such an argument is an individualistic, competitive attitude that feminists understand as being mythical because of the cooperation necessary within a whole community of people to assure individual success.

## Reconceptualizing the Curriculum of Teacher Education

Unfortunately, the discussion of professionalization of teaching within the frameworks of social structure evades several more important issues. First, the teacher as an intellectual who works to transform the classroom, school, and society is bypassed by the discussion of teacher professionalization based on the technocratic teacher who masters a knowledge base and develops curriculum accordingly, controls classrooms, attains high evaluations, and helps students to perform well on competency tests. Schon's (1983) teacher as reflective practitioner within the postmodern framework can recognize and pass on to students the importance of the revolution of science and new understandings of knowledge, as well as literacy and its relation to power and knowledge. Yet, the teacher education programs proposed by the myriad of reforms seek to develop technocrats who do not address ideas beyond the limited borders of specialized sciences or disciplines. Positivism as it dictates bodies of knowledge or the limits of research, particularly, has produced internal censorship of educational issues of knowledge as determined by the exercise of power (Bourdieu, 1977; Foucault, 1972; Labaree, 1992).

In 1989, reconceptualists in the *Journal of Teacher Education* announced what was needed in order to align the curriculum of teacher education and public schools with the work that has become well known in postmodern academic circles. Shaker and Kridel pointed to the bankruptcy of present efforts to go far enough in reforming education. Grumet called for more theory in order to give pre-service teachers many windows through which to view social reproduction in schools. Pinar denounced the feeble attempts to make teacher education professional in comparison to other professions. Reconceptualizing literacy and making teacher education more critical are necessary to align teacher education with contemporary anthropological, sociological, and psychological insight into existing oppressive structures of education.

## Reconciling Professionalism and Social Critique

The attainment of teacher professionalization without critical and feminist pedagogical components will not necessarily in and of itself produce only positive results. Several viewpoints on such an outcome vary from different political perspectives. For example, Marxists see two such scenarios—one being an extension of class control by educators and a second as a euphemism for proletarianism (Labaree, 1992, p. 128). Apple (1989) sees the interconnectedness of ideology and the curriculum as a way to view the role of teachers in social production.

A lack of awareness of the power of ideological control or hegemony by the narrow definition of what counts as knowledge does not support a critical approach or transformative effort from teachers. A Foucaultian consideration of such a professionalization movement indicates both a technology and a measure of disciplinary biopower and knowledge to extend social control (Foucault, 1972, 1965, 1978). Bernstein's assessment supports Foucault's notion of harnessing biopower through the state's pedagogic discourse. His view is that "The training requirements of agents (especially dominant agents) within the field of symbolic control will influence the 'what' and the 'how' [of teacher preparation]" (1990, p. 194). Prepared in this manner, the teacher is in a powerful position to teach in a manner deemed ideologically acceptable by the state.

Weberian sociologists see the negative effects of teacher professionalism within these contexts as a mechanism for self-interest (Labaree, 1992). Labaree argues that the teacher professionalization movement can have a detrimental effect on "U.S. education, and on the teachers, students, and citizens who have a stake in seeing this institution carry out its goals effectively" (p. 125).

Two explanations for his assessment are the augmentation of the influence of the university over primary and secondary schooling by reinforcing the authority of those who teach teachers and the increase in the rationalization or positivistic nature of a research-based model of teaching practice (Labaree, 1992, p. 125). Labaree feels that upholding the role of the expert is not a move toward democracy in schools, but rather away from it (Kincheloe, 1993, 1995).

## Teacher Education: A Power Struggle

The area of teacher education reform, besides being rife with projects, is also still widely contested terrain (McWilliam, 1994; Britzman, 1986; Zeichner, Melnick, & Gomez, 1996; Stringer et al., 1997). The politics of teacher education reform not only is a college departmental issue, but also has been established as a state concern (Prestine, 1991). Prestine's work describes the negotiations that endured over time between the flagship campus education department at Madison, Wisconsin, and the state board of education. Her account exemplifies how state politics influence teacher education reform in the ways policies are formulated.

Thus, the special interests of teachers and teacher education institutions are not alone in legitimating the professional status of teachers. Such an uplifting of the profession would also require public approval. The public would have to acquiesce to such a movement, thereby producing a double result of teachers' feeling some benefit from the movement and the public's legitimizing the movement through the reward system. As expressed by several commissions that have supported more excellence in education, the teacher population is responsible for the link between social efficiency, perpetuating the structures and functions of society and preserving an American culture, in addition to raising the gross national product as the United States competes within a global economy (U.S. Department of Labor, 1987; U.S. Department of Education, 1983, 1984a,b).

**A Postmodern Perspective of Teacher Educational Reform**

To comprehend how teachers, policies, and technologies of control construct students as subjects, we must ask how the existing knowledge-power relations construct teachers. It appears that, beyond the rhetoric of professionalization of teaching through higher standards, more rigorous and practical training, and technological education, human capital literacy and education are the foremost objectives of both national and state policymakers. The rapid growth and evolution of technology have necessitated in-service and pre-service teacher education for technological pedagogical skills (U.S. Department of Education, 1983, 1984a,b). This social revolution, along with "Reaganomics" laissez-faire leadership of the 1980s, shifted educational focus on equity to market solutions that would displace government centralization and bureaucracy (Spring, 1996). Throughout the discussion of the failures of the educational system and the need to improve *both* teacher and public school education, the focus of several public discourses of human capital development requires that *both* the teacher and the student be technologically literate subjects as well as possess basic skills. Following Reagan, the Bush presidency looked ahead to the twenty-first century and marked the passage of the *National Literacy Act of 1991*, legislating that literacy be tied to the requirements of business. Although the first and second Clinton administrations employed rhetoric of opportunity, the focus of new educational policies is human capital literacy tied to modern technology as well as market concerns. Social and educational policies are intent on solving economic problems rather than social and human problems.

*Feminisms* propose various policies to voice women's concerns within academic, economic, and sociocultural domains of life. *Postmodern literacy* encompasses the precepts of critical and feminist theories. It enables voices to articulate the previously discussed problems associated with the feminization of teaching, its de-skilling, and its continued disparagement by the business management and policymaking sectors of society.

## Discourses of Human Capital Literacy

The official pedagogical discourse ties the professionalism of teachers to the needs of the state. The testing fetish that the United States is currently experiencing has sparked much discussion about the inadequacies of the state's competency test to measure the important kinds of learning that need to be going on in classrooms. Tying teacher evaluation to student scores on these reading, writing, and math competency tests is the newest development in a series of more recent attempts to link classroom work to the purposes of the power blocs in the state. The *National Literacy Act of 1991* reveals the actual legislation of literacy projects to respond to the needs and desires of the business community: "to enhance the literacy and basic skills of adults, to ensure that all adults in the United States acquire the basic skills necessary to function effectively and achieve the greatest possible opportunity in their work and in their lives" (p. 1). According to the text describing the background and need for such legislation, the measure was taken to formulate primarily "workforce literacy" through adult education (p. 10), provided for in a grant for national workforce literacy strategies that meet the criteria of basic skills training, that are specific to program offerings, and that make appropriate assessments of the literacy and basic skills required by business. According to the law, literacy goals recommend cooperative arrangements with other organizations involved in providing literacy and basic skills training, including adult education organizations, vocational education organizations, community and junior colleges, community-based organizations, state-level agencies, and private industry councils. These organizations would develop appropriate assessments of the literacy and basic skills needs of individual workers and the skill levels required and specified by business.

We see in this proposal for stronger links between literacy instruction and work the market incentives and neo-conservative ideology of the Reagan era. Such an outgrowth of scientific rationalization and technicization of teaching through a professionalized teaching force, in the words of Labaree, "pushes technical questions into the foreground and political questions into the background as either unscientific or unproblematic" (1995, p. 148). The contested terrain of curriculum, teacher preparation, and what counts as literacy demands a critical view of literacy, particularly as the rise of testing (begun early in the twentieth century) led to a rise of the corporate state, tracking, and more testing. Again, the so-called scientific method as practiced by educational psychologists has been utilized to test basic literacy, thus allowing little time for students to develop more critical and feminist literacies.

The rationale is that more time spent in public school, more attention to basics and competencies, and more testing will result in better test scores that ought to reflect better prepared workers. The policy treatment for the illiteracy problem assumes that the domain of literacy instruction is related to time spent on task in school and accruing credit hours and more technological preparation (U.S. Dept. of Education, 1983, 1993a). As the state calls for more professionalism in teachers, it also has suggested tying teacher evaluations for accountability to student performance on exams. Thus, the professionalism is hollow because it does not allow autonomy and informed decision making about the best manner in which to teach and test students.

**Teacher Education Versus Postmodern Theory**

The movement to improve teacher education has been grounded in more requirements across the gamut of teacher licensure or credentialing requirements. In addition to more course requirements in specialty concentration, more fieldwork, and more competency tests, the field of education has not acknowledged social theory as a way to better pre-service teacher programs. If teachers are not educated about social theory, hegemony, ideology, and discourse analysis, they will likely be unable to deal with the complexity of knowledge and power relations present in the classroom. Looking to the work of European theorists cited in this work, as well as to feminists whose work will be reviewed in upcoming sections of information, we see that the concept of reconceptualizing teacher education depends in large part on redesigning the curriculum.

Curricular reconceptualists targeted scientific simplifications of disciplinary instruction for failing to address epistemology and evading interpretive inquiry in the 1980s. Shaker and Kridel (1989) trace a history of the use of the word "reconceptualist" to the 1960s and 1970s. They found that Klor applied the word to curricular change in the kindergarten through twelfth-grade classrooms during the mid-1960s and early 1970s, and they cite Pinar's use of the term also during the 1970s. Macdonald's elaboration of three camps emerging in curricular research is described by Shaker and Kridel as follows: One camp pursued efforts to develop curriculum, whereas the second worked to develop theory within a scientific and empirical framework, and a third approached unexplored theoretical arenas. The third stood on the "fringe of educational orthodoxy" (Shaker & Kridel, 1989, p. 3). What they found most disturbing was that colleges of education appear to be controlled by government in a manner that excludes popular culture from the curriculum (p. 6).

In the field of curriculum the Tyler rationale dominated during the 1940s until challenged by Schwab's ideas in the 1960s. Schwab promoted efforts to understand the curriculum as well as develop it (Pinar, 1989). Such efforts, according to Pinar, were "informed by history, political theory, aesthetic theory, phenomenology, gender research and feminist theory" (p. 9). The emphases of rethinking curricula emphasized the school as a microcosm of society and the school as experienced by the individual (Pinar, 1989).

As the Holmes Group began to reconceptualize teacher education at the outset of its mission, the concern was whether the new programs would become more standardized, behavioristic, and technical or manifest the critical and reflective content and goals of the curriculum (Pinar, 1989). Perhaps what has finally resulted is a relenting to the other political forces that ultimately determine what the complexion of teacher education is to be

(Labaree, 1995). However, the postmodern movement to redefine literacy is part of the contemporary attempt to re-envision the curriculum.

## Reconceptualizing Literacy and Curriculum

At this moment the reforms that pervade educational bureaucracies speak of children as "human resources" to be developed. Maxine Greene's feminist perspective informs this communitarian comment on the state of such educational focus in the following:

> This is a moment when great numbers of Americans find their expectations and hopes for their children being fed by the talk of "educational reform." Yet the reform reports speak of those very children as "human resources" for the maintaining of our nation's economic competitiveness and military primacy in the world. Of course we want to empower the young for meaningful work, we want to nurture the achievement of diverse literacies. But the world we inhabit is palpably deficient: there are unwarranted inequities, shattered communities, unfulfilled lives. We cannot help but hunger for traces of utopian visions of critical or dialectical engagements with social and economic realities. (Greene, 1986, pp. 427–428)

The need for more human capital literacy and technological skills expressly surfaces in the Information Age restructuring efforts. Undeniably, technological skills are necessary, as is some degree of cultural literacy to be able to function as an enfranchised citizen. The power relations within communities, schools, and classrooms are not elaborated in discourses of cultural or human capital literacy. The remainder of this research will attempt to connect critical and feminist pedagogy to the reading and writing instruction that goes unquestioned. These discourses are most important in their relationship to the democratic classroom, school, and society—a utopian vision. As far as my research has discerned, advances in more democratic visions of schooling have been made in the work of the reconceptualists, criticalists, and feminists. In some cases, their nomenclature distinction separates their purposes; however, many of their missions are similar—striving for more democratic ways of learning and using knowledge. Unfortunately, it is more by accident than by design that educators would encounter these radical politics of education—the primary reason being that they represent change, rather than adherence to status quo operations of schools.

It has not been until the rise of multicultural education classes and awarenesses that race, class, gender, or place has mattered to teachers as they taught reading and writing skills. As previously discussed, the focus on present-day practices built from Newtonian and Cartesian understandings of science and reality has led to technicist teacher education (Kincheloe, 1993). Jesse Goodman (1995a), in his historical treatment of the school reform and restructuring movements, says that much of the reform that has materialized has been articulated by the loudest voices. The technologists, in the ongoing reform movement of the recent past and present, have been most vocal. They represent the future of expansion of capitalist markets, both domestic and foreign. They do not question the merit of more technology for society; rather they assume that technology is good and that the power and knowledge relations among business, capital, and knowledge production are cemented in technocracy as the newest embodiment of progressive liberal ideology. Forming technocratic teachers who can in turn influence technocratic students is good for expanding the economy (Shutkin, 1994). Thus the utopian vision becomes blurred by the technological exigencies of entering the Information Age.

## Teacher Education Reform: Forming Teacher Subjects

Zeichner (1996a) asserts that the teacher education reform movement that has spanned the last decade has probably received more attention in this decade than in any other in its history. However, he argues that "despite the lofty rhetoric surrounding efforts to help teachers become more reflective, in reality reflective teacher education has done very little to foster genuine teacher development and to enhance teachers' roles in educational reform" (p. 201). Furthermore, he laments that "[a]n illusion of teacher development has often been created that has maintained in more subtle ways the subservient position of the teacher" (p. 201).

Omnipresent are signs that indeed the teacher is subservient. The historical and ongoing assumption that teaching is a second-class job because a majority of teachers have been and are female is not analyzed beyond the surface or seen as somehow rectifiable (Spring, 1996; Tozer et al., 1998). A state's passage of the new proposed curriculum without the input of the public or the teacher population at large assumes that the experts in lofty positions indeed know better than those who perform the work of teaching what is needed to make education "right" or correct.

Ongoing media coverage of teachers as somehow lacking and therefore needing more credentials is present in newspapers sometimes weekly and at least monthly. Even the band wagon of "reflective teacher" discourses is overflowing with ideological conflict as the definition of *reflective teacher* ranges from moral responsibility, to technical effectiveness, to behavioral mastery of prescribed practices, to critical science seen as a means toward emancipation and professional autonomy (Zeichner et al., 1996).

## Encouraging Skepticism in Teacher Education Through Policy Analysis

The crux of this research is a method for questioning mandates for human capital and cultural literacy development made in educational policy statements. Through discourse analysis, the meanings of words, the manner of their positioning, and their intention become suspect. Educators who have postmodern understandings of culture, values, and reason can look at the bigger picture with knowledge of social reproduction. They can understand that both cultural and human capital literacy are limited in what they enable individuals to think, read, and write. With postmodern literacy, teachers can assess what they learn in their practical and field service experiences as important, but they also see the value of theoretical orientation to analyze ideological orientation and management excluded by new teacher education (Spring, 1996). As teachers begin to decipher their relationship to hierarchical social structures, constructions of school, and social successes and failures, they can make decisions about teaching their students powerful literacies that enable looking at the world and word to determine the relationship between their own lives, their students' lives, and the written word (Freire, 1970).

The hegemonic forces forming the macrocosm in which arguments for cultural literacy and human capital literacy prevail inspire counter-discourses inviting educators to understand their roles in reproducing social inequities, as well as social and political obliviousness, that occur in classrooms. As teachers engage in postmodern thought, they will consider the post-Enlightenment scientific and modernist philosophies of social engineering descended from binary views of reality developed by Newtonian-Cartesian assumptions.

With understanding of present practices, a historical view of literacy policies deployed in *A Nation at Risk*, 1983; *America 2000*, 1991; *A*

*National Literacy Act of 1991*; and *Reaching the Goals: Goal 5*, 1993, within the present historical moment of restructuring education, becomes more meaningful. After the foundations of cultural and human capital literacy discourses are illustrated, they will provide the backdrop against which poststructuralist critical and feminist discourses will be discussed. Additionally, Freirean literacy as an emancipatory activity will be defined and contrasted with tenets of human capital and cultural literacies.

## Understanding Literacy as Modern and Postmodern

Modern literacy has its roots in the modernization movement originating in post-Enlightenment Europe. Intellectual thought espoused scientific objectivity as both its goal and the means to attain knowledge outside of the individual. Scientific literacy practices emerged from the moral and cultural beginnings of literacy instruction in the United States. At the turn of the nineteenth century, Noah Webster's addendum to his dictionary outlined morals that were acceptable in the formation of the American character. At the turn of the twentieth century, McGuffey readers were utilized to teach students both civic, moral, and literacy instruction. Now on the brink of the millennium, various textbooks, testing agendas, and basic skills determine the curriculum of literacy instruction. As Shannon depicts in *Broken Promises: Reading Instruction in Twentieth-Century America* (1989), teachers reify through enactment of the scripts of teacher guidebooks and textbooks the nature of modernistic literacy practices. Such coverage of reading and writing as that prescribed by textbook publishers and conservative coalitions of textbook adoption procedures proposes that the reading and writing curriculum follow the book, avoid controversy, and assure accountability as measured by tests of reading comprehension. This rigidity endures despite critical examination of the curriculum over the past twenty years bringing to the forefront of philosophical reconsiderations of education the non-neutrality of knowledge and the non-neutral manner in which knowledge is legitimized in the curriculum proper and in the hidden curriculum (Greene, 1986; Apple, 1989; Giroux, 1988a,b, 1991, 1993; Lankshear & McLaren, 1993; Kincheloe, 1993, 1995; Luke & Gore, 1992). Yet, scientific and positivistic manners of educational research and measurement reign despite the objection of relativists, who see knowledge as part of individual development rather than separate and existing outside of the individual, waiting to be attained.

## Banking Education as Formulated by Freire

At the heart of the "banking" view of education lies the argument of knowledge as something that can be deposited by the teacher into students' accounts and given back to the teacher to determine if the students' accounts measure up to what was dispensed to them (Freire, 1970). The important consideration of future educators within this framework is the role of the teacher as a reflective practitioner versus a technocrat. Postmodern literacy education leads to the former, and scientific or modern literacy enables the latter. The two approaches to learning and instruction come from opposite paradigms (ways of thinking about reality).

As federal and state governments describe a national crisis in education, economy, and the moral fabric of society, they cite dropout rates, low SAT scores, ethnic and racial inequities in education, and the low prestige of the teaching profession as contributing to the overall failure of education in the United States. An Enlightenment view of human progress seeks to rationalize the manner in which education should embrace technological progress as a means to harness the human intellect to a Hegelian view of social change and universal truth (Shutkin, 1994).

The present emphasis on cultural literacy to maintain a tradition of American life and human capital literacy as a technological preparation for the world of work encompasses the efforts of the established power bloc to move the United States into the Information Age while solving its social problems, many of which were created by modernism. Modernism followed the Enlightenment mode of intellectual thought and envelops various social, cultural, political, and economic structures that have contributed to segmentation, centralization, capitalism, and bureaucracy in the liberal democratic state (Kincheloe, 1993). Like the modern factory, the modern school proposed techniques of control to assure that the student would emerge from the assembly line able to read and write in the manner deemed important for promoting social and cultural morals and mores.

In contrast, postmodern thought seeks to address the problems caused by the attributes of modernism. Rather than embracing segmentation, postmodern approaches to politics and education seek holistic approaches to social and political life. The disengagement promoted by objective knowledge has constructed the social fabric within which segmentation, centralization, capitalism, and liberalism have proved to promote and perpetuate undemocratic social and power relations, as well as other social malaise.

A theory of postmodern literacy teacher education presupposes debating the problematic nature of modern scientific literacy formulated by social and power relations of knowledge as they have been and continue to be reduced, produced, and reproduced in the educational system. The analogy made between schooling and learning to play the game of life indicates that there are winners and losers in the game—that is, in the school game and in the game of "real" life. Such binarisms have contributed to the dichotomies that have served to polarize understanding of male and female, physical and mental, work and play, and many other concepts that come to color our lived experiences. I would argue that for teachers the binarisms of Cartesian-Newtonian logic initiated by *"scientific practice"* have displaced the *theoretical* as more important for teaching. As priorities are decided, test scores have predominated over aesthetic discussion, and the uncontroversial takes precedence over the political consideration of many issues revolving around race/ethnicity, language, gender, and class.

Because of its legitimacy, science supersedes controversy. Science has traditionally been a male enterprise. Although teachers are predominantly females, the science of education has been traditionally pursued by the university professoriat comprised predominantly of males. Although the discourses of feminism and critical theory are present in the academy in other departments and colleges, pre-service teachers have been excluded from such discourses. Knowledge and power relations in the university have constructed the discourses of knowledge bases as the foundation for teacher education, but feminist ways of reading the school, academy, university, and the world are not considered legitimate or scientific, with the exception of liberal feminism. Ironically, such feminist literacy would question the knowledge and power of the structures, disciplines, and criteria that are utilized to decide the merit of credentialing.

**Feminists, Foucault, and Body Politics Inform Educators**

Wexler (1992) states that feminists have become extremely sensitive to their arguments becoming public discourse, as opposed to jargonistic, complex, and fine-grained. In *Up Against Foucault* (Ramazanoglu, 1993), women reclaim the understanding of body politics for feminists. Ramazanoglu convincingly argues that although Marx argued that economic class affected the experience of the body, Foucault showed us theoretically and painstakingly how the politics of the body have been normalized and can be resisted. In the women's movement of the 1960s, control of the woman's body was more political and considered, even by feminist writers, less theoretical (p. 184). Thus, feminist writers were drawn to Foucault's work that described inscription of the body, something Wollstonecraft (1792/1992) had written about two centuries ago.

Politics of the body are personal and public politics. They are engaged in schools, pervade the life of human research, and determine the socialization processes of all students who learn to read and write. Understanding the body as the site where power is exercised over readers and writers gives us postmodern, poststructural, critical, and feminist understandings of how we are conditioned to be literate in schools and how traditional modern literacy practices might be transformed. Foucault tells us that as the sciences and social practices came to regulate individuals, truth as power and knowledge impinged on bodily freedom of individuals. His understanding of power through normalization procedures helps to perpetuate male dominance over females. However, as stated by Ramazanoglu, socialization is produced through self-normalization to habits of masculinity and femininity (1993, p. 190). As female teacher politics—intellectual and bodily—are controlled by the state, postmodern literacy is not encouraged.

The initial Foucaultian influences on feminism concentrated on concepts of discipline, docility, normalization, and bio-power. A second wave, more postmodern perhaps, emphasized contestation and subversion. In Foucault's view, resistance and transformation are continual and must be exercised to overcome the grip of institutions on individuals. Feminist and critical reactions to such debate are concerned that the assumed "best practices" in education privilege males (usually white) and are less optimum for most females and many males of other backgrounds, particularly those from diverse backgrounds (Shakeshaft, 1986).

The work of poststructual criticalists and feminists seeks to reveal the various unquestioned practices of the liberal democratic and late capitalistic state, including those of the present educational reform movement. The manner in which these two groups achieve critical analysis of language and policies that are taken for granted invokes discourse analysis.

To comprehend how teachers, policies, and technologies of control construct students as subjects, we must ask how the knowledge-power relations construct teachers. Yet for Foucault, a discourse from authorities on high did not guarantee agreement from all actors. Departure from control through discourses lay in the individual's power to submit or reject the discourse in one's locale. The refusal to submit or acquiesce is a power of all individuals.

## Questioning Literacy Policy

Literacy policy as it relates to curriculum often targets problems (in this case, teachers and students), seeks to solve the problems (such as dropping out, ill-preparedness for work, test failure) from a range of policy choices, inculcates policy initiatives into existing programs, or superimposes them on existing philosophies of educators and then attempts to affect change in the target problem population (Scheurich, 1994). Macedo (1991) argues that literacy cannot be viewed as simply developing skills and acquiring dominant standard language. Such a notion of literacy sustains ideology that systematically disconfirms rather than legitimizes the cultural experiences of the subordinate linguistic groups who are affected most by such policy.

Likewise, those literate individuals who acquire little capacity to analyze the political economy are educated illiterates. Attention to doublespeak and discourses of freedom informs the intent listener and reader that freedom is often disguised as control. Through educated stupidification, literate individuals can be easily controlled as well as become controlling through pernicious practices that hardly qualify as democratic (Macedo, 1994a). Brodkey asserts that

> [b]ecause all definitions of literacy project both a *literate self* and an *illiterate other*, the tropics of literacy stipulate the political as well as cultural terms on which the "literate" wish to live with the "illiterate" by defining what is meant by reading and writing. (1991, p. 161)

Brodkey, whose work was inspired by Foucault, acknowledges that literacy is a figure of speech (trope) that can be used to "justify or rectify social inequity" (p. 161). Brodkey asks what we mean when we say "functionally illiterate." Whether we are talking about young or older students or adults, literacy policies separate people from each other on what is usually arbitrarily assigned criteria determined by an ideology or an ideological discourse.

In Freire's view, reading always involves three steps: (1) reading, (2) critical perception and interpretation, and (3) rewriting what is read (Freire & Faundez, 1989). What is not discussed in teacher training programs is the nature in which literacy is a social construction of white male-dominated knowledge and power that has built all the structures within which we operate. As educators are taught such literacy and then teach it as they learned it, many important characteristics of "official" literacy are not emphasized. Some of those aspects of literacy that are taken for granted include the traditional, but arbitrary, knowledge bases that are deemed scientific and therefore valid, including textbooks, disciplines that segment knowledge, and the exams that determine students' and teachers' success or failure. And finally, consideration of the political nature of defining literacy is not deliberated as part of the project of restructuring of schools beyond part of the necessary requirements to move into the Information Age and global economy. In sum, creating and testing for standards in the midst of cultural wars, as well as filtering literacy programs through local school official or mainstream cultures, diminishes the advantage of those whose gender, language, experience, and economic situations do not fit with the "scientific method" of traditional school reading programs (Shor, 1986a,b).

The point of this project is to look at discourses that formulate and define ways of being literate, and to encourage educators to go beyond the simplistic or tightly defined parameters of literacy to embrace a critical approach to teaching students to read and write. Such critical pedagogy requires some postmodern outlooks, including poststructural and feminist theoretical orientations that give teachers new ground from which to analyze what they are being asked, through formal as well as informal policies, to teach students.

## Changing the Way That Educators Regard Literacy

The present mainstream change mission of state education policy has not re-envisioned literacy, nor its teaching, despite all of the good scholarship done on school-based curriculum and reading and writing pedagogies from critical-revisionist historical, ethnographic, feminist, and sociological perspectives. The critical discourse of literacy is overpowered by two discourses that center on functional and cultural literacy (Green, 1993, p. 1), feminist literacy being unknown to most people.

Green's literacy research drew three conclusions. First, major revision is required in our traditional assumptions about literacy as both a human accomplishment and social phenomenon. Second, there is a rich collection of text about and for pedagogy. Third, unfortunately, given these findings and resources, the outlook for socially critical literacy education in the near and distant future is unfavorable (Green, 1993, p. 1). In order to advance a more socially critical literacy education, teacher educators and teachers need to know how tradition and social milieu contribute to narrow interpretations of modern literacy which are usually bound to positivistic evaluation that reduce knowledge(s) to multiple choice exams.

## Reviewing Discourse Formation of Literate Subjects

Literacy statements included in the texts of broader educational policies, such as *A Nation at Risk*, *The Nation Responds* (U.S. Dept. of Education, 1984b), *Alliance for Excellence* (U.S. Dept. of Education, 1984a), etc., serve to define and measure the attributes of the literate. Literacy policy statements, broadly defined, become the discourses through which educational rhetoric and practices structure reading and writing, as well as instruction in other disciplinary areas. Literacy discourses not only structure aspects of self-, social, and political development, but are also structured by other sociocultural and historical forces in the society.

Educational discursive practices among those working within the field of education, the family, the media, and private business serve to construct the populace through knowledge and power relations that render the individual as both the object, or the recipient, of the policy and the subject of the policy. As subject of the policy discourses, those who internalize the prescribed values and norms reproduce society as discourses shape them (Foucault, 1972).

Because of political, social, and economic forces, modern literacy practices are undemocratic, yet they predominate. State-adopted textbooks and literature chosen by the teacher comprise most of the literacy curriculum. Reading and writing curricula define many courses, including reading and writing, language arts, children's literature, secondary composition, ESL, and literature. Of course, the literacy connections made or not made between these language courses and the rest of the curriculum are crucial for understanding the social, cultural, and historical ways of thinking about knowledge. Nonetheless, traditional segmentation of knowledge dominates the syllabus, teachers' lesson plan books, and departmental politics in schools and universities for the most part.

The transmission of compartmentalized knowledge is the assumption on which official pedagogical discourses rest. Thus, unless we are intent on changing literacy interpretations and the knowledge and power relations they signify, we become complicit in the work of the state to control people's lives through how we teach reading and writing. The moneys spent on testing a limited definition of literacy do not address social conditions that create other kinds of literacies. If testing proposes bell curve results in success and failure, then we commit symbolic violence against those whom we are teaching and testing to become illiterate by not enabling their success and/or development of more analytical skills (Cochran-Smith, 1991; Edelsky, 1991a). We ensure their failure by not making the policy changes significant enough to affect real change. Given the nature of the way we account for knowledge and literacy in present-day curricular and testing practices, those reforms occurring over the last fifteen years have been, in the estimation of some, an exercise in changing to keep things the same in schools and colleges of education (Goodman, 1995a; Borman & Greenman, 1994).

In the next chapter, I will set forth my methodology—an eclectic, hermeneutical way of interpreting rhetoric from critical perspectives. It is my goal, in setting forth such a method, to inspire interpretive and intellectual thought and to promote reflective and critical literacy classroom practice by teachers.

# NOTE

1. Dewey is often associated with the Progressive Education Movement. His ideas were borrowed heavily by the movement and to a large degree misinterpreted and misused. Dewey eventually disassociated himself from the movement, although he never abandoned his philosophy of child-centered education nor the concept of education through schooling as the practice of democratic life (see Cremin, 1964; Dewey, 1916).

# CHAPTER III

# DOING AN ARCHAEOLOGICAL GENEALOGY

## Beginning the Work

### Narrowing the Study

In the first conceptualization of this study, the goal was to explore a recent history of the discourses of literacy. However, the uses of the term literacy are prolific and generative, so that such a history would have proved to be problematic in two ways: (1) it would have been too extensive and (2) it would not necessarily have probed the issue of teaching pre-service teachers critical and feminist literacy so that they could, in turn, teach critical and feminist literacies in their classrooms. By focusing on four discourses of literacy, I concentrated on educational policies whose objectives include educating "literate" subjects. Beginning with a critical rupture in human capital and cultural literacy practice, Freire's *Pedagogy of the Oppressed* (1970), this research focused on literacy policy from 1970 to the present.

Although Freire's work is important to what has ensued in critical literacy discourse, his ideas are not practiced by mainstream teachers. Within the mainstream discourses of literacy policy, I focused on official policies and scholarship related to fostering the development of literate subjects in the field of education through human capital and cultural literacy discourses. Assuming that the discourses of literacy are constituted by knowledge and power relations, I looked for literacy discourses that produced truth in literacy and teacher education. As I proceeded with this analysis, my guiding assumption was that the human capital and cultural discourses of literacy are dominant because they emanate from positions of power where speakers prescribe educational policy in the United States.

Most salient of the regimes were four academic and political positions relating to human capital, cultural, critical, and feminist literacy. For the sake of discussing paradigm shifting of literacy, I differentiated between modern and postmodern discourses of literacy. Official policy statements and academic discourse about human capital and cultural literacy fall into a modernist, conservative, educational paradigm. In contrast, Freirean and feminist literacy policies occupy an emerging postmodern paradigm that promotes radical change in literacy definitions and practices. The shifting paradigm is a metaphor that attempts to capture the differences between modern and postmodern foundations of knowledge, the way we research the knowledge in either paradigm, and, consequently, the manner in which we teach literacy. This research seeks primarily to understand the discourses of literacy within the two paradigms and their implications for teaching. Ultimately, this chapter outlines a method to promote postmodern literacy practices in classrooms informed by prior pre-service conscientization (Freire, 1970) of the relationships among ideology, political economy, and schooling.

## Identifying the Discourses

Identification of human capital, cultural, critical, and feminist discourses of literacy represents an important component of this research. Particularly important in this identification process is locating how literacy discourses became manifest as they connect to notions of democracy, citizenship, and economic wherewithal. Establishing the connections between and among the discourses locates the political dissentions that give rise to the dialogue and debate that occurs between them (Spring, 1996; Weisburd, 1994; Jackson, 1994). Following the intertextual and intratextual dialogue that occurs in educational policy, educational research and theory engages participation in the conversation among the political positions expounded by their proponents.

**Defining Discourses of Literacy**

Discourse as defined by Foucault's work refers to rhetorical representations that develop and mediate disciplinary technologies of the self (1965, 1972, 1978). I concentrated on educational policies as disciplinary technologies whose objectives include educating literate subjects. Consequently, I searched for official policies related to notions of educational theory and policy that promote development of literate subjects and that are constituted by the state. Bureaucratic specifications and reifications of literacy operate through the credentialing of schools and universities to legitimize knowledge and power relations. Early in the research process, looking to the antitheses of these official discourses, I defined critical literacy within a critical and feminist pedagogy framework. However, the more I read feminist educational and poststructural theory, the more I realized the necessity to make a distinction between critical literacy and feminist literacy.

## My Relationship to the Study

**Personal Conscientization**

My experiences in schools as a teacher of language arts taught me that in order to have a broad picture of how to educate literate subjects, pre-service teachers need to know more possibilities than are represented by modern literacy as embodied by the two dominant discourses of literacy. Such possibilities exist within the postmodern framework. Unaware of these alternatives early in my teaching career, I found myself in personal/professional conflict about how I was teaching literacy. On the one hand, I believe that education is aesthetic, experiential, and political. However, the manner in which I was evaluating my students was tied to measures of knowledge as exhibited on tests. Such evaluation reduces literacy to factual, operational, and scientific manipulation of information. The latter may be the norm as literacy is practiced, but what was not clear in my own practice is that normalized practices, such as literacy testing or limiting literacy to a patriarchal view of history and culture, for example, are not necessarily ethical. What my quest for understanding in literacy has ultimately taught me is that such practices are reversible.

In the classroom, I saw the need for holistic literacy practice; however, several years passed before I knew that postmodern literacy was what was missing from my teaching methods. What I found problematic about standard literacy practice was its focus on quantitative assessment of reading and writing, when so much more was involved in literacy. My faith in scientifically measurable literacy waned as my classroom teaching experiences showed that important knowledge did not always produce good test scores or brilliant expression through written composition. My classroom research through dialogue revealed that my "illiterate" students possessed reasoning skills and abilities to read the world that were as brilliant as those of students who were college bound to become professionals. At that point, I decided that there is something inherently wrong with a system that bases social position, future economic rewards, and potentials for upward mobility on a written code of language and social comportment associated with that code.

Upon realizing my role in reproducing social hierarchy through literacy classroom practices, I returned to the university to better understand how to teach high school students who had not yet mastered paragraph writing. After I was well into my study program for a master's in language arts education, I was introduced to Freire's *Pedagogy of the Oppressed* (1970). It was then I realized the teacher's power in legitimizing literacy. As outlined carefully by Freire, teachers can oppress students through literacy practices that do not acknowledge student knowledge. Upon this realization, I began to prepare myself to educate students to be engaged, political self-advocates through various media including the reading and writing curriculum.

My position in the pursuance of this research is one of a critically literate teacher who has analyzed human capital and cultural literacy discourses to find them lacking in cultural diversity and representation of the majority of the populace. I have also traced the origins and consistencies of critical and feminist literacies within larger frameworks of critical and feminist pedagogies.

Through an archaeological genealogy, which this chapter is about to present, pre-service teachers can look at present modernistic literacy practices to understand the history of literacy. By better understanding the history of literacy policies and practices, teachers can begin to make differences in their classrooms. They will care more about the manner in which they do and do not approach literacy pedagogy by incorporating more critical analysis into classroom discourses from a postmodern perspective. They will be more prepared to address females, minorities, and the poor, who have traditionally been marginalized by textbook-driven curricula grounded in modernistic literacy practices.

The journey to critical and feminist literacy took many years. It was not until I began this research of the discourses of literacy that I came to understand much of my gendered socialization, the exclusion of a female perspective in philosophy, history, literature, and most educational disciplines, as well as gender discrimination in socioeconomic life. Although I had been a politically critical thinker for years, those details escaped me through the literacy that I developed. I thought that by introducing educators to postmodern literacy discourse analysis they might be more cognizant of the teachers' role in social reproduction of academic tracks and subordinate female literate subjects by the time they entered the classroom. Seeing the need to take some action to make pre-service teachers aware of the effects of dominant ideology on teaching thinking, I began to formulate this study. I pursued the study so that it could be utilized as a tool to move teachers from modernistic to more postmodernist literacy practices.

**Coming to Voice Through Praxis**

This method chapter has three purposes: (1) to provide the vehicle through which I can present this research; (2) to model critical and feminist analysis of literacy policies; and (3) to frame an approach by which teachers can interpret literacy policies that will affect the curriculum, instruction, and student performances, and consequently their classroom practice. This project represents my coming to voice and praxis in the discourses of literacy.

Praxis, as envisioned by Freire (1970), is the action required to make the message of this literacy policy analysis tool for teachers more than words. Praxis will be the practical application of what this work says; practicing this method with teachers will enable them to practice postmodern literacy with their students. However, I have no doubt that postmodern praxis is difficult given the pervasive, externally imposed curriculum and assessments that originate in the scientific modern paradigm. Because control is exerted through literacy discourses, this postmodern discussion represents a counter-discourse and practice to the dominant discourses of literacy.

Such counter-discourses can represent conflict in identity formation of teachers. Because teachers become literate subjects in a system driven by dominant discourses of literacy, this method may not resonate well with them. Another potential negative outcome of this method is that forcing this issue of understanding the subject formation of literate subjects in order to broaden the scope of discursive considerations of literacy may become controlling, thereby producing the opposite of its intended effect. Foucault reiterated that there is little stability in discourses and that they are constantly in flux with social changes. Given that this method might produce controlling rather than emancipatory effects, it is with some reservation that I promote teachers' actively addressing inequality, oppression, sexism, classism, and racism through literacy practices. Yet, changes are needed in classroom literacy practices, and changing teaching practice cannot occur without information. With the following information, pre-service teachers can critique literacy policies and consider their own actions within a larger critical project for literacy transformation.

## Limitations of the Study

Although this study extends to the political, social, economic, public education, and teacher education discourses about literacy, it seeks to concentrate on literary discourses in four official policy statements and other discourses that have surrounded and responded to those policies. As recommended by the Foucaultian genealogy, the concentration in this work is to look at why, how, when, and for what purpose these specific literacy policies were enunciated to produce the effects of truth (Foucault, 1972).

Additionally, as Foucault's theories inform social education, it is important to locate the "ruptures, fissures, and breaks" in the science of literacy education discourses. Unlike Foucault, who was working within expansive time frames of hundreds of years when he located the fissures in his effective histories of the prison, asylum, and sexual practice, I will be focusing on the thirty-year period described earlier.

The breaks in literacy policy and practice will not reveal the dramatic discourse evolutions documented by Foucault's studies. Nonetheless, during the thirty years of intertextual and intratextual discourses of literacy discussed herein, there has been change. Dramatic breaks changed the course of knowledge and power relations for educators who expanded the definition of literacy from reading the word to reading the world. Alongside a prolific body of scientific treatment measuring populations' reading and writing growth, we find a history of literacy scholarship that describes literacy as social practice (Heath, 1983) and a history of literacy as political practice (Freire, 1970; Giroux, 1983; Lankshear & McLaren, 1993; Willinsky, 1990; Shannon, 1990b; Olson & Hirsh, 1995; Stone, 1994). Engaging teachers in discussion of these changes is the focus of this work. The rest of scientific literacy research and pedagogy is beyond the scope of this work, except in my treatment of the problems with modern literacy as exhibited in human capital, cultural literacy, and testing.

Although numerous policy discourses exist, I will focus on four educational policies as archaeological monuments: *A Nation at Risk*, *America 2000*, *National Literacy Act of 1991*, and *Goal 5: Reaching the Goals: Adult Literacy and Lifelong Learning*. Within these monuments, the serious statements or relics of literacy will be considered.

## Overview

This method combines aspects of Foucault's archaeological genealogy, feminist scholarship, and hermeneutics. These theories ground a field of social relations in which one can question the sociopolitical relations produced by focusing on certain discourses of literacy and teacher education discourses. Foucault's work supposes historical research of serious statements of policy discourses, which he refers to as textual "relics." The feminists' perspective on literacy discourses utilizes positioning questions to discern the scope of reform versus the rhetoric of reform as non-neutral. Hermeneutical interpretations of the discourses of literacy are infinitely possible, and therefore the conclusions which one reaches at the end of deliberation are neither definitive or correct. They are interpretations which may be further interpreted.

Such generative interpretation presumes an aspect of change as "becoming." Through discourse analysis, pre-service teachers will better understand their roles as interpreting control agents versus change agents. In essence, postmodern literacy, as developed within the genealogical, feminist, and hermeneutical interpretive process, allows teacher internal change through interpretive transformation which then can be expanded to transform external classroom literacy practices.

Chapter 4 will comprise my construction of the representation or exclusion of human capital, cultural, critical, and feminist literacies from these official educational policies. In the analysis, questions that arise in deliberation of the social and power relations imposed or suggested by discourses of literacy will be addressed. In chapter 5, the same method of discourse analysis is implemented to interrogate teacher education discourses.

## Data Sources

In addition to the four educational policies (monuments) identified above, I have researched political statements, scholarly books and journals, as well as best-selling books by E. D. Hirsch (1987), William Bennett (1984, 1986a,b, 1992a,b), and Alan Bloom (1987) to find what appear to be important influences on mainstream discourses of cultural literacy policies over that last twenty years. The "relics" of educational policy discourse statements include published statements in professional educational journals, one city newspaper, and policy statements, each from its own sociocultural position. For example, the discourses of critical pedagogy and literacy will emanate from poststructural and critical theorists; the feminists' discourses originate in several positions of feminism, but will focus on feminist educational discourses. The news coverage of literacy usually emanates from the larger community's discussion of skills, testing, and accountability.

## Representation

At the heart of paradigm shifting occurring in the present moment within the social sciences (Denzin & Lincoln, 1994), the problematic nature of representation of human experience surfaces as one of the most salient research issues. With respect to representing the effects of literacy on individuals, the postmodern critic identifies problematic aspects of human capital and cultural literacy discourses' impact on workers, women, and "others." As social policymakers decide on public policy, there is a two-way exchange between government and society. Powerful voices from the mainstream of society articulate the kinds of literacy that are important;

their representations are mirrored in policymakers' desires for literacy education. The reverse is also true. Yet, as normalization occurs, the manner in which policies become controlling is not often questioned systematically. Often the policies emanating from high levels of expert decision making and the social practices that they engender become taken for granted. Reification of literacy practices becomes substantiated by compliance to banking educational practices that measure quantitatively the reading and writing skills of students.

The existing political economy provides an environment where scientific, quantifiable measurement of reading and writing achievement is easily justified. Maintaining equilibrium in the system becomes an easier proposition if researchers and teachers of literacy accept the recent policymakers' discourses of attainment of higher standards, credentials, and test scores as forefront in their educational agendas. When accountability by test scores is not attained as specified by the scientific expectations and measures of reading and writing abilities, the problem lies with the teacher, student, or community, not the system that perpetuates such literacy practices. By the same token, the system is more likely to remain at status quo if workers accept the "givens" of such economic and political practices than if workers question their place as cogs in the machinery of postindustrial capitalism (Kincheloe, 1995; Spring, 1996; Aronowitz & Giroux, 1985).

On the other hand, upsetting the rhythms of literacy as a quantifiably measurable skill and the reproduction of social structures through schooling practices involves questioning the knowledge and power relations of bourgeois democracy and the nature of work (Kincheloe, 1995; Freire, 1970; Lankshear & McLaren, 1993). Because the discourses of the women's, multicultural, Afrocentric, and critical educational movements exist in opposition to the existing dominant discourses of education, they threaten the knowledge and power structures as they exist. The overarching goal in this literacy policy analysis is to look at policy statements and around them to discern how literacy is utilized as both a means and an end to discipline students, teachers, and the citizenry at large, allowing politically conservative information to deploy literate subjects. The archaeologist-genealogist's task is to discern how literacy discourses represent truth and to interrupt that truth.

## Policy Analysis Procedures

In the following framework, these words are used interchangeably: analyst, policy analyst, postmodern critic, postmodern educator, critic, and postmodern analyst.

### Naming the Policy

The naming procedure of executing critical literacy discourse policy analysis involves four steps. The first is the selecting of the policy to be analyzed. Analysis of each of these four monuments in educational policymaking in the last fifteen years will follow: *A Nation at Risk*, *America 2000*, *A National Literacy Act,* and *Goal 5: Adult Literacy and Lifelong Learning*. The first two are broad-based, landmark meliorative educational policies addressing what national officials represent as an educational crisis in the United States. In *A Nation at Risk*, officials sought to improve secondary education in the United States, whereas *America 2000* established broad-based educational objectives for elementary, middle, and secondary schools. The third, the *National Literacy Act of 1991*, is a law passed by the United States House of Representatives, following policy suggested in and since *A Nation at Risk*. The fourth serious policy statement discussed is *Adult Literacy and Lifelong Learning,* as a more narrowly based document addressing literacy issues for adults.

After policy selection, the analyst must do careful and close readings of the policies that are intended to improve education. Textual and rhetorical interrogation allows the reader to discern who is doing what to whom to improve education. Several rereadings afford a backward and forward knowledge command of the policy.

Analyzing the text is the next task in policy analysis. Sentence by sentence, the reader determines upon what foundation the arguments within the policy are based. Here is where symbols, metaphors, and rationales are notated and interrogated. The analyst determines intertextual meaning within the document. To accomplish intertextual explication, the critic extrapolates on the potential meanings suggested by relationships between the signified (the written word) and their signifiers (the ideas expressed by the words) across several policies.

In the capturing stage, the main points of the policy are determined. A holistic determination summarizes journalistic guiding questions to describe who, what, when, where, why, and how the policy was made. After the actors and their settings are located, simple questions are used to elaborate on the information. In a consideration of power, the analyst identifies the official position that allows exclusivity of officials to enunciate such a policy. The text is then extended into the sociocultural and political environment to describe the network site that prompted such a policy to be made at that point in time.

In sum, the first phase of this analysis process involves the four steps taken to name the policy: selecting, reading, analyzing, and capturing. This part of the process requires that the analyst develop a working acquaintance with the document. Such familiarity comes from sentence by sentence analysis, as well as from gathering outside information about the politics of the social milieu that produced it.

## Fixing Discourses of Literacy Statements

After the analyst has done textual analysis, fixing the discourses of literacy is necessary. This step requires isolating literacy statements. The relics (archival references to the discourses of literacy) become the focus of the study. As the official recommendations for literacy are made, one asks, This policy is suggesting literacy for what? Literacy for reading, writing, and work are common referents. In this case, allusions to workers, citizens, cultural socialization, and critical literacy are isolated. Now, the analyst is particularly concerned with official policy statements about human capital and cultural literacy. The necessary task is to locate signifiers or words that signify human capital, work/workers, or related meanings to the reader (the analyst in this case). Quotations are recorded and documented as they appeared in the original document.

Next, the analyst locates rationales for articulating such a policy within the policy and the political milieu surrounding the policy. The critical eye focuses on justifications for literacy identified in the economic, political circumstances that surround the policy. The analyst questions the rationale of the proposed policy within the discourse of literacy, work, and economic conditions. Key words to look for in this stage of the analysis are literacy objectives such as achievement of wealth, work preparation, social improvement, national wealth, economic well-being, national security, cultural socialization, community, democracy, and empowerment.

Because part of the postmodern project involves determining how cultural myths or discourses become taken for granted, the analyst must determine who benefits from such social arrangements that are unquestioned. For example, the analyst determines for whom national wealth and power are most meaningful. Further, the poststructual critique searches for grand narrative statements or metanarratives. A metanarrative overgeneralizes experience or cultural conditions such as history, progress, prosperity, and individualism.

The analyst's objective in locating myths is to reveal how the romanticized notions of American culture are perpetuated through metanarratives that undergird policy. In such a deliberation, the critic asks how the policy constructs the people in the margins in relation to the middle and upper echelons of elite literati. Such consideration contrasts idyllic rhetoric and realistic experiences of literate subjects on the lower end of the social hierarchy.

In sum, looking to the signified and the signifiers, the postmodern educator asks how policy constructs literate subjects. Locating sociocultural myths and metanarratives, the analyst distinguishes between the ideal and real potentials for educational improvement advocated in the policy.

### Framing the Discourses

The policy analyst at this point asks what the isolated statements about literacy say, ascertaining the prescriptions of the policymaker. Now the critic questions how the discourses deploy critically literate students, teachers, and other subjects. Repeated references to preparation for the world of work are classified as official discourses of human capital literacy. As *A Nation at Risk* or other policies construct literate subjects, the critic asks what kinds of literacy are promoted through the education at all levels. Projecting a scenario into the future, the analyst surmises what kinds of literacy teachers and students will develop if policies are carried forward as articulated in the statement. The analyst now seeks to determine three things from the discourse: first, how teachers and students fit into the larger sociopolitical framework; second, for whom reproduction of certain discourses are beneficial; and third, how literacy is constructed as scientific truth.

Now, the postmodern reader asks if truth is constructed through empirical argument for certain practices. If numbers are used to depict the scientific nature of an argument, the postmodern critic finds his or her own numbers or looks beyond the numbers to describe the people that have been averaged. The analyst then dialogues with the text to find omissions that are not revealed through scientific discussion of literacy. If arguments are made in favor of certain kinds of literacy, the analyst conjectures what other kinds of literacy are omitted.

In sum, in the framing stage of research, the analyst looks for the weaknesses in the arguments supporting certain kinds of literacy, locates teachers and students in the network of discourse, and articulates what has been omitted from the policy such as consideration of gender, class, and race. The teachers' and students' positions within the context of gender, class, and race constitute the basis for policy counter to that articulated.

**Tracing Discourses' Proliferations**

After discerning which discourses of literacy are given credence over others, the analyst traces the discourses. In this tracing stage, the policy is followed to other social, economic, and cultural articulations. In a broad view, the critic locates in mainstream media the same arguments for literacy. Now looking back to education, the critic arrives at rationales for such depiction of literacy and follows such depiction to the curriculum of teacher education as well as the general curriculum.

Heibert tells us that classroom practice is educational policy in action (1991). If policies originating as official pedagogical discourse become law and are promoted through professional practices, these discourses have attained a status of scientific truth. As an example, motifs of accountability testing promoted in *A Nation at Risk* have surfaced in various other official policies, in law, in state-defined curricula, in teacher assessment instruments, and in competency testing. These and other locations of literacy indicate proliferations to the analyst and should become part of the analytical construction.

Overall, the critic is interested in tracing the consistencies of included or excluded signifiers of testing, workers, citizens, and/or critical thinkers within the network of discourses of literacy. A chronology allows tracing history readily.

## Tracing Discourses' Transformations

From the postmodern critical perspective, the policy analyst now examines how the discourses of literacy articulated within various sociopolitical, educational, and cultural milieus are transformed. For the critical educator, the task engages thought about how the transformations in the discourses also transform literate subjects from the environment of discourse. Such transformation depends on how the discourses are altered, perpetuated, or transformed into law.

Transformation occurs in the discourses as well as the subjects who engage them. The analyst asks how literate subjects are expected to conduct, discipline, and promote the discourses of literacy to form the conscience and social consciousness. For the educator, the primary concern becomes awareness of discourses that interrupt conformity in literacy practices or promote transformation in classroom practices.

In essence, transformation occurs in two locations—in the sociopolitical milieu and within the individual. Tracing those transformations is important to a postmodern understanding of literacy discourses and in constructing an effective history.

## Positioning of the Teacher Subject

In this step of the literacy policy interrogation, the analyst looks for power through control. Such an inquiry probes how the forces exerted by law, social, economical, and educational institutions through the literacy policies position the teacher. An important consideration is again the race, class, and gender of teachers versus policymakers, school administrators, and students. Taking into account this information, the analyst traces institutional expectations to literacy practices by determining how controlled the teacher is by institutional force.

In so doing, the postmodern critic is better able to explain how the curricula and social structures broadly or narrowly contribute to the positioning of teachers within a limited field of literacy knowledge. All in all, the analyst ascertains how pedagogy as prescribed by the literacy policy constructs a field of knowledge and truth development.

**Teaching Student Subjects**

In this phase of the analysis, the postmodern critic attempts to determine how the literate student is formulated from within the field of literacy discourses. The modern practices of literacy have focused on Western cultural development, as well as a host of scientific developments. Such developments in mathematics, science information technology, and basic skills have been particularly important to the development of the range of literate students. Determining the resources allocated to the ends articulated is also important to the postmodern analysis. The educational policy analyst must determine if the political desire enunciated by the formal policy is supported with the resources to make the policy a reality for all.

Another important goal of the analyst at this point is to surmise what discourses of literacy and educational enterprises are de-emphasized when others are emphasized. In general, recognizing how silencing or exclusion of other literacy policies limits the range of literacy in the individual body, the student body, and the social body is the utmost consideration in the formation of literate subjects.

**Forming Postmodern Literate Subjects**

Foucault proposed and discussed at length the deployment of discourses by the dominant power holders at various locations in society (1972). He asserted that the presentation of one argument always negates another. The modern scientific arguments for literacy, improved teacher preparation, and a better prepared labor market negate the postmodern, critical, feminist, and multicultural discussions about literacy. Focusing on one side of an issue or assuming, for example, that all progress is positive fails to illuminate the negative effects of modernization. In the case of the newest emphasis on teacher accountability by quantitative measure, the logic of teacher accountability to teach ethical and democratic behaviors to students becomes lost in the bureaucratic procedures that serve to further impose quantifiable literacy skills. Such imposition becomes oppressive to individual students who are not allowed to pursue questions that respond to their problems, needs, and interests. The allusions to self-directed learner or child-centered learning are little more than rhetoric espousing democratic progressive education that rarely is practiced. Promoting the dominant discourses of literacy may oppress learners; however, such domination does not obliterate the subordinate viewpoint.

As discussed by Foucault (1972), discourses from various academic or political positions do not destroy the other. The analyst discovers the tensions between the discourses that respond to each other by locating where power is exercised in many locations. The desire to expand the self beyond the limiting frameworks of schooling requires looking to the borders, margins, and what is rendered invisible by what we take for granted about literacy policy. The postmodern critic is familiar with what critical feminists' and multiculturalists' dimensions add to the literacy formula. The postmodern teacher uses this information to deliberate, exercise, and promote democratic literacy as power.

**Writing the Analysis**

At this stage, the discourse analyst constructs an interpretive narrative about the literacy policies. Throughout the narrative, the writer attempts to converse with the various discourses and to formulate convergence on the four representations of literacy discourses and how such representations can be used more and less democratically to form literate subjects. From the teacher's perspective, the questions indicated in the preceding steps of the analysis, and the consideration of literacy as controlling or emancipating, frame the discussion.

## Conclusion

This chapter is framed so that the policy analyst can isolate the tasks of policy study. This method of study involves a nine-stage template. As one goes through the process of this analysis, some steps can be combined. Several readings of literacy statements within the four documents were necessary. The readings cannot be depicted here, except in the isolation of passages and in writing my reactions to them as I have deconstructed the relevant passages within the policies. The steps that occur after reading become parts of the analyses and are reflected in various sections of chapter 4. When it was possible to differentiate between the steps, I did so; however, some of the steps ultimately overlap in interpretive analysis reflected in the upcoming narrative.

# CHAPTER IV

## LITERACY POLICY ARCHAEOLOGY

In this chapter, official (from the state) and foundation-recommended literacy policy statements and the rationale for specific kinds of literacy will be discussed. Passages from those educational policy movements which focus on literacy will be summarized. The discussion format will be divided into nine steps: (1) naming, (2) fixing, (3) framing, (4) tracing literacy discourses' proliferations, (5) tracing discourses' transformations, (6) positioning the teacher subject, (7) teaching student subjects, (8) forming postmodern literate subjects. The ninth step is writing the narrative. In this archaeology, literacy as promoted by official policies and academic non-mainstream policy statements will be elaborated.

### Naming the Policies

**Selecting**

Foucault (1972) said that the timing of events is important to discourse formulation of truth effects. In keeping with an archaeology, this analysis attempts to be chronological only insofar as it looks from literacy policy texts made in the last seventeen years to the environmental conditions that led to the articulation of the literacy policies by the U.S. Department of Education and the United States Congress within *A Nation at Risk*, 1983; *America 2000*, 1991; the *National Literacy Act of 1991*; and *Reaching the Goals: Goal 5: Adult Literacy and Lifelong Learning*, 1993. The focus here will be on policies as they exist in textual forms across several networks of governing agencies, including central government, universities, and schools. According to Foucault (1972), the discourses emanate through various networks to society at large via governing agencies. Through such consideration, the analyst relates the social, cultural, and economic climate that led to national and state control of literacy to be exerted over the populace through policy discourses. Rather than focusing on linear historical development, this archaeological genealogy or effective history seeks to explain how the effects of truth are utilized to develop literacy as knowledge and power relations.

As a policy analyst, I located literacy statements within the more general policy monuments to ascertain the emphasis of those who produce and articulate the official pedagogical discourses (Bernstein, 1990). In the manner in which Foucault thought it necessary to look for the breaks, ruptures, and fissures in science, this exploration moves beyond the smooth patterns of understanding literacy policy history. As Foucault recommended, this study proceeds to consider and reconstruct power and knowledge relations as they are formed by the policy statements. Such a task is accomplished by contrastive analysis of official literacy statements in generic governmental literacy policy as they might be interpreted from gender, race, and class perspectives in a poststructural fashion.

**Reading the Policies**

In order to develop this discussion, I read the policies several times, then isolated passages prior to analyzing and capturing components, which are including in this first step of policy analysis.

**Analyzing the Policies**

Analyzing the policies is a long-term and iterative process. It begins on the first reading of a policy and continues through the construction of this framework. Searching for signifiers that allude and refer to literacy is the initial component of this policy study. In this search, one finds the overall terms established in the documents which follow.

**Policy Summary**

*A Nation at Risk.* A journalistic summary of the policies helps to contextualize the discussion at this point. The *Nation at Risk* policy statement was made in 1983 by members of the National Commission for Excellence in Education, authorized by provisions of part D of the General Education Provisions Act (P. L. 90-247) and the Federal Advisory Committee Act (P. L. 92-463) which set forth standards for the formation and use of the advisory committee. The exclusivity established by President Ronald Reagan and this commission to be able to make national policy objectives and then implement them at the state level follows in a long line of national attention given to education, particularly since the 1950s. Traditionally, education was a power reserved to the states; however, the nation-state has considered education a priority in national security issues and under that rubric works with corporate support to highly influence the curriculum (Spring, 1996; Tozer, Violas, & Senese, 1998).

Four stated purposes and functions of this commission guided the effort behind the publication of *A Nation at Risk*. First, there was a review and synthesis of data and scholarly literature on the quality of learning and teaching in schools, colleges, and universities, with concern for teenage youth. Second, there was an examination and comparison of United States curricula standards with those from other advanced nations. Third, a study of college admission standards, successful programs, and entrance exams was conducted. Fourth, a review of the major social and economic changes that have occurred in America over the last quarter century was related to the educational goals, problems, and proposed improvements (U.S. Dept. of Education, 1983, p. 39).

The commission consisted of at least 12 but not more than 19 public members appointed by the secretary of education. Four meetings were called by the chairperson with advanced approval of the designated federal official. The commission charter began August 5, 1981, and finished activities in 18 months, followed by a report of findings finalized in two years (pp. 40–41). Meetings of the commission were held mostly in Washington, D.C., but also in other parts of the country, including Stanford, California; Philadelphia, Pennsylvania; Houston, Texas; Atlanta, Georgia; New York, New York; Chicago, Illinois; San Diego, California; and Cambridge, Massachusetts. The hearings and testimony came mostly from California, the president's home state, whereas teacher preparation programs in the whole country were researched (U.S. Dept. of Education, 1983, pp. 46–47). No rural issues or locations surfaced as important to the nation's expressed crisis.

An overview analysis of the particular policies discussed herein reveals concerns articulated through vocabulary pertaining to national affairs such as wealth, national security, global economy, competitiveness, and reorientation of labor to an Information Age economy versus an industrial one.

*America 2000.* *America 2000* represented educational priorities articulated by President George Bush. The policy states its challenge: "These National Education Goals are not the President's goals or the Governor's goals: they are the nation's goals" (U.S. Dept. of Education, 1991, p. 47). From a position of exclusivity, the goals of the nation are voiced as emanating from the people. Fifteen points stated in the policy include world-class standards, American achievement tests, encouragement to use the tests, presidential citations for educational excellence, presidential achievement scholarships, report cards on results, report card data collection, choice, the school as the site of reform, a merit schools program, governors' academies for school leaders, governors' academies for teachers, differential pay for teachers, alternative teacher and principal certification, and honor teachers.

In a *Phi Delta Kappan* review, Doyle (1991) states that *America 2000* is the "first serious policy initiative in the nation's history to address the issue of whether the federal role in education ought to be enlarged—and if so, in what manner and serving which children" (p. 185). In what Doyle refers to as a "congenial" program, President Bush, his administration, and his secretary of education, Lamar Alexander, called for "hard work, private initiative, self-reliance, [and] freedom" as the basis for this educational policy (p. 185). Doyle cited Gallup and *Phi Delta Kappan* surveys showing strong national support for underlying concepts of *America 2000:* choice, high standards, radical reform, and national testing.

As a means to the goals of *America 2000*, President Bush requested a not-for-profit foundation be established. The New American Schools Development Corporation committed to raising $150–$200 million to design and implement a model program, such as a prototype design requisitioned in private business (Doyle, 1991, p. 187). Members of the committee included Chairman Thomas Kean, president of Drew University and former New Jersey governor; Vice Chair Louis Gerstner, chief executive officer of RJR Nabisco and chairman of RJR Nabisco

Foundation; Treasurer Roger Semerad, president of RJR Nabisco Foundation; and Secretary Bob Schneider of Xerox.

The foundation raised $38 million by October 1, 1991, and planned to raise another $120 million in "venture capital" for the nation's public schools. Doyle called this the biggest philanthropic effort of its kind in history as the nation "chart[s] new directions and prepares new ground" (1991, p. 190). In the 535-plus parts of this program, Congress was asked to appropriate $1 million per congressional district for a school to lay out and implement in a model school program what was learned from New American Schools Development Corporation.

Literacy was one of the goals of *America 2000*. As stated in the foreword of this policy statement, the "six broad Goals serve as a framework for much of the current reform movement" (U.S. Dept. of Education, 1991, p. iii): (1) readiness; (2) improved graduation rates to 90%; (3) competence testing in grades 4, 8, and 12; (4) international predominance in science and math; (5) adult literacy and skills for citizenship; and (6) drug-free and violence-free schools.

*National Literacy Act of 1991.* The terms which establish the foundation of this literacy bill to become law are discussed in an upcoming section titled "Tracing Literacy Discourses' Transformations." As the effects of truth produced by the aforementioned literacy policies are inculcated into practice, an official imprimatur is granted to the business community's requirements of literacy by passing a national law that decrees reading and writing be developed in the populace for human capital literacy.

## Capturing the Political Climate

One of the major products of Reagan's educational efforts was *A Nation at Risk* (1983). This document was a wake-up call for the United States, whose predominant role in world trade was jeopardized by the aggressive growth of European and Japanese markets. For Reagan, who de-emphasized civil rights and the women's movement, importance was placed on educating workers. His administration focused on perpetuating power and knowledge relations of the Anglo-Eurocentric political economy. Human capital issues became foremost in his programs (Tozer et al., 1998; Aronowitz & Giroux, 1985).

## Constructing Children Workers

The work ethic advocated for literacy acquisition is also proposed for childhood education. Hillman (1989) in *Phi Delta Kappa Fastback 292* advocates early childhood activities that foster health, happiness, and life skills in young children. According to Hillman, the play that children do is also their work: "Doing a wooden puzzle of a nurse holding two newborn babies is play. It is also work" (p. 14). Besides preparing children for school life, educators must also prepare them for work. As will become apparent in the discussion of these documents, school life as preparation for the world of work should be extended from childhood to adulthood.

## Constructing Workers

*A Nation at Risk* expresses policymakers' fear of Japanese cars, South Korean steel, and German tools, which "signify a redistribution of trained capital throughout the globe" (U.S. Dept. of Education, 1983, p. 7). Important in the twenty-first century will be "knowledge, learning, information, and skilled intelligence" (p. 7). The new commodity in the current and future economy is knowledge.

In order to connect children-students with the work world, career orientation is emphasized in auxiliary and principal documents discussed here. Teachers and schools are expected to better prepare students to desire careers. After preparing children for work, educators and other policy implementers must prepare them all the way through school life, and that school life should be extended. In *Career Beginnings*, Bloomfield (1989) says that because minorities do not test well on the SAT, they need academic preparation for college. Statistics show that black and Hispanic students are twice as likely to score below 400 on both the verbal and math portions of the SAT as are white students. "Job projections for the year 2000 will require a labor force whose median level of education is 13.5 years as compared to 12.8 years now" (U.S. Department of Labor, 1987, p. 13), making education beyond the secondary level more important. One way to accomplish this is through a mentored experience for the communities, as outlined in the *Career Beginnings* program, that would help students "to understand the demands of the workplace punctuality, regular attendance, taking responsibility" (p. 13). Here, human capital literacy is explicitly defined. Such literacy learning extends from childhood through adult life.

A bold statement on adult literacy was made in *Reaching the Goals: Goal 5: Adult Literacy and Lifelong Learning:* "By the year 2000, every adult American will be literate and will possess the knowledge and skills necessary to compete in a global economy and exercise the rights and responsibilities of citizenship" (U.S. Dept. of Education, 1993a, p. 1). The essence of the message is that adults will be increasingly "learning at all ages" (p. 1). The reason that adults will remain a learning community is that "ever-changing work environments require recurrent education for workers to upgrade skills and knowledge" (p. 1). As the focus on self-sufficiency and corporate socialism is portrayed, preparation for work and work for economic productivity are the citizens' responsibilities.

*Reaching the Goals: Goal 5: Adult Literacy and Lifelong Learning.* With exception to the call for critical thinking as a last objective, the goals of *Reaching the Goals: Goal 5: Adult Literacy and Lifelong Learning* are a reiteration of the *America 2000* policy statement. The five goals follow: (1) involvement of every major American business between education and work; (2) worker opportunity to acquire basic and highly technical skills; (3) increased quality in programs (including libraries) to meet the needs of part-time and mid-career students; (4) increased numbers of minorities who enter college; and (5) advanced ability of college graduates to think critically, communicate effectively, and solve problems. *Reaching the Goals: Goal 5: Adult Literacy and Lifelong Learning* was prepared by the Goal 5 Work Group of the Office of Educational Research and Improvement. This policy follows from President Bush's and the nation's 50 governors' adoption of six national education goals (later expanded to eight goals).

## Fixing Discourses of Literacy

### More Skills Testing

*America 2000, Goal 5: Adult Literacy and Lifelong Learning*, and the *National Literacy Act of 1991* follow many of the recommendations set forth in *A Nation at Risk* (U.S. Dept. of Education, 1983, pp. 18–22). The conservative and corporate politics that inspired the tipping of the scale in favor of excellence over equity came in reaction to a two-decade period of gains in civil rights and recognition of multicultural issues. Conservative discussions in several domains erupted in favor of a redefinition of nationalistic policies, a rethinking of language in an environment of rapidly growing minority populations, and a reevaluation of curricular rigor as *A Nation at Risk* and *America 2000* inform future workers. Testing, as proposed in the two documents, would ensure more serious attention by teachers and students toward their work (U.S. Dept. of Education, 1983, pp. 18–29).

## Anti-Teacher Unionism and Smaller Government

As one examines the political interworkings at the national level during the 1980s more closely, one finds an environment hostile to teachers' unions. Teachers' unions did not support President Reagan in his 1980 campaign. There were few if any discussions between the White House and the unions about educational and teachers' issues (Spring, 1996). Intent on promoting school choice in various forms and dissolving the Department of Education, Reagan designated conservative appointees to educational research and development posts.

## Growth of Poverty and Upper-Crust Assets

Much work has been done to reveal the augmentation and feminization of poverty during the Reagan-Bush years in the presidency (Frazer, 1989; Shakeshaft, 1986; AAUW, 1995). Also conspicuous was the omission of female educational issues within a broader general framework that has traditionally been and continues to be based on male educational constructs and needs (Frazer, 1989; Shakeshaft, 1986). Noticeably missing from the policies discussed herein were gender politics which have resulted from a proliferation of research findings on gender inequity and female poverty.

Also casually dismissed are the politics of class as the speakers from upper echelons construct conditions for the lower classes. Thurow documents the new and unforeseen class disparities, the likeness of which is present in no other postindustrial nation other than the United States.

The share of total net worth of the top one-half of 1 percent of the population rose from 26 to 31 percent in just six years, between 1983 and 1989. By the early 1990s the share of wealth (more than 40 percent) held by the top 1 percent of the population was essentially double what it had been in the mid-1970s and back to where it was in the late 1920s, before the introduction of progressive taxation. Behind these changes lie technological shifts that demand a more skilled work force, competition from lower-paid but well-educated workers in the rest of the world. (Thurow, 1995, p. 78)

This new economy wherein the masses possess fewer possibilities for economic stability and the upper one percent have developed wealth far beyond that which Rockefeller and Carnegie managed to accrue during the Progressive Era is the new environment wherein education must be reconstructed. Throughout the documents cited here, issues of human capital are linked with teacher professionalism and state building explicitly and implicitly. National wealth is the justification.

## Teacher Professionalism and State Building

Popkewitz (1991) surmises the social and economic transformations that occurred during the nineteenth and twentieth centuries as complex networks of the modern state or problems of governance. State educational institutions produced dynamic effects in the interrelationships among professional organizations, schooling, pedagogy, teacher education, and university work in the social sciences. Through these avenues, proposals for the re-formation of the industrial worker-individual developed. Particularly within the stratified organizational relations between administration and teachers, school reform and professionalization evolved, or at least was paid lip service (Popkewitz, 1991). However, the professionalization of teachers is, as chapter 5 will indicate, a tenuous classification (status). The manner in which teacher professionalization works within the system, as recommended by *A Nation at Risk*, is that teachers at the bottom of a hierarchy are asked to instrumentally pass the knowledge formulated and produced at the top of the educational hierarchy by commissioned studies, knowledge research and development, and other formal and informal educational organizations' work (Popkewitz, 1991; Bernstein, 1990; Spring, 1996). Teachers are specified as competent stewards of the United States' talent, entrusted with the duty to educate generations of workers.

## Rally Around the Flag—Union and Self-Reliance

*A Nation at Risk* begins with a rallying call, in which the people are beckoned to contribute their fair share to building and rebuilding the nation. The call to rearm the country begins:

All, regardless of race or class or economic status, are entitled to a fair chance and to the tools for developing their individual powers of mind and spirit to the utmost. This promise means that all children by virtue of their own efforts, competently guided, can hope to attain the mature and informed judgment needed to secure gainful employment, and to manage their own lives, thereby serving not only their own interests but also the progress of society itself. (U.S. Dept. of Education, 1983, p. 4)

Although the rhetoric is targeted to public appeal and is made on the supposed basis of equity issues, President Reagan's other cutback policies and statements counteracted much of the equality and civil rights won through long struggle during the 1960s and 1970s (Shor, 1986a).

### Controlling Workers—Workers Controlling Themselves

Renewed interested in promoting worker literacy was evident in a national forum uniting President Bush and all state governors to discuss educational issues in September 1989. Similar goals were also articulated in 1993 in the *Goal 5: Adult Literacy and Lifelong Learning* statement. Literacy objectives included commitment to human capital literacy for "achieving maximum returns from educational investment in English, and to compute and solve problems at levels of proficiency necessary to function on the job and in society, achieve one's goals, and develop one's knowledge and potential" (p. 8). Work-life education and training was defined as

a process whereby individuals, 17 years old or older who are moving into, through, or out of the workplace, undertake formal or organized instruction/activities with the intention of bringing about changes in information, knowledge, understanding, or skills. (p. 23)

With respect to educating minorities who traditionally achieve lower levels of higher education, postsecondary institutions need to "do a better job of recruiting, retaining, and graduating minority students, primarily for reasons of economic competitiveness, but also for the welfare of the individual" (p. 25).

Such a consideration of work as it relates to economic competition and the individual does not take into account the built-in unemployment policies to assure that labor costs do not rise too quickly and to keep inflation down. Perhaps these policies are successful in attaining the equilibrium desired by economists or policymakers; however, the underemployed, unemployed, and minimum-wage workers who lack economic security do not profit from such taken-for-granted practices of laissez-faire and government-regulated approaches to social and fiscal policies.

The reference in *A Nation at Risk* to the need for citizens to develop the ability to manage their own financial affairs (U.S. Dept. of Education, 1983, p. 3) is possible to a certain extent. Yet, workers' affairs are always at the mercy of employers and investors whose decisions set minimum wages, close down plants, move production overseas, divest, or buy out other businesses with little or no notice. Thus, the rhetoric in this statement is optimistic, but superficial as far as it describes workers whose lives are regulated by a dynamic, corporate, capitalist economic market rapidly moving to highly technical operations and a large service industry (Levin & Rumberger, 1983; Thurow, 1995).

## Framing the Discourses

### Literacy Relics in a Sociopolitical Framework

A flurry of activity to improve schools, teachers, and colleges of education, as well as the rigor of the American curriculum, followed on the heels of the cry for attention because other postindustrial nations surpassed the United States in a world economy. *A Nation at Risk* was concerned with the "characteristics, habits, curricula, and spirit that typify the best schools in any geographic or socioeconomic setting" (1983, p. 3). The four policies discussed in this book fix literacy in a work context—work that needs to be done more effectively or education that will prepare workers better. Other policies cited herein were also work related. Specifically, *A Nation at Risk* states that all schools up until the present have not been able to teach school literacy to all children. The directive was "Every elementary can and must teach all its students to read" (p. 2) and writing must be more than filling in blanks and should be taught across the curriculum. Parents were called upon to read to their children or find someone else to read if they could not. Thus, "schools must address parents who are failing their children" (p. 9). In this case, parents' not doing their job necessitates that the schools teach basic skills.

*A Nation at Risk* defines the New Basics as the "foundation for success" and "essentials of a strong curriculum" (p. 24). New basics are included in English and across the curriculum to some degree, equipping graduates to

> (a) comprehend, (b) write well-organized effective papers, (c) listen effectively and discuss ideas intelligently, (d) know our literary heritage and how it enhances imagination and ethical understanding, and how it relates to customs, ideas, and values of today's life and culture. (p. 24)

Today's life and culture are discussed in the singular, yet poststructural and feminist awareness informs us that neither concept can be singular. We are a nation of many cultures, and we are individuals who experience many different lives. The nation responded with statements from many sectors—librarians (U.S. Department of Education, 1984a), the states (U.S. Department of Education, 1984b; Department of Labor, 1987), the university (Holmes Group, 1986, 1990), and foundations (Carnegie Task Force on Teaching as a Profession, 1986)—all committed to help Americans acquire better literacy and work skills, in keeping with an American identity.

**Cultural Literacy—Literacy American Style**
Also in keeping with an American identity, cultural literacy became an important topic. From the view of several elite academics, cultural literacy was lacking in our society and that was the source of social problems. E. D. Hirsch (1987), Alan Bloom (1987), William Bennett (1986a,b), and others equated cultural literacy with a reminiscence of better American morals, values, and knowledge. Subsequently, through his position as secretary of education, and since that time, William Bennett has been a firm and influential advocate of cultural literacy. Both he and Hirsch have directly and indirectly influenced the recent American curriculum, capitalizing on cultural literacy. Schools across the nation have adopted the Hirsch curriculum and its new and improved version that is supposed to incorporate more multicultural elements into the lexicon that guarantees cultural literacy (Hirsch, 1990). Bennett has influenced American opinion about cultural literacy at large with at least two best-selling books: *The Book of Virtues* and a children's series teaching traditional values and morals through Greek mythology.

From his cabinet position in education, William Bennett oversaw several documents about the state of American education, and it is his influence on literacy that is present in this discussion. In *First Lessons* (1986a), he stated that there had not been an extensive report on elementary schools since 1953. He said that the overarching goal of elementary education is "to build for every child a strong foundation for further education, for democratic citizenship, for eventual entry into responsible adulthood" (p. 1). He advocated that the home and school relationship must be seen as a covenant with a goal. Additionally, cultural literacy, a common body of knowledge for all students, is important: our education system must embrace a "knowledge," "moral," and "intellectual discipline" in order to create a "civil nation." Elementary schools must provide the "fundamental skills with which to manage a lifetime of learning . . . enabling disciplines" (p. 21).

In a subsequent document, *What Works: Research about Teaching and Learning* (Bennett, 1986b), he harkens back to Madison's emphasis on knowledge for self-government. The report is meant to provide accurate information to parents and the American people about what "works in the education of our children" (p. v). The curriculum is extended to the home; reading, speaking, and listening, as well as early writing and phonics, reading comprehension, and storytelling are components of his recommendations. Also included are cultural literacy and preparation for work. The message related is that what parents do to help their children learn is more important than the family's financial and social status. Reading to children often is important, as is encouraging children to scribble stories at an early age. Through hard work, then, literacy can be acquired, so that literacy can be utilized in adulthood to work hard.

Within the *Goal 5: Adult Literacy and Lifelong Learning* document, there are internal contradictions which support literacy for social and economical advancement on the one hand, and, on the other hand, state that such skills are no guarantee for economic recompense. Simultaneously, the document explains the need for more worker literacy while it also states that

> Lack of economic rewards for studying and learning is a fundamental problem since the U.S. labor market fails to reward effort and achievement in high school. Although studies have shown that competence in reading, mathematics, and science are strongly related to productivity in almost all

jobs, employees' wages do not reflect this. . . . Wages of employees who
demonstrate such competence are only slightly higher than employees who
lack these skills. (U.S. Dept. of Education, 1993a, p. 15)

The Department of Education also states that although the relationship
between communication skills and the workplace has been made, the
application of communication skills in workplace and citizenship capacities
must be found and taught. Yet, there is a "lack of faculty commitment to
relate those skills to the workplace and citizenship" (1993a, p. 33).

## Teachers Performing Badly; They Need Higher Standards

*A Nation at Risk* both declares teachers' inadequacy and describes
their working conditions as unacceptable (U.S. Dept. of Education, 1983,
pp. 22–23). Despite these conditions and low pay, the document
nonetheless prescribes that educational standards for teachers and all
students need to be raised and more teacher professionalism needs to be
developed. Closely aligned to teacher professionalism is the prognosis that
by recapturing a patriotic mission the American people can educate and
reeducate themselves in order to compete in the international market.
Economic welfare is the principal message of human capital educational
documents (U.S. Department of Education, 1983; 1984a,b; 1993a,b). The
effects of literacy policy contained within the larger general educational
recommendations are expressed as the necessity to incorporate more
reading, writing, foreign language, technological literacy, and math into
the curriculum. As recommended by *A Nation at Risk*, English
requirements for high school graduation were raised from three to four
years and students were expected to take at least one course in
technological literacy. For college-bound students, the recommendation has
been and continues to be four years of English studies. Literacy policy as it
is practiced in the curriculum has changed very little.

## Curriculum Archaeology

Looking at the various course names utilized to describe literacy in the
contemporary curriculum (Hiebert, 1991), we see a slightly different
picture of literacy instruction in the United States. Subject areas in which
public school students learn literacy include English I, II, III, IV, language
arts, reading, resource reading, computer reading skills, English as a
second language, bilingual education, foreign language, and basic skills.[1]

Recent attempts to foster academic improvement across the curriculum have looked to enhance reading skills. Strategies and multiple techniques for engaging learners in language through skills orientation and whole language have been implemented to enhance reading skills (Block, 1995; Willinsky, 1990).

Isolated skills that are used to teach literacy include a myriad of combinations of drills and exercises that attempt to teach reading and writing. The curriculum in Texas has added a Texas Assessment of Academic Skills (or the new version Texas Essential Knowledge and Skills) component to the curriculum. Reading passages and formulaic writing are utilized daily and/or weekly to enhance students' test-taking abilities. Other literacy curricular practices include spelling, vocabulary, paragraph writing, grammar, reading, literature, discussion, composition, and finding main ideas. More advanced literacy work is done in writing research, debate, group problem solving, speech, and drama. Added courses, particularly in technology, math, science, and English, attempt to impose rigorous standards on students. Although little time is left for creativity, and the word creativity does not appear in *A Nation at Risk*, some creative writing occurs around novels, poetry, and short story studies.

At the post-secondary or university level, some of the course parameters that define the preparation of pre-service teachers of literacy include reading, methods, strategies, approaches, language, literacy, culture, multicultural education, bilingual and foreign language, English, English as a second language, grammar, and linguistics. In some colleges of education, some attempts to unite the study of the sciences and humanities in interdisciplinary studies have been made.[2]

Despite the several facets to the teaching and learning of literacy, investigation reveals that the course requirements and the curriculum taught in those courses in schools across the country have remained the same since *A Nation at Risk* (U.S. Dept. of Education, 1984a,b; Hiebert, 1991). Although some efforts have been made to integrate the curriculum, knowledge at all levels of education is disseminated through differentiated means and is generally reduced to "factoids" (Kincheloe, 1993). The disciplines of study are isolated from each other with little connection made between subjects (Pinar, 1995; Grumet, 1995). Curriculum reconceptualists, including Pinar and Grumet, have proposed aligning teacher education with professional intellectual programs such as those common in law schools where "professional" means exercising informed decision making. Critical pedagogical curricula advise using more life experiences of students tied to skills rather than skills developed for skills' sake. Political dimensions of critical and feminist pedagogy attempt to gear classroom literacy activities to student questioning of knowledge and power relations (Maher & Tetreault, 1994; Kincheloe, 1993).

## Molding Student Subjects

Two important points about students surface in the policy statements, particularly *A Nation at Risk*. One is concerned with what students study and the time they spend studying. The message of the policy is that they have not been studying a rigorous enough curriculum, that they take a smorgasbord of courses, that they opt for simplicity over difficulty, and that they do not spend enough time on task at school, nor on homework (U.S. Dept. of Education, 1983, pp. 17–21). Another expressed concern in the policy is the performance of American students in contrast to students of other industrialized countries. Perhaps as a way to cause fear in those concerned with international dominance, it was stated that American students do not fare well in comparison of international test scores. Of course, Berliner and Biddle (1997) inform us that on the contrary, Americans do quite well when compared internationally.

The idea of forming generic students who excel in all areas ignores important information that differentiates between the poor and middle-class students. The poor are constructed as illiterate, having few resources and parents who do not do their job of teaching their children to read. Little mention is made of the differences between middle-class and poor students' access to reading material, time to read, and a place to read. In broad strokes, *A Nation at Risk* glosses over shortage of supplies and the unsuitable living and learning environments that many people face daily. The document clearly states that impoverished schools and/or inner city schools are also lacking certified teachers, particularly in science and math (pp. 22–23). We find upon closer examination that standardized course requirements across the country do not necessarily guarantee the same or equal opportunities. More salient perhaps, in the words of Spring, equality of educational opportunity means little if students are taught that they are inferior or unequal (1996). Readily apparent in Jonathan Kozol's *Savage Inequalities* (1991), the requirements of the curriculum make little difference because some schools, for lack of funds, have neither textbooks nor access to computer technology. On the opposite end of the spectrum, wealthy schools promote technological access to students in classrooms and have richly stocked libraries, textbooks, and other supplies. In between the two ends of the country's spectrum are varying levels of wealth and need.

## Excluded Discourses

Due to funding shortages, the poor are at risk for both dropping out of school and not getting a proper education should they remain in school. According to critical work done by women's studies departments and research across various disciplines, the female gender is also at risk, particularly poor females (Shakeshaft, 1986; Fraser, 1989). The American Association of University Women's study (1995) illustrates how schools shortchange girls typically, and girls and young women "miss out on educational opportunities routinely afforded males" (p. 11). Girls and women, who had been excluded from university life until late last century, historically have been silenced.

At the primary and secondary levels, even girls who study similar curricula as boys are not allowed the same educational opportunities that boys possess. However, the issue of gender inequity was never mentioned in 65 pages of *A Nation at Risk*. Perhaps authorship of the document determined the emphasis given matters of consequence within education. A preponderance of male members of the thirty-five commissions, task forces, and boards of directors would help to explain why female issues did not come to the forefront of educational improvement considerations suggested within the report (U.S. Dept. of Education, 1983, pp. 10–11). The 1995 report *How Schools Shortchange Girls* documents salient deficiencies in the system which ostensibly promotes equity and then teaches all students as if they were male (American Association of University Women, 1995).

## Literacy Practice Makes Literacy Policy

Within the curriculum itself, very little has changed about the way that language arts skills are conceptualized in classrooms (Hiebert, 1991). For the most part, elementary school students do combinations of phonics and whole language learning with trade books. Such practices have generated heated debate, as decision makers in some locales like California, Texas, and Florida have blamed low test scores on whole language. In the middle school, some innovation has occurred by incorporating reader response into the reading and writing activities (Wells, 1996). At the high school level, the textbook is the source of literacy activities, along with some classic American and English novels in some schools (Shannon, 1989; Goodman et al., 1988; Shannon & Goodman, 1994). Thus, the materials which teachers and students utilize to develop literacy have not changed very much during this century (see Hiebert, 1991).

However, what has changed noticeably in classroom curricula since the 1980s has been the reduction of literacy to skills mastery for test success (Shannon, 1990a,b). Utilizing practice test schema takes time away from other reading and writing curriculum. With some individual successes, schools have raised their literacy, as measured by reading and writing test scores. Yet, the overall picture shows the nation's achievement level in a holding pattern as depicted in *The National Education Goals Executive Summary* (National Education Goals Panel, 1995b). Although issues of race, class, and gender are most salient to literacy issues as discussed by Mitchell and Weiler (1991) and Heath (1983), the focus in policy statements only alludes to race and ethnicity when dropout statistics are cited. Moreover, these issues rarely enter mainstream discussions of policymakers as they make expert decisions about how to improve literacy (Fraser, 1989).

## Tracing Literacy Discourses' Proliferations

### Tectonics of Literacy

Just as the earth's plates shift and push one against the other, anthropologists, sociolinguists, curricularists, literary theorists, reading, language, literacy, and culture academic positions push and nudge each other to redefine and refine literacy. Literacy skills are important to all these theorists; however, literacy skills do not guarantee comprehension, nor do they preclude literacy as being used to repress or manipulate individuals (Willinsky, 1990; Spring, 1996; Tozer, Violas, & Senese 1998). Willinsky, along with others, has defined new literacy as political practice (Block, 1995; Edelsky, 1991a). Shannon (1989), in pursuit of more holistic language practices, described the reliance on textbooks for literacy instruction as breaking the promise of education. Sociolinguists have explored the realms of linguistic differences and their relationships to society, locating obvious political aspects of language characteristic to groups of people in their various locations (Hudson, 1980). Cook-Gumperz (1986) described the social construction of literacy as both school and socially related. Heath (1983) found different kinds of literacy practices in communities that related to their needs.

Mitchell and Weiler (1991), incorporating the poststructural works of criticalists, linguists, and feminists, rewrote literacy as related to discourses and social, cultural, and gender experiences. In a study relying on poststructural theories of Michel Foucault and Pierre Bourdieu, Luke (1992) has related the classroom furtherance of literacy as an exercise in bodily, temporal, and thought control of students as they learn literacy as self-control. Gutierrez (1994) has researched classroom literacy discourses to locate differential access to learning based on the relationship between language, context, and literacy teaching. These and other breaks, ruptures, and fissures in the science of literacy research lead us to a better understanding of literacy as a project of social, cultural, and linguistic domination or empowerment (Brodkey, 1991).

Freire (1970) and critical theorists influenced by him—curriculum reconceptualists, poststructuralists, and feminists—associate literacy as defined by the state with projects of domination. "New literacy" projects are described in the words of Haraway as "freedom projects" (cited in Olson & Hirsh, 1995, p. 50). Freedom projects promote social and economic justice within politically oppressive regimes. Such freedom projects, in varying degrees, attend to literacy and political engagement as necessary for coming to voice in a world where many experts and representatives, especially corporate policymakers, speak for others (Foucault, 1965; Kincheloe, 1993; Stone, 1994; Luke & Gore, 1992; U.S. Department of Education, 1983, 1991).

## Significant Signifiers of Literacy Policy Statements

Contrary to advocating literacy for freedom projects, as those advocated by proponents of critical/feminist literacy, the *A Nation at Risk* text makes several references to literacy as related to "skill" and "training." The first excerpt that follows below incorporates both skill and training as necessary for full participation in national life. It is interesting to note the use of the word "disenfranchisement." This term usually connotes a participation in government. Following an introductory discussion about opportunity, in which individuals are asked to prepare themselves "on their own efforts" to "secure gainful employment, and to manage their own lives, thereby serving not only their own interests but also the progress of the nation itself," the first reference to literacy in *A Nation at Risk* is made:

> The people of the U.S. need to know that individuals in our society who do not possess the level of skill, literacy, and training essential to this era will be effectively disenfranchised, not simply from the material rewards that accompany competent performance, but also from the chance to participate fully in our national life. (U.S. Dept. of Education, 1983, p. 7)

In Foucaultian discussion of bio-power, technologies of control, and the union of the state and notions of wealth, the state prepares students through measures of control to be worker-citizens (Foucault, 1980, 1984; Spring, 1980). Such rhetoric, referring to the gross national product and productivity, is articulated to inform the populace how the state's interests, which are also the interests of propertied elites, are best served. In considerations of new anthropology and sociology present in Marx's and Foucault's work, the notion of "progress" is questioned. They felt that "an onward march of progress can no longer be assumed" (Gubrium & Silverman, 1989, p. 5). It is common for statesmen to make statements about social progress, particularly in their associations with policy as socially ameliorative (Weisburd, 1994; Shutkin, 1994; Scheurich, 1994; Jackson, 1994).

As Foucault (1972) theorized about the rise, appropriation, and comingling of discourses, we see that although *A Nation at Risk* is predominantly about worker education, such human capital literacy is tightly and inextricably linked to cultural literacy: "A high level of shared education is essential to a free, democratic society and to the fostering of a *common culture* [emphasis mine], especially in a country that prides itself on pluralism and individual freedom" (p. 7).

Common culture, as it is related to Anglo-European white male supremacy set forth within the *Constitution* and *Federalist Papers*, has been the subject of much discussion, disseminated by the works of Hirsch (1987), Bloom (1987), and Bennett (1984, 1992a,b) as discussed earlier.

Each has described the works that ought to comprise a focus on Western social, historical, and philosophical foundations. Viewed from the postmodern criticalist perspective, such foundations originate in archival footholds reflecting Anglo-Eurocentric, patriarchal-centered knowledge, or the Western canon. If we view the canon as an anachronism, as do some civil rights and women's advocates, we see the canon as obsolete, undemocratic, elitist, exclusionist, racist, and sexist in both overt and covert manners (Stone, 1994; AAUW, 1995; Shakeshaft, 1986).

In *A Nation at Risk*, we see a revival of the canon and revitalization of the educational system with its precepts of male domination and meritocracy. This philosophy, used to advance the concept of competition and individual merit to explain academic and/or financial success, supports the needs of capitalism and leaves status quo knowledge and power relations in place. Such educational policies also attempt to render power invisible (Popkewitz, 1991). Human capital and cultural literacy adheres to Industrial Age power relations and the elite base of what counts as knowledge. Multicultural and gender awareness calls these principles into question. In a conservative backlash, however, nationalistic forces construct "the culturally different" and "illiterates," as determined by skills competency testing, as social pariahs.

## Literacy Anxiety

The conditions under which policymakers wish to make the illiterate literate have been considered a traditional social and economic necessity, particularly for immigrants and culturally different groups (Luke, 1995; Weisburd, 1994). As revealed in *A Nation at Risk*, cultural difference and "functional illiteracy" are threats both to national security and identity: "[Twenty-three] million Americans are functionally illiterate by the simplest tests of everyday reading, writing, and comprehension" (U.S. Dept. of Education, 1983, p. 8). The concern with such a large percentage of illiterates is illustrated below to represent just over one-sixth of youths in general and almost half of minority youth as illiterate: "About 13% of all 17-year-olds in the U.S. can be considered functionally illiterate. Functional illiteracy among minority youth may run as high as 40%" (p. 8).

As indicated by the *A Nation at Risk* discussion, the concern for creating balance in the socioeconomic system is not one fashioned around notions of re-formulation of policies that led to the redistribution of wealth to the top one percent of the population and creates more poverty than in the past (Lamb, 1993; Thurow, 1995). Rather, reform focuses on achievement through higher testing standards that historically have discriminated against those who do not read and write standard English (Edelsky, 1991a).

In essence, the anxiety about functional illiteracy of minority youth expresses imminent unemployed or underemployed future adults as a question of balance that might pit the "have-nots" against the "haves" within society. Insofar as the colonized or dominated groups in this country (whose populations are growing) are unable to pay their way, policymakers project that the political system will encounter instability in the future if such minority groups do not learn to read and write in the manner prescribed by policies. With such an underclass, the United States might be fighting domestic unrest as well as attempting to maintain preeminence within the world market. Workers who are unprepared for the twenty-first century will render the country unable to compete. As of 1983, when *A Nation at Risk* was released, the attitude of the Reagan administration was that "We are raising a new generation of Americans that is scientifically and technologically illiterate" (p. 10). As will be elaborated in the upcoming section, literacy is transforming to become equated with technical skills. Because of rapidly evolving technology, technical and computer literacy become critical skills. Other notions that interrelate with this new emphasis on skilled workers are reflected in the law of literacy. Bound up in the success of business are technical and cultural literacy as they inform and form an American identity.

## Tracing Literacy Discourses' Transformations

Several kinds of literacy transformations have occurred: cultural literacy became multicultural understanding, cultural literacy became nationalistic, and technical literacy and work skills as advocated by business became law. In the 1970s, several scholarly papers described cultural literacy. For example, in *The Cultural Literacy Laboratory: A New Dimension in Multicultural Teacher Education* (University of Arizona, 1973), cross-cultural communication between teachers and students was encouraged. Allen and others (1980) developed the *Tucson Desegregation Model for Teacher Training*. This model defined cultural literacy as an insight into one's culture, a comprehension of frustration and toleration levels, and, finally, as the ability to work with culturally different people.

Bowers (1977) defined "cultural literacy" as tripartite with relation to education. Three definitions include (1) how public education transmits the cultural values that make up the technological world view, (2) how the school socialization process transmits social reality in a way that obscures underlying assumptions of the cultural belief system, and (3) how to alter the socialization process to transmit culture at a more explicit level of awareness.

By the 1980s, cultural literacy in literacy policy was concerned with passing American history, heritage, and culture to public school students. Understanding one's place in the world, known as cultural literacy as conceptualized by Paulo Freire in the 1970s, was quickly displaced by the 1980s with efforts to Americanize and impart middle-class values to public school students. Intercultural understanding became known as multicultural literacy. Freire's conscientization became known as critical literacy.

The literacy advocated by corporate-state government in the policies discussed here became law in the *National Literacy Act* (1991). Technical literacy and work skills became critical as a national crisis was portrayed to the public and teacher educators. Discourses for human capital literacy as dictated by knowledge and power relations came to be regarded as law.

The national literacy legislation was passed into law on March 18, 1991. The Committee on Education and Labor sponsored a bill appropriating $200 million to be spent from 1991 through 1995 on literacy training, particularly for adults. The law entailed establishing vehicles "to enhance the literacy and basic skills of adults, to ensure that all adults in the United States acquire the basic skills necessary to function effectively and achieve the greatest possible opportunity in their work and in their lives" (*National Literacy Act*, 1991, p. 1).

According to the text describing the background and need for such legislation, the measure was taken to formulate primarily "workforce literacy" through adult education (p. 10). The *National Literacy Act*, a federal law, provided a grant for national workforce literacy strategies that meet the following criteria through

(A) *Basic skills training that is—*
   i. *cost effective;*
   ii. *needed by employees; and*
   iii. *required by employers to establish a trainable workforce that can take advantage of further job specific training and advance the productivity of the labor force on an individual, industry, or national level.*
(B) *Specific program offerings, which may include—*
   i. *English as second language instruction;*
   ii. *communications skill building;*
   iii. *interpersonal skill building;*
   iv. *reading and writing skill building; and*
   v. *computation and problem solving.*
(C) *Appropriate assessments of the literacy and basic skills required by business.*
(D) *Cooperative arrangements with other organizations involved in providing literacy and basic skills training, including adult education organizations, vocational education organizations, community and junior colleges, community-based organizations, state level agencies, and private industry councils.*
(E) *The establishment as appropriate of technology-based learning environments, such as computer-based learning centers.*
(3) *Any partnership described in subsection (a)(1) that desires to receive a grant under this subsection shall submit a proposal to the Secretary. The proposal shall contain a plan specifying a strategy for designing and implementing workforce literacy and basic skills training for workers, and justifying the national, statewide, or industry-wide importance of this strategy. The proposal shall include—*
   (A) *a demonstration of need for literacy and basic skills training;*
   (B) *a description of the business or industry for which the strategy is to be established;*
   (C) *a statement of specific, measurable goals and participant outcomes;*
   (D) *a strategy for achieving the goals, including a description of the process to identify literacy and basic skills required by employers and the skills of individual workers, and a description of the specific services to be provided;*
   (E) *a description of the costs of the activities to be undertaken. (1991, pp. 26–27)*

This literacy law inculcates the business community's needs for labor force skills into the context of how to train people to be literate. Although there is some reference to personal skills development, the focus on such skills is to promote worker literacy from the perspective of the business community. The omnipresent concern for expenditures on education necessitates monitoring student achievement from a criterion of productivity and investment payoff (Becker, 1993). Such considerations have been promoted by policymakers as a way to ensure accountability that falls into economical frameworks within a rather amorphous category of human capital theory (Sweetland, 1996). Sweetland traces the genealogy of the concept of human capital theory during a time period from 1776 to the 1960s. The overarching assumption of human capital theory, in the words of Sweetland, "suggests that individuals and society derive economic benefits from investments in people" (p. 341). Since liberal arts studies, and particularly philosophy, have been replaced by profit motives for class mobility, the contemporary focus on what an education is worth hinges on the payback to the individual as well as the nation (Becker, 1993).

Another admonition from the *A Nation at Risk* message was the warning that because "[w]e are raising a new generation of Americans that is scientifically and technologically illiterate" (p. 10), our workers will be unable to compete scientifically, mathematically, and especially technologically with other nations in a new international economy. The nation's workers, or human capital, must be developed with cutting-edge equipment and information.

Science and technology come to the forefront of consideration of the nation's and states' literacy project (Shutkin, 1994). Computer technology is touted as the way to a sounder future throughout the arguments made within *A Nation at Risk*. Many policy initiatives since that time reflect the same necessities (Shutkin, 1994; Spring, 1996; Kincheloe, 1993). According to Shutkin (1994), such political and educational efforts to create technologically literate subjects are applied in schooling, media, play, leisure, and work, so that the students desire technological expertise. This exposure leads to expansion and development within the high technological arena (Shutkin, 1994). The needs of industry, translated into the needs of the state, also become the needs of the individual. The school can begin to meet those needs, driving the economy forward. Yet the big technological revolution can neither correct the errors of inequality nor the trend that is occurring toward inflated credentialing (Levin & Rumberger, 1983). Higher standards of education for lower wages and benefits for many United States' workers, as well as worker reeducation, are described as necessary within a dynamic economy (Kincheloe, 1995; U.S. Department of Education, 1991).

Advocacy of worker literacy through business insights is also traceable in the following five objectives from *Goal 5: Adult Literacy and Lifelong Learning:*

Every major American business will be involved in strengthening the connection between education and work.

All workers will have the opportunity to acquire the knowledge and skills, from basic to highly technical, needed to adapt to emerging new technologies, work methods, and markets through public and private educational, vocational, technical, workplace or other programs.

The number of quality programs, including those at libraries, that are designed to serve more effectively the needs of a growing number of part-time and mid-career students will increase substantially.

The proportion of those qualified students (especially minorities) who enter college, who complete at least two years, and who complete their degree programs will increase substantially.

The proportion of college graduates who demonstrate an advanced ability to think critically, communicate effectively, and solve problems will increase substantially. (U.S. Department of Education, 1993a, p. 5–6)

Much of the success at the attainment of these goals relies on teacher efficiency, which brings us to the next discussion of teacher positioning by these policies.

## Positioning the Teacher Subject

An articulation of the limits to growth in *A Nation at Risk* stated the following:

Each generation of Americans has outstripped its parents in education, in literacy, and in economic attainment. For the first time in the history of our country, the educational skills of one generation will not surpass, will not equal, will not even approach, those of their parents. (p. 11)

On the same page of the document, the following reference to literacy classifies the extent to which the present generation is more educated than the one that preceded it:

> It is important, of course, to recognize that the average citizen today is better educated and more knowledgeable than the average citizen of a generation ago—*more literate* [emphasis mine], and exposed to more mathematics, literature, and science. . . . Nevertheless the average graduate of our schools and colleges today is not as well-educated as the average graduate of 25 or 35 years ago. (p. 11)

Inflation of job and educational credentialing makes more rigorous demands on students and workers presently than in the past, and, in the argument of *A Nation at Risk*, puts more obligation on teachers to teach to the test. Such education results in less well-educated students.

The teacher is responsible for bringing students up to high levels of literacy and will be held accountable to do so. The literacy which teachers are expected to develop in their students is advanced, problem-solving, and oriented to the post-capital society. Although policymakers advocate more education, higher standards, and quantifiable improvements in score attainment, such increases do not ensure better education, nor do they guarantee job security or high wages. What workers on the bottom of the hierarchy have experienced is that education is no longer a guarantee for a comfortable existence, nor is work within the field of high technology necessarily predictable or a panacea (Spring, 1996; Levin & Rumberger, 1983).

Looking to explain low achievement of culturally different students in particular, the *A Nation at Risk* report points to poor management in some California classrooms, revealing that some students get one-fifth the instruction of others in reading comprehension (p. 22). Perhaps, with California's high minority and immigrant populations, it would have been important to explore if such a discrepancy was more an indication of language and cultural discrepancy rather than a lack of intellectual ability or desire. Foucault (cited in Gordon, 1991) explained important connections for centralization of national power located within discourses that unite the purposes of the individual with those of the state. Connecting the individual with the nation necessarily requires socialization, language mastery, and identification with the greater polity (Weisburd, 1994).

The teacher's work becomes synonymous with harnessing the desire of the populace along with the interests of the state to deploy the child as a disciplined student who will become a disciplined worker-citizen (Shutkin, 1994). Such discipline is learned as the controls of rhetoric affect and determine the actions or inactions of individuals as discussed by A. Bennett (1991).

When Bennett explains the rules of exposition, she points to how the parameters around the discourse lead to conclusions within the guidelines prescribed by the speaker or writer. Through representation of values and norms within exposition and reliance on rhetorical strategies, the positioning of the speaker or writer is privileged over the listener or reader. Essentially, the writer is in control, the reader is controlled. Hence, there is no negotiation between what the writer sets forth as truth and what the reader must interpret as truth. The writers of *A Nation at Risk* lead us to their logical conclusion: to reform education by expecting more of teachers, who will transform the non-English speakers, the immigrants, the unemployed, and the future underemployed, as well as the political economy. Teachers, as subalterns, are not allowed to speak or are minimally acknowledged.

## Teaching Student Subjects

In a society that is unequal, undemocratic, and rife with problems caused by lack of community that enables people working together (Putnam, 1995), the teacher is held accountable to teach students cultural literacy and literacy skills for work and citizenship. Students, both in the public school and the university, who learn these kinds of literacy might not be prone to question the economic forces that Thurow described in the new great disparities of wealth in the country.

Such information, as provided by Thurow (1995), sheds new light on what it means to an educated worker at the present time and into the twenty-first century. In *Adult Literacy and Lifelong Learning* (U.S. Dept. of Education, 1993a), the worker is encouraged to develop human potential through the

> ability to read, write, speak in English, and to compute and solve problems
> at levels of proficiency necessary to function on the job and in society,
> achieve one's goals, and develop one's knowledge and potential. (p.8)

Yet, the constraints of work and the low-salaried workers who develop job skills are not readily comprehensible unless one analyzes critically what is considered acceptable to question within the domains of the classroom (Gutierrez, Rymes, & Larson, 1995).

With a growing multicultural population of students and a shrinking population of multicultural teachers, teachers are being held accountable to teach objectives that differentiate knowledge. Students are not, in most cases, asked to make connections between economics, history, and language in their learning. Students are being asked to develop into problem solvers who do not question the most obvious problems that exist all around us: classism, racism, sexism, and economic exploitation, as they are constructed in a system whose purpose is to inspire consumption.

**Forming Postmodern Literate Subjects—Reading Word and World**

Two contradictory ideas of economic and human progress are omnipresent in *A Nation at Risk*. The reality of the limits of growth and progress and the contradiction of the ever-expanding capitalist economy fueled by the ideal of the rank-and-file worker rising up through ranks from the lower class to the upper class bespeak contradiction. A critical perspective by Aronowitz and Giroux (1993) holds that the closed frontier of the middle nineteenth century left little opportunity for social and economic advancement. The exception was the school, where those who labored could hope that the discrepancies and contradictions between the American dream and reality would be corrected. By interrupting the rationale of the *A Nation at Risk* rhetoric, teachers can symbolically subvert the conclusions to locate the power plays that define teachers' work.

Over the last twenty-five years, with the development of poststructural reader response theories, extensive scholarship has described the role of the teacher as interpreter of text versus the reader as meaning-maker (Butler, 1995; Barthes, cited in Sontag, 1982; Kristeva, 1988). Also, as revealed in Mitchell and Weiler's *Rewriting Literacy* (1991), the narrative style and interpretive abilities of readers vary, so that conventional literacy might be sidestepped for more profound understanding or expression. Such expression might be inappropriate according to standard assessments of expository speech and writing. Sociolinguists have studied speakers in their respective communities and found that many groups resist standard language as part of their political reaction to the speakers of standard language (Hudson, 1980; Tozer et al., 1998).

With specific relevance to rhetoric as a curricular requirement, *A Nation at Risk* asserted the importance of learning rhetoric as part of the literacy campaign. Although the reason given for rhetorical development is one of learner empowerment, the rules of rhetoric also enable complacent or docile acceptance of discourse with little or no argument (Bennett, 1991).

## Reading the World

The postmodern critique of such practices raises the world citizens' consciousness on two levels. The first is that actions of all citizens in the world extend beyond their borders. Second, within the borders of the nation, to train only a "few good men and women" is discriminatory and elitist, and thereby unacceptable in a democratic society. The framers of *A Nation at Risk* bemoan that the United States, having come of age, is no longer "isolated from malignant problems of older civilizations" (U.S. Dept. of Education, 1983, p. 6). This malignancy represented the tyranny of a corrupt king and royalty to the founding fathers. In the late nineteenth and early twentieth centuries and throughout the Cold War, political malignancy was personified in socialism and communism. Now, the threat of economic inferiority to advancing postindustrial nations affects the educational goals by demanding more technological know-how and competitive interaction in an international economy.

To what degree, the criticalist must ask, is the average worker going to participate in the international economy? The corporations that move readily beyond national borders will benefit by international expansion, while the average workers will be unemployed because of outsizing, downsizing, and divestitures. How will technological education avert such losses? A postmodern view of the role of education in a corporate-controlled state brings to light the predatory and colonial policies and practices of postcapitalism.

The postmodern feminist or criticalist moves beyond the borders of nationalistic ethnocentrism. Teachers must help students progress beyond the myth of predominance of the United States economy, as well as the preeminence of the postmodern consumer society. As far as standard of living goes, the United States ranks eleventh by various indicators

(McLaren, 1998). With little international conscience or conscientization about worker abuse and oppression, American workers might have formerly accepted their working conditions in exchange for comfort. They might not have questioned the myth of meritocracy critically. In a meritocracy as established by Eliot and Thorndyke, equal education and rewards are bestowed upon the fittest. Unequal education might not have appeared pernicious because workers could earn more than adequate wages. Now, workers have more reason to be critical because neither extensive education nor hard work will guarantee financial success. However, a more enlightened view is that workers around the world have historically earned less and consumed fewer resources—many of them under the domination of U.S. political and economic policies. With respect to the American worker, lack of competitive edge with foreign economic strength is not due to poor productivity, but rather to United States postwar foreign policy. After World War II, development in Europe and Japan through the Marshall Plan put the United States behind because those overpowered in war rebuilt themselves anew in the American image in order to develop capitalism around the world.

A schizophrenic attitude toward the world has had American policymakers looking abroad for commerce yet demanding that Americans remain provincial in their views toward language and foreigners. Familiarity with the outside world brings us to greater realization that in the global village one can no longer practice linguistic isolationism. Ironically, elite politicians and statesmen have historically learned foreign languages in order to develop themselves personally and socially through international relations. At the same time, they have promoted English-monolingualism and Anglo-centric cultural dominance for the masses. Through their associations, elites had access to lavish indulgence in foreign opulence and culture; at the same time, they prohibited foreign ideas such as communism and socialism (malignant problems) from the mainstream market of ideas. Classist views have traditionally advocated poor immigrants' forgetting their language and culture, whereas the wealthy were encouraged to be multilingual.

Ironically, now that corporations seeking higher profits exploit cheaper labor outside of the borders of the United States, the economy is "global." Workers, on the other hand, may not trespass borders to enter other countries' jurisdictions for work. Perhaps, if upholding the freedoms of democracy were at the heart of the message articulated in *A Nation at Risk*, the global economy would be reconceptualized to include what a truly global economy would entail.

Scholars from many persuasions of feminist theory consider the experiences of women from around the world. They listen to these women's voices to reframe the vision of what social, political, and economic life might be like if there were serious considerations being taken for women and children around the world. In this respect, Maxine Green quotes Merleau Ponty, who said, "The world is not what I think but what I live through" (cited in Stone, 1994, p. 17). Because patriarchal decision-makers in positions of power can more easily articulate to the many what our reality is, we interpret our realities through what Green terms a stock of knowledge at hand. Yet, the American ideology of optimistic democracy and progress does not easily accept elite political and economic dominion as oppressive. Lather, citing Giroux, says that "the very fact of domination has to be proven to most Americans" (Lather, 1994, p. 246).

The omission of women's issues and input into *A Nation at Risk* is not obvious unless we look closer at the panel who wrote the document. The American Association of University Women's report (1995) says, "Sixty percent of the education-reform-report commissions reviewed for this study had less than 30 percent female representation. Only two were at least 50 percent female" (p. 10). Lather (1994) looks to the role and economic exploitation of women. She says that teachers, who are generally women, continue to bear the brunt of educational critique in reports like *A Nation at Risk*. In general, women also deal with the stress of double days (responsibility for work outside and inside the home, as well as childcare). The message of progressive policy prescription sends women dual signals as they attempt to participate in public life, often at the expense of children, and as they participate at home, raising children with no compensation. Women "daily witness the rhetoric of America as a child-centered society versus the reality of our culture's devaluation of care and raising children" (Lather, p. 247). Correction of the vulnerability and exploitation of women and children around the world in corporate as well as home life depends on reexamination of the global effects of more children growing up with primary care given by neither father nor mother. The key message of *A Nation at Risk* brings overcoming language and cultural difference to the forefront of educational importance. As promoted by postmodern literacy insight, the basics of literacy formation are much more basic to respective life concerns of all learners. Rethinking the basics means transformation of the curriculum and what we call "basic skills."

## Conclusion

Literacy, as spelled out in *A Nation at Risk,* means worker skills and technological know-how. Reeducation, particularly to conform to the necessities of the technological revolution and progress, is defined and outlined by policymakers. Such progress necessarily depends on scientific measures of attainment, rather than on the needs of citizens. Women's, children's, and struggling low-wage earners' issues fall outside the consideration of educational policy discourses framed by mathematical, scientific, and technological focus (Scheurich, 1994). Through required scientific measures of basic skills by experts, literacy for control of the masses is accomplished for nationalistic and corporate purposes and not for the larger purposes of a democratic society.

The degree to which teachers consciously or unconsciously play the part of passing the torch of established knowledge and power regimes to the next generation in the classrooms has been seriously pursued by continental and American scholars. The Marxist notion of social reproduction is often cited as the foundation for the criticalist view of capitalist society and schooling (Freire, 1970; Giroux, 1983, 1988a,b; Aronowitz & Giroux, 1985). More recently, feminists have broached the subject, not only from a collective perspective but also from personal experience, dependent on individuals' own voices to express how such knowledge and power relations are taught through the traditional curriculum. In some locations, the university curriculum has been the location of experimentation in feminist classroom and feminist pedagogical innovations. Such attempts to alter the androcentric foundations of knowledge have met with their own difficulties as the position and power of the professor remains an issue in any learning situation where the students must perform according to the professor's standards.

The United States Department of Education admits, in *Reaching the Goals: Goal 5: Adult Literacy and Lifelong Learning*, that "There are multiple definitions of literacy" (1993a, p. 1). In spite of this acknowledgment throughout the document, literacy is linked to training for work-life. Such training is defined as

> a process whereby individuals, 17 years old or older who are moving into, through, or out of the workplace, undertake formal or organized instruction/activities with the intention of bringing about changes in information, knowledge, understanding or skills. (p. 23)

As outlined by the Department of Education this policy advocates achieving more and better education for workers' literacy in the United States by tracking nationwide progress.

The Department of Education, incorporating the findings of a 1989 policies and practices study, cites that participation in "worklife education and training" is related to factors including age, race/ethnicity, prior education level, income, employment status, and type of education. As reasoned in the document, the least likely to participate are "those 55 to 64 years old, black and Hispanic, having less than a high school education, incomes of less than $10,000, unemployed, or in lower paid, lower skill occupations" (1993a, p. 23).

Some of the barriers that they encounter, according to the document, include "personal problems, lack of confidence, education costs, lack of interest in organized education, or lack of interest in available courses. Education costs and lack of time were the most often cited [barriers]" (p. 24). Critical analysis of this phenomenon suggests that people who possess low-paying jobs realistically possess few opportunities to better their lot in life. Yet, altering social and economic structures that perpetuate the low-paying status of some work is not considered as a viable option. Persons with low-paying positions are expected to raise their salaries by getting more education.

The *Goal 5* document spends several pages on the ways that work and school can be related through communication. The document emphasizes how communication skills relate to work issues. In a critical mode, teachers must question how we teach students to be compliant students and workers. By educating citizen-workers rather than worker-citizens, we will teach them to question public and community policies. If they learn to write well-organized papers about literature and other language arts–related subjects, will they also learn to write well-organized papers that speak to the problems in our society? If students are from privileged backgrounds and they see no blatant problems in their own experiences, are they made aware of and expected to discuss social life and its pressures? Are home and family concerns related to social and political issues that have traditionally limited and defined women's work? What kinds of ideas are students allowed to discuss intelligently? Are there political, social, and economic subjects that can simply not be discussed? As the new curriculum for economics education has been reduced to the study of free enterprise, are students apprised of the kinds of socioeconomic issues that they face with shrinking full-time job opportunities, shrinking incomes, and few benefits? Are they intelligently allowed to think and write about why their lives will be affected by governmental policy that forms them into economic beings or *homo economicus*? In a consumer society, it is often difficult to discern other reasons for being.

Certainly citizenship ought to be first and foremost for living in a democratic country. Citizens' roles as parents, workers, community builders, and political beings capable of transforming society are the roles of postmodern literacy education for teachers. Shor (1986a) found that although policymakers pay lip service to equity, the focus has still been on excellence, particularly following the impetus of policies such as those implemented during the Reagan era that channeled resources into educating an elite segment of the population. In "Lifestyles of the Poor and Working" (Lamb, 1993), reading the world suggests a different picture of poverty than that which paints welfare queens:

> In 1991 the Census Bureau reported that nearly 36 million Americans were living in poverty, write John E. Schwarz and Thomas J. Volgy in *The New Republic* (Nov. 23, 1992). But Schwarz and Volgy, authors of the recently published book *The Forgotten Americans* (Norton, 1992), say the real figure is actually much higher. They claim that "during 1989, 56 million Americans—or 22 percent of the American population—resided in households with incomes that could not realistically provide for basic necessities." (Lamb, 1993, pp. 19–20)

Such poverty gives new insight into the postindustrial, Information Age dream of national grandeur. Teachers, among some of those poor, cannot correct the problems of modern capitalism. Let us now turn to how teacher education discourses construct pre-service teachers' literacy.

# NOTES

1. Although literacy also is taught in all the disciplines as well as in the hidden curriculum, literacy per se is limited to the study of language and literature focusing on reading, writing, speaking, listening.

2. At the University of Texas at San Antonio, there is an interdisciplinary studies major that connects the sciences and humanities in preparation for elementary school teaching. At the secondary level, students are required to major in a discipline and then take 18 credit hours of education courses.

# CHAPTER V

## DISCOURSES OF TEACHER EDUCATION

The goal of this chapter is to focus on some well-disseminated discourses of teacher education reform. Along with school restructuring, teacher professionalism has been one of the most salient features of the recent reform movement. However, the reforms that have made the most impact on changing teacher education programs and restructuring schools have not made teacher education as professional as other professions, as discussed in chapter 2. The discourses on which I will focus have involved initiatives to improve education by "recruiting, preparing, and re-training competent teachers by better utilizing their knowledge and talents over the course of a reshaped career" (Darling-Hammond, 1990, p. 17).

### Fixing Discourses of Teacher Education

A hierarchy of power beginning at the national level descends to the state level, where teacher education discourses are controlled by laws and university governance procedures. Power over teacher education also exists in colleges of education, as well as in schools where students do their interning and student teaching. Within universities, the disciplines in which secondary education majors learn the subject in which they will specialize are often dictated by a host of traditions in programs in which majors and minors are required to study traditional content area. Knowledge dissemination in teacher education depends on history, past decisions, and policies within respective disciplines (Cherryholmes, 1988). Cherryholmes believes that these discursive practices are partially anonymous and that they are enforced by power structures. Postmodern teacher education engages students in understanding those power structures and helps pre-service teachers articulate critique of normative practices and power arrangements that perpetuate existing knowledge and power relations defining and forming teachers.

### Statements Construct Inferior Teacher Subjects

Official policy statements about teacher inferiority and "unprofessional" teacher education at the national level have been explicit and implicit over the last seventeen years. *A Design for a School of Pedagogy* (Smith, 1980) elaborated on the shortcomings of teacher education from several perspectives, including professionalism, knowledge bases, and scientific grounding of pedagogical theory. Explicit references to pre-service teacher education in *A Nation at Risk* are concerned with meeting higher academic and test-score standards. One statement asserted that

> Persons preparing to teach should be required to meet high educational standards, to demonstrate an aptitude for teaching, and to demonstrate competence in an academic discipline. Colleges and universities offering teacher preparation programs should be judged by how well their graduates meet these criteria. (U.S. Dept. of Education, 1983, p. 30)

Other statements about teacher education in *A Nation at Risk* refer to in-service teachers. Concerns are expressed about raising salaries; rewarding good teachers; scheduling time for curriculum and professional development; implementing career-ladder incentives that would reward master teachers; addressing math, science, and English teacher shortages; assisting areas of financial need; and designing teacher education programs (pp. 30–31). Discourses of teacher education improvement also emanated from colleges of education and consortiums of teacher educators over the last fifteen years (Goodlad, 1983; Goodlad, Soder, & Sarotnik, 1990; Holmes Group, 1986, 1990, 1995b; Murray & Fallon, 1989).

## Framing the Discourses of Teacher Education

These official statements about teacher education occur within the late twentieth century in three paradigms of teacher education, described by Kincheloe (1993) as (1) behavioristic, (2) personalistic, and (3) traditional-craft orientations, as they exist in colleges of education. The *A Nation at Risk* guidelines for teacher education are grounded in Newtonian-Cartesian scientism, behavioral psychology, and liberal arts traditions. As suggested by *A Nation at Risk,* teachers need to be better test-takers, teach to tests better, and pass on the traditions of Western canonical knowledge. The document also sets into motion a propensity to monitor teacher work which has intensified through present administrative procedures.

Through state teacher appraisal systems developed since *A Nation at Risk*, teacher surveillance has increased. Most recent efforts to hold public school teachers accountable will measure teacher performance by student test achievement. Taking the surveillance one step further, newest reforms in Texas education will hold colleges of education accountable for prospective teachers' performance on the ExCET Exam ("Teacher Prep Programs," 1997). Newest federal executive articulations of monitoring teacher work include President Clinton's proposed education standards. He has forcefully recommended state adoption of policies that would create exams designed by the leadership of the Department of Education to measure fourth graders in reading and eighth graders in math beginning in 1999 ("Clinton Lashes Out," 1997).

As pre-service teachers currently prepare themselves to teach in public schools, they understand how in-service teachers are being evaluated by test achievement and thus think that they will be compelled to teach to the test. Most recent efforts to bring low-achieving schools up on standardized tests include implementing curricula that promote practice of test items in all classrooms, to the point that all teachers must cover the same page and problems on the same day. Pre-service teachers can prepare themselves to deal with these testing requirements that can easily disempower teachers (Schon, 1983). They can follow the rules, becoming more technocratic rather than tempering the technical abilities with attributes desirable of reflective practitioners.

An alternative to being controlled to teach to the test is to prepare students to achieve results by practicing test procedures, as well as by developing critical literacy with students. Many pre-service teachers who will not be engaged in transforming classrooms into democratic communities with their mentor teachers will succumb to technocratic teaching because of their fear of not presenting themselves as accountable (Cochran-Smith, 1991). Surveillance of test scores and close classroom observations by school administration promotes control of knowledge, as well as teacher and student behavior.

**Surveillance of Teachers**

Monitoring of teacher behavior is accomplished through several strategies—some originate in scientism and behavioral frameworks of assessing educators and others emanate from more recent attempts to improve teacher professionalism. Outright normalization occurs instrumentally as students and teachers are allowed little personal freedom to explore learning outside of the tightly controlled curriculum. Assessment scales, designed to measure teacher effectiveness on site in classrooms by administrators or outside reviewers, rate teacher efficiency. Ironically, even more progressive teacher preparation also promotes surveillance of teachers. Such surveillance occurs as collaboration as mentor teachers guide interns or new teachers. Although innovative in respect to forming learning communities intent upon improving themselves, such cooperation still accomplishes surveillance over teacher work. In a Foucaultian analysis, the surveillance of teacher work is a technology of control that teachers eventually impose upon themselves. The idea of some control of teachers is not unfounded; however, the degree to which discourses of teacher accountability reflect the necessity of teacher compliance with little discussion of alternatives indicates how surveillance becomes part of authoritarian regimes whereby knowledge and power relations are not questioned and therefore can become oppressive to both teachers and students.

## Tracing Teacher Education Discourse Proliferations

The Holmes Group, a consortium of teacher educators from nearly 100 research universities, formed in 1983. The consortium was committed to three ideals: (1) making programs of teacher preparation more rigorous and connected to liberal arts education, (2) doing research on learning and teaching, and (3) promoting wise practice in the schools. Three reports by the Holmes Group influenced teacher education across the nation to some degree: *Tomorrow's Teachers* (1986), *Tomorrow's Schools* (1990), and *Tomorrow's Schools of Education* (1995). Specific attention was given to improving colleges of education by making public schools a more integrated part of teacher education. In a report of the Holmes Group, *Tomorrow's Schools: Principles for the Design of Professional Development Schools* (1990), the group promoted more serious links between the school and university education departments. As articulated by a Holmes spokesperson, "The more we talked, the more we realized that teacher education represents a mesh in a very wide net that stretches from the universities to the schools and out to the wider society" (1990, p. vii).

In 1988, with Ford Foundation money, the Holmes Group prepared a report to describe the reform movement. Their vision tied professional programs to the concept of the professional development school. Important to the success of this reconceptualized system are bonds that must be formed between universities and schools. These partnerships would consist of peers including practicing teachers, administrators, teacher educators, and administrator educators. According to the precepts of this system, tomorrow's teachers would gain experience in areas that address the reciprocity between research and practice, acquire willingness to try new forms of practice and structure, and approach systematic inquiry or commitment to the development of teaching strategies for a broad range of children with different backgrounds, abilities, and learning styles (Holmes Group, 1990, p. viii).

The Holmes Group plan developed as ideas emerged from the educational community. Representatives from business, state governments, and national education policy experts collaborated "to offer their views on the future structure of schools and work of educators" (1990, p. ix). As defined by the Holmes Group, the professional development school's mission entails six initiatives:

1) Promoting more ambitious conceptions of teaching and learning on the part of prospective teachers in universities and students in schools;
2) Adding to and reorganizing collections of knowledge about teaching and learning;

3) Ensuring that enterprising, relevant, responsible research and development is done in school;

4) Linking teacher advancement in knowledge and status with efforts to improve schools and better prepare new teachers;

5) Creating incentives for public school and university faculties to work mutually;

6) Strengthening relationships between schools and sociopolitical and economic communities where they reside. (1990, pp. 1–2)

Six guiding principles of the professional development school included:

(1) Teaching and learning for understanding might require a radical revision of the schools' curriculum and instruction;

(2) Creating a learning community;

(3) Teaching and learning for understanding for everybody's children;

(4) Continuing learning by teachers, teacher educators, and administrators;

(5) Thoughtful long-term inquiry into teaching and learning;

(6) Inventing a new institution. (1990, p. 7)

Several education analysts, theorists, and practitioners have tackled several of the Holmes Group's concepts in the contexts of their own educational discourses (Stone, 1994; Shaker & Kridel, 1989; Grumet, 1989; Kincheloe & Steinberg, 1995).

In a critique of what Holmes innovations have accomplished, Murray and Fallon (1989) describe three "disturbing trends" in the greater national reform arena. The following are cited: (1) several of the strongest universities in the country omitted their colleges of education "as a means of strengthening their other, presumably more worthy, professional schools," (2) the education of teachers became entrusted to universities less than the nation's best, "many of them unaccredited and impoverished," and (3) none other than colleges of education thought or thinks much of their abilities to live up to their responsibilities in the past or the future (p. 28). The areas of proposed change in the 1995 Holmes Group report included new faculty, new instructional arrangement, new students, new scholarship, and new partnerships.

Labaree and Pallas (1996) attack the newest Holmes report on the grounds that the proposed innovations should occur within the professional development school prism. They assert that to disregard the importance of graduate school research questions about education is to "narrow the mission of the education school and limit its possible contributions to American education" (Labaree & Pallas, 1996, p. 47).

Other articulations of improving teacher education have come from corporate foundations. Aspects of improving teacher education with respect to liberal education are advanced in Carnegie Corporation's *The Reform of Teacher Education for the 21st Century* (Murray & Fallon, 1989). The crux of the policy is a challenge to replenish teacher education with more liberal arts courses, as well as some awareness of multicultural and gender issues. However, these references are superficial and do not recommend serious social reconsideration or reconstruction of undemocratic educational and social practices.

If we look for reversal in policy statements about education reform, we find no discussion about teacher education in *America 2000* (U.S. Dept. of Education, 1991). In fact, no references to teacher education are made in *America 2000*. Instead, the goals of the plan invoke finances and expertise of corporations, the business community, and corporate foundations. Thus, the business and political community bypass and override the educational community in this project. Support of 535 excellent schools, one in each congressional district, is the main thrust of *America 2000*. The policy's promotion of competition and choice with no mention of race, class, and gender issues assumes that all students are operating with the same level of resources at home and at school and that excellence is optimal over equity, thereby promoting highly technical school meccas where ostentatious equipment overshadows what most schools are able to offer their future teachers and students.

## Tracing Transformations in the Discourses of Teacher Education

Empowerment of teachers through site-based management and technological prowess has overpowered mainstream policy discussions of teacher education. Such technological focus has had positive results in some settings, yet the politics of restructuring schools have not accounted for reconceptualizing teachers' work. Restructuring has meant little change in teachers' work. On the contrary, concern with de-skilling of teachers as educational technology and testing drive desires and accountability in education is discussed at length by Darling-Hammond and Wise (1991); Smith (1980); Apple (1989); and Aronowitz and Giroux (1993). Smylie (1996) evaluates standards and assessments as they have been employed to improve education through action as "technically complex and philosophically and politically contentious; and they are problematic as singular mechanisms for change" (p. 10).

Extending the economic definition of human capital to the promotion of teacher work as human capital, Smylie defines human capital in education as "the knowledge, skills, dispositions, and social resources of adults in schools that can be applied to promote children's learning and development" (1996, p. 10). In order to achieve such objectives, teachers need "to be flexible, innovative, critically analytical, and reflective" (p. 10). Such empowerment of teachers promotes change through teacher professionalism and autonomy, supported by creating the environment conducive to such change, as opposed to "bureaucratic work rules and procedures" (p. 9). In a nutshell, Smylie surmises that "While the primary change mechanism of regulatory policy is control, the crucial mechanism for building human capital is learning" (p. 10).

Approaching teacher learning through the concept of human capital building is presented by Smylie as a potentially positive endeavor. In some places, teacher learning is addressed weekly through staff development meetings (Sam Houston High School, San Antonio Independent School District). In this way, teacher learning is facilitated. However, despite promotion of teacher learning, if teacher appraisal is built around student achievement on standardized tests, the net result is still regulatory control. Thus, the idea of teacher work enhanced by teacher learning often becomes tied to the concept of teaching teachers how to teach students how to perform successfully on exams, rather than how to be critical readers and writers.

**Discourse of Teacher as Technocrat Predominant**
Wolcott (1977) describes the rise of teachers as technocrats whose work has been molded by a combination of forces: predictability, control, management, and data-based decisions fit into structures formed by rules and regulations. In a counter-discourse, Giroux (1988b) discussed teachers as intellectuals, providing a counterpoint to the abundance of discussion

about education as technocratic and teachers as subservient state-serving clerics.

The emphasis on technicism became prominent after progressive liberal ideology led to the efficiency model of schooling as opposed to Dewey's democratic developmentalism (Tozer, Violas, & Senese, 1998). If we consider the efficiency model as a dominant discourse of teacher education and school management, the theory of reversal invites us to question what discourse is excluded by emphasizing the efficiency and technicist domains of achievement. Such critique reveals a feminist domain of human interaction, pedagogy, and literacy insight. Feminist ideology stands in opposition to the technocratic approach to bureaucratic efficiency and management. Contrary to modern education practices exists an ethic of care, concern for community, and promotion of human relations and more democratic social practices (Martin, 1994; Stone, 1994; Gilligan et al., 1988).

Freire (1970) responded to the rise of the teacher as technocrat with the emancipatory curriculum based on the lives of learners. The teacher for Freire is not a technocrat, but rather a politically engaged learner who mobilizes with students to strive for democratic social transformation.

In the United States, where many assume that because we call ourselves a democratic society we are one, it is common practice for teachers to implement directives as they are articulated from above. Often it is difficult to convince teachers that they must contextualize teaching and learning in the social setting where it occurs (Kincheloe, 1993). The postformal teacher practices within the emerging postmodern paradigm of knowledge construction and critique with students. He/she rejects the curriculum of power and authority to question with students the foundations of knowledge as well as the network of control which the power and knowledge form throughout schooling. Questioning the presentation of history, the origins of literature, and the foundations of classical, liberal, democratic thought redefines the mission of an inquiring teacher. Patterson, Stansell, and Lee (1990) have examined the empowerment of teachers as researchers who gain power as they research within their teaching environment. Firsthand creation of knowledge, upon which teachers may reflect and make informed decisions, becomes the work of the reflective practitioner.

Interestingly, the discourse of reflective practitioner has been employed by critical educators and most recently has been appropriated by state proficiency guidelines as articulated by the Texas Education Agency (1994). The state guidelines encourage reflective instruction on the part of teachers to address issues of student-centered education and equity. However, the issue of equity as envisioned by the state does not encourage questioning the knowledge and power relations that formulate knowledge. Rather, it encourages implementing standards and giving some semblance of equal opportunity to students to master the preordained curriculum and the required state exams. Therefore, the emphasis in teacher learning as it is developed in teacher education discourses remains a technical venture, one tied to test scores and accountability instruments, rather than one committed to uniting teacher and student learning to most effectively address problems, needs, and interests of both teachers and students as learners.

## Positioning the Teacher Subject

Modern teaching relies on the authority of bureaucracy, assessment, basic skills, and decontextualized social settings to pass knowledge to a new generation of student learners. Teachers, who are not able to articulate their needs for themselves or to decide what school and social goals ought to be, are managed and are part of the human capital development project initiated with *A Nation at Risk* (U.S. Dept. of Education, 1983). To the degree that teachers are faced with more requirements and accountability based on test performance by students, they are de-skilled and disempowered. They become subjects of modern educational policy that serves to differentiate and thus exploit workers in a capitalist system. Teachers are used as the scapegoats for the ills of the capitalist economy as articulated by the neo-conservative movement. They are expected to behave as professionals with few benefits afforded other professionals, including livable wages. The teachers, in turn, because of their compliance with authority that specifies curricula and standards, expect standard performances from students who come from lower sectors of society where blue-collar wage earners are often unappreciated and are regarded as socially inferior. Tracking, as it is imposed in schools and within classrooms, helps to further the hierarchical power relations that value elite knowledge and is scornful of native knowledge and cultural differences. In the words of a student of mine, teachers are often the "exploited, vilified, and underpaid." Yet, they teach the knowledge deemed appropriate by the exploiter. Those who advocate corporate control over social and public issues are considered exploitative of the masses by postmodern critics who question the use of power for economic gain at the expense of women, minorities, or low-wage earners. Teachers who teach respect for the knowledge and power relations as they exist in a corporate-dominated society can be considered in collusion with knowledge and power relations that are often socially unjust and economically undemocratic.

A few teachers will benefit from existing undemocratic knowledge and power relations. For example, those teachers who teach in *America 2000* schools may enjoy cutting-edge technology and curriculum enhancement. They are teaching privileged students—elite learners who will become the designers of technology—rather than less privileged students who are controlled by technology (Levin & Rumberger, 1983; Levin, 1985; Kozol, 1991). Teachers themselves will also be controlled by technology unless they formulate the use of their own technology programs in classrooms (Apple, 1989).

Unless teachers question how they are positioned in the social hierarchy within schools with varied resources, they will be easily controlled. As evaluations of teachers reflect student test achievement, teachers will adapt and do better jobs of teaching their students the required curricula contextually, or they will be punished for not having disciplined themselves and their students adequately. However, teaching skills in the context of literate critique of real issues, textbook knowledge, and school policies need not preclude basic skills and test competence because such basic skills enable further development of more critical skills. As teachers question their place in the social hierarchy, they can better understand how they become agents of the state to perpetuate the existing knowledge and power relations that can exploit some learners and exalt others who will become the future beneficiaries of a hierarchical, sociopolitical, and economic system.

## Teaching Student Subjects

Reformed teachers within the modern mode ask their students to conform and perform. When teaching jobs are dependent on student performance, teachers are more manageable. Similarly, when students comply with the regulations set forth in tightly controlled classrooms, there is little room for advancement of critical thought or for reconceptualizing what a democratic society or classroom might look like. According to Foucault's (1980) explanation of reversal, that which is emphasized in classrooms de-emphasizes other kinds of knowledge or activity. In the case of a classroom where the established order of knowledge and power is perpetuated by reading groups focused on the classics (which concentrate on the lives and histories of elite white males), little, if any, attention is given to girls, who need to develop more feminist understandings of their inferior position in the knowledge and power hierarchy, as well as within the socioeconomic order.

A refocusing on the classics and a liberal education, while preferable to dwelling solely on scientific and technological domains of human development, does not necessarily get to the root of the problem of redefining knowledge. As Kincheloe (1993) described the notion of teacher and student construction of knowledge, it is the last boundary of examining formal knowledge versus other ways of knowing. Modes of thought and the setting in which they occur constitute knowledge that is highly valuable for critically engaged students and teachers. A redefinition of knowledge and literacy demands understanding paradigms and how within given frameworks certain knowledge is more important. On the contrary, if the paradigm shifts, the rules change, and certain knowledge is considered less valuable because the priorities have changed (Barker, 1992). A postmodern educational framework demands that teachers become adept at questioning the knowledge and power relations that can lead to the oppression of students by not encouraging political engagement through literacy development.

## Forming Postmodern Literate Teachers

Inquiry-oriented teacher education within feminist and critical poststructural frameworks engages in four areas of deconstruction of the taken-for-granted public school discourse and practice: (1) examination of power, (2) the uncovering of deep social and educational structures, (3) desocialization through ideological reckoning, and (4) deference to community knowledge as the most powerful pedagogy (Kincheloe, 1993). A discussion of these four processes follows.

Moving past awareness of power and knowledge relations in various dimensions of teaching and professional education demands defining how power is represented in schools as well as in the curriculum. Teachers can develop local means to respond to legislatures that formulate educational policy around business and industrial leaders. In essence, to look at the social construction of schooling and knowledge and how they formulate literacy is to begin to understand how to deconstruct them and to reconstruct them more democratically.

As pre-service teachers proceed from their understandings of knowledge as a social construction, they can uncover the deep structures that shape society and education. Such excavation can occur in action research. Through practicing analytical habits of reading, writing, and thinking, students with teachers engage in textual analysis of the methods that comprise much of pre-service teacher education and then apply what is found in field experiences.

As postmodern practitioners, pre-service teachers with their teacher educators look at tacit knowledge and assumptions about education and render them problematic. Kincheloe refers to this process as "desocialization via ideological disembedding" (1993, p. 197). Such an enterprise requires explanation of how "myths, behavior, and language dictate school practice and teacher expectation" (p. 198). Moving past the myths and grand narratives of progress and toward reading the world, we discover how much work there is to be done in the building of democracy. Britzman (1986) recommends that student teachers' personal, social, and cultural experiences hinge on education that privileges some students while exploiting others. Postmodern teacher education allows pre-service teachers to consider and reflect on the forces that have formed them as students and as future teachers and how those forces will be reproduced or interrupted by them as future classroom teachers.

Knowledge and power relations of literacy and democracy inform the postmodern, literate pre-service teacher. Linking democracy and literacy practices promotes recognition of the role of "self-organized community groups" and "powerful pedagogy" (Kincheloe, 1993, p. 198). Educational change in the emerging postmodern paradigm looks beyond the demands of business and industrial elites to become part of a transformative social movement. Such a movement relies on reconceptualizations of democracy and consciousness building. For Giroux (1988a,b), Shor (1986a,b), Kincheloe (1993), and McLaren (1998), "postmodern knowledge becomes a product of democratic cooperation, a manifestation of what happens when experience is interrogated in the light of historical consciousness intercepting personal experience" (Kincheloe, 1993, p. 198).

In *Community-Based Ethnography* (Stringer et al., 1997), the roles of theory and experience are expanded. In Stringer's project, community-building precedes knowledge construction. The sharing of experience brings common goals and visions, which in turn result in democratic knowledge-building. When community-building happens democratically, personal, professional, social, structural, and community knowledges culminate in polyphonic expression of many voices. In a learning community, members share discourse in ways that often are overlooked in the modern approach to professional development or teaching in classrooms.

## Conclusion

### Reformed Subjects

The area of teacher education reform has evolved through studies funded by corporate foundations, school-university partnerships, and grant projects, usually under the leadership of university departments or site-based initiatives. Although most critics of education agree that there is a long way to go until optimal reform is achieved in educational programs, they disagree about the substance of educational reform. The discourses about what ought to constitute curricular reform occur in a widely contested terrain (Kincheloe, 1993; Kincheloe & Steinberg, 1993; Stone, 1994; Greene, 1986). Efforts to reform education that followed *A Nation at Risk* and *America 2000* to affect the politics of teacher education eventually became affairs to be settled between and among state legislatures and university educational departments (Prestine, 1991). Year 2000 initiatives by the state legislature and Governor George W. Bush have sought to reform education by promoting change in the colleges of education across Texas; in turn, the colleges have responded by restructuring their programs according to state mandates. The decentralization of power structures from the state board of education and the college of education to the site of the school, however, does not necessarily untangle the networks of power relations in colleges of education, much less those in classrooms.

The flurry of existing policy formulation within the Clinton administrations has responded to the rhetoric of shortages of math and science teachers. During the Reagan and Bush presidencies, much discussion centered on the rise of teachers who scored in the lowest quartile on college exams, thus threatening international competition in math and science (Shor, 1986a). College students who perform well on the Scholastic Aptitude Test often go into more technical areas of study rather than becoming science and mathematics teachers. Levin (1985) indicated that 15 to 50 percent of all scientific personnel are employed directly or indirectly by the Defense Department. Such understanding leads us to question the policies that promote such strategical expertise at the expense of the populace. Liberals and conservatives might argue that such use of scientific and mathematical skills helps to maintain our freedom and democracy through national defense—therefore promoting the belief that protecting the populace is a more important mission than teaching math and science. On the other hand, radicals argue that were there not as many economic and human resources expended on defense, the focus of mathematical and scientific progress might be on human problems rather than economic or strategic arms development (Levin & Rumberger, 1983; McLaren, 1998; Aronowitz & Giroux, 1993).

In sum, the politics of promoting science, math, and technology during the Red Scare of the 1950s has carried over into Information Age ideology. Many of the problems of critical teacher shortages as articulated by federal policy have in essence been caused by federal policies that have long promoted highly paid, professional status for those scientists and mathematicians who work in private industry that profits from large government contracts. Such power arrangements will not restructure schools and teacher salaries at the expense of powerful corporations. With critical literacy skills, teachers can see the links between shortages in one social sector as related to the knowledge and power relations that encourage innovation in highly technical systems of national defense rather than as incapacity on the part of those who choose to teach.

## Really Reformed Subjects

Postmodern teacher education provides future teachers opportunities to question tacit knowledge. Deconstructing oppressive knowledge and power relations necessitates rethinking self-formations within a postmodern paradigm. Such reconsideration questions the knowledge and power relations of gender, class, and race as undiscussed aspects of socialization through education. Teachers who understand how race, class, and gender socialization affected their own literacy can promote political awareness and democratic literacy practices in their classrooms. Such practices entail engaging teachers with students in understanding the larger social system in which teaching and learning occur, as well as questioning the focus on developing certain kinds of knowledge as politically, economically, and socially connected to knowledge and power relations of the macrocosm.

In this chapter, I have attempted to show how the discourses of teacher education are grounded in human capital ideology. The teacher is positioned as the disseminator and assessor of student knowledge in a banking model of education. Although many references are made to developing well-rounded educators through liberal arts education, the focus in that liberal education is in a tradition that is more conservative than liberal. As postmodern discourses of teacher education are juxtaposed against the official and university-directed initiatives to improve teacher education, we see that the difference between well-prepared teachers within the two frameworks lies in the emphasis put on content knowledge, accountability, and scientific efficiency. In contrast, the postmodern discourses of teacher education attempt to deconstruct the knowledge and power relations that help to hold the political economy steadfastly at the status quo. Change for the policymakers proposes more work for teachers, hierarchization within teacher ranks, and explicit attention to traditions of the existing power and knowledge relations. One progressive attempt to move teacher education to more postformal understandings of knowledge was the Holmes Group's attempt to re-envision teacher education in the professional development school. However, if we look closely at the rhetoric of the proposal, the existing public school structure ultimately dictated what the professional development school and educational research would be like, rather than the reform itself. Settling for such a state of affairs offers little hope to improve the lives of teachers and students in public schools by transforming classrooms and schools, much less for social transformation.

The final chapter discusses research, postmodern developments, and awareness within the field of education as instructors have reconceptualized literacy instruction. An example of a classroom application will be suggested.

---

# CHAPTER VI

## PRACTICING CRITICAL AND FEMINIST LITERACIES

### Implications for Classroom Practice

In the last chapter, I recounted some of the discourses that are prevalent within the recent wave of teacher education reform. Examining those teacher education discourses, I looked to mainstream, critical, and feminist perspectives of what has ensued from alterations in teacher education following *A Nation at Risk* (U.S. Dept. of Education, 1983). In the discussion, I reported some critical aspects of teacher empowerment. In this chapter, I attempt to tie literacy policy formulations and their counter-discourses to the discourses of classroom practice.

### Overview of Discourses of Critical Literacy

Teachers who become sensitive to critical discourses of literacy question the nature of power relations as social, cultural, and sociopolitical relations in the many ways that they originate in text, language, and history (Willinsky, 1990). By calling on personal power to construct and deconstruct text and speech acts, postmodern literate teachers can encourage literacy development of students in ways that interrogate how traditions and practices empower and disempower individuals. Willinsky contends that "The educational experience of literacy is not a period of preparation, but the actual practice of a personal and public power" (1990, p. 86). As indicated by Willinsky's *New Literacy*, in order for students to practice literacy as public power, pre-service teachers' comprehension of literacy must expand.

Reforming education in classrooms involves teacher engagement in precepts of the emerging paradigm of scientific research as it becomes relevant to classroom literacy practices. Teachers can begin to transition from technocrats to reflective practitioners as they pursue quests for truth(s) through relevant curricula. Contending with literacy as a large component of democracy, the postmodern educator understands that unless democracy is practiced in classrooms through literacy, democratic schools are not possible. Herein lies the importance of poststructural understanding of knowledge with respect to the curriculum.

Poststructural applications of understanding the curriculum and classroom practices replace atomistic skills and practice as literacy is expanded into holistic notions of knowledge. The current knowledge base that predetermines disciplinary knowledge production maintains the dominance of an elite knowledge–based curriculum by restraining questions and assertions through linguistic control of tightly defined areas of discussion. Scientific rationalism thus promotes accountable teaching and learning in modern schooling practices. Deviating from the modern model allows students to explore their needs and interests through literacy practices (Willinsky, 1990; Kincheloe, 1993; Block, 1995). In such practice(s), teachers help their students make meaningful assessments of language and real lived experiences. These critical endeavors engage critical teachers with their students in critical literacy practice (Tozer, Violas, & Senese, 1998). Such practice might run counter to what counts as knowledge, or epistemological determinations within scientifically rational knowledge bases (Foucault, 1980; Willinsky, 1990). However, the postformal paradigm of knowledge as represented in the domain of qualitative research and epistemology is as legitimate as the dominant scientific paradigm, although it lacks scientific credibility.

Interparadigmatic change to embrace postformal knowledge becomes the key to the transformative potential of literacy practices. Most of the discussions of personal, social, and political enhancement in literacy relate to feminist and criticalist policies associated with critical and feminist theories and notions of epistemology (Giroux, 1983, 1988a,b; Martin, 1994; Kincheloe, 1991, 1993; Stone, 1994). Moving beyond the Newtonian-Cartesian precepts of truth, postmodern knowledge interrogates the foundations of knowledge and truth as contextual, arbitrary, and grounded in narrowly constructed discourses (Foucault, 1972; Dewey, 1916).

Postmodern insights into literacy provide new lenses from which to think about knowledge development. Literacy as explored within the realm of politics has been defined as political practice (Block, 1995; Edelsky, 1991b; Willinsky, 1990; Freire, 1970). The feminists have asserted the personal as political in all social networks (Stone, 1994). From this perspective, teachers and students working on personal and public issues through language development engage personal and social power (Willinsky, 1990; Giroux, 1988a,b). However, the politics of language is multifaceted. Views of language as spoken text, communicative acts, and discourses have affected various academic positions on literacy.

Sociolinguists have explored linguistic differences and their relationships to society. By locating differences in language characteristics of groups of people, the power of elite forces to control literacy becomes clearer when contrasted with the contentiousness over what constitutes "standard language" (Hudson, 1980). The differentiation between literacy as a school and a social construction manifests personal versus scholastic literacies. Gee informs us that when differences between primary and secondary discourses are pronounced, the linguistically disadvantaged student encounters difficulty with school literacy (Gee, 1991a; Cook-Gumperz, 1986).

A practical historical application of teaching learner-centered literacy has occurred historically as individuals have struggled to utilize reading and writing instruction in the modern mode (Shannon, 1990b). Yet, the tenacious practice of textbook literacy instruction and other modernistic teaching and learning techniques persists (Shannon, 1989, 1990b). Shannon and Goodman (1994) concluded, after looking at textbooks that contain more storybooks and other embellished activities, that a textbook in a new package is still a textbook.

Enabling literacy that is more than textbook-centered learning, from a poststructural perspective within the critical and feminist academic positions, utilizes text construction and deconstruction from perspectives of social, cultural, and gender experience (Mitchell & Weiler, 1991; Cherryholmes, 1988; Davies, 1989, 1993). In indicting studies of literacy for disciplined control of individuals, poststructural theories of Foucault and Pierre Bourdieu (1977) have inspired a new look at literacy as temporal and physical, as well as a form of thought control over individuals, as they are mastered by (conform to) external discourses of literacy through reading instruction (Luke, 1992). Responding to the external discipline of literacy, through socialization and conditioning, literate subjects later reproduce desired literate behaviors in self-disciplined behavior (Luke, 1992). Hence, literacy in itself becomes a form of social and cultural control. When the control extends to de-legitimize students' identities, literacy becomes oppressive (Freire & Macedo, 1995).

The oppressive nature of literacy instruction can be unintentional and sometimes subtle. Gutierrez (1994) has studied classrooms as discourse networks, where talk, context, and script shape contexts for learning. McLaren and Gutierrez (1994) discuss how social control and teacher knowledge determine the acceptable literacy and its practice. They inspire pedagogy of dissent and transformation to move classroom literacy beyond control to more proactive realms of literacy development.

Gutierrez, Rymes, and Larson (1995) have deconstructed classroom discourse to reveal the repressive potential of teachers to control knowledge. In their study, knowledge was narrowly defined, particularly from a middle-class or patriarchal perspective, as the teacher expected students to guess or know current events from the newspaper, which neither the students nor students' families read. Interrupting the controlling patterns of the literacy development in classrooms, such as relying on textbook or newspaper text, is the mission of the postmodern literate teachers. Some guidelines provided by postmodern scholars who have blazed the trail of critical literacy can help pre-service teachers approach the task of critical literacy instruction.

**Educators Meet Postmodern Literacy**

As Foucault discussed, the regimes of truth as they are established in mainstream classrooms establish knowledge and power relations. Contributing to classroom regimes of literacy are components including the curriculum, the instruction that occurs advertently and inadvertently within that curriculum, and literacy practice that results from that instruction. In a modern classroom, knowledge is differentiated, fragmented, and presented as factoids in textbooks. Differentiation of knowledge assumes knowledge bases of essential facts and information to be mastered. Unlike modern literacy, postmodern literacy is holistic, student-centered, and critical. Critical literacy applies critical thinking and analytical writing to promote opportunities for extending self-development, power, and expression (Willinsky, 1990, p. 24). Extending some power and initiative to students enables them to direct their literacy rather than be subjected to literacy formation under the guises of classroom control.

### Classroom Management Makes Regimes of Literacy

Modern teachers often construe their power in classrooms as "in control," or they attempt to master classroom control through classroom management. A general belief among neophyte and experienced teachers is that mastering classroom control through classroom management signifies good teaching. Postmodern teachers concern themselves with good instruction and creating community in classrooms which ultimately empower students. Often when power is not shared with students, distortions of knowledge and power occur through authoritarian views of what comprises knowledge on the teachers' part and reluctance to value what the teacher deems important knowledge on the part of students (Gutierrez et al., 1995). *Resistance* is the term utilized in critical theory to describe students who fail to respond in desired manners to formal instruction (Tozer et al., 1998; Corcoran, 1989; Giroux, 1983). Accommodation occurs as teachers modify instruction and requirements so that students can simulate, within varying degrees, formal performance in content area knowledge. If rational, scientific guidelines of textbooks and modern curricula are sterile, impersonal, and irrelevant to students, teachers must modify curricula to appeal to and consequently engage students.

Making curriculum modifications to engage learners can help alleviate the resistance that many students feel when teacher and textbook-transmitted knowledge drives classroom literacy practices. Resisting and accommodating curricula and administrative management can also be accomplished by teachers (Millman & Darling-Hammond, 1990).

As discussed in chapters 4 and 5, teachers are the objects of directives, rendering them subjects of discourses who then act on their students as objects of discourses. Awareness of subject-object dynamics of discourses can empower teachers to share power effectively in classrooms. Such modifications in power-wielding can also approach paradigmatic changes that look beyond tightly controlled development of knowledge and literacy. Shifting literacy practices whereby students are allowed to express themselves, construct knowledge, and exercise their literacy as personal power involves teachers' power sharing.

## Moving Toward Student-Centered Learning—Power Sharing

Postmodern teachers are unafraid of power sharing in classrooms and encourage power sharing through open communications with students. Hence, postmodern teachers expect to share power in classrooms and encourage power sharing through discussion of important issues in students' lives. These issues can often be obscured by formal curricula. The teacher's enforcement of knowledge regimes can allow or disallow student knowledge to emerge. Self-awareness of how the teacher's stance determines what counts as knowledge and can marginalize student knowledge must be considered by reflective practitioners. However, teacher awareness of new literacy practice (Willinsky, 1990) is not sufficient to engage classrooms in postmodern literacy. The postmodern critical practitioner is aware of the knowledge and power relations constructed with literacy but also engages students in unofficial spaces wherein students are encouraged to be critics and articulators of their realities.

As articulations of meaning construction and deconstruction occur with student interaction through literacy as power of individuals in personal and public domains, power networks can be examined. Postmodern teachers understand that power relations are learned, produced, and reproduced. It is through personal experiences that students shape their identities and consciousnesses. If unequal power relations are sustained around their identity formations, students become convinced that the social construction of reality is irreconcilable rather than reconstructable.

As social spaces are created in moment-to-moment interaction, postmodern teachers and their students understand how competency-tested literacy is stilted and skills based. Teachers help students differentiate between necessary skills and literacy for basic literacy and literacy for personal, social, and political engagement. Embracing a democratic model for literacy practice, teachers and students can begin to struggle for democratic classrooms—connecting student voice with participatory democracy.

When the teacher moves beyond the teacher monologue or script, student counterscript, or what Gutierrez, Rymes, and Larson (1995) refer to as "underlife," can emerge. Student resistance to teacher-dominated discourse can handily become part of the transformation of dominant curriculum and skills-based literacy script. Critical and feminist perspectives become the vehicles through which teacher and students are able to transcend the dominant scripts to merge their views in newly constructed critical knowledge. Giroux (1988a) calls this process a struggle for public life. The focus on traditional curricula does not promote a meaningful engagement of students and teachers in public life. A reconceptualized curriculum can do so, but not as a panacea.

**Tropics of Postmodern Literacy**

Although public life is squelched in public schools and business interests control much of educational innovation, the postmodern literate teacher harnesses the energy of life that most students bring to school (Giroux, 1988a,b). As discussed by educational theorists, power relations, as they are sublimated or emphasized by media and communicative forces, must be considered and discussed seriously in the interest of furthering democracy in classrooms, schools, and society. Bringing race, class, and gender to the forefront of teacher education discussions and literacy practice is one vehicle for debating present unequal power relations (Kincheloe, 1993, 1995; Fiske, 1993).

Adapting techniques set forth by Freire (1970, 1973) constitutes a large part of critical conscientization. These techniques include codification and problem posing. As all learners understand their place in the world or understand the world that puts them in their place, they can better begin to transform themselves and their immediate environment. Utilizing the canon of literature in high school, for example, can be a beginning or a means to question present cultural practices rather than a manner in which to edify them.

Shor (1986a), who used many of Freire's ideas, utilized problem-posing approaches to teaching and learning. The steps of Freire's and Shor's process include listening, dialogue, and action-based activities. Unlike more conventional assessment of teachers' facilitating students' learning, the critical application of the three-step process involves listening, dialoguing, and acting as determined by students' needs to develop language, self-expression, and some degree of control over their own lives (Shor, 1986a). Such control does not mean foregoing all authority and rules, but rather learning how to work with and against authority to accomplish goals. Students also learn to formulate rules and articulate why some rules are necessary or advisable. Postmodern understanding comes through deliberation about the intentions of those who formulate rules and about the effects of the rules on those most affected by them. The give and take of power as actor and acted-upon helps to guide postmodern conscientization.

Student-centered learning about students' experience becomes more a focus of critical and feminist literacy practices than a by-product of the curriculum with guidance from a postmodern literate teacher. As students come to understand their own needs and desires and the impact of power on those needs and desires, literacy can become an interrupting activity—one which furthers social and cultural critique. In poststructural fashion, students, rather than learning technological literacy as compliant automatons, question the effects of media, including computers and highly technical equipment, on their learning. They begin to question the dialectics of what concentration and development in one area or discipline negates in other aspects of their personal development. Questioning the knowledge and power relations that are formulated in highly technical learning and working environments can inspire critical thinking rather than serve to further deify technology as structurally and functionally indispensable.

Part of the agenda of critical and feminist educators involves struggling with other teachers for teacher curricular input and community connections. Understanding how modern educational practices that assume expert and hegemonic knowledge are more appropriate, more reliable, and more "true" than suppressed knowledge has shown how alienating the educational system can be to groups and individuals (Shaker & Kridel, 1989; Pinar, 1989, 1995; Foucault, 1980). In reconsiderations of Ebonics and in criticisms of bilingual education, English as a second language, and test-focused language drills, researchers find the cultural deficit still at work in elite and middle-class teachers' and policymakers' views (Hudson, 1980). Building on the native intelligence of learners and teachers enables them to work with their assets in literacy building rather than supplant elite and middle-class book knowledge in place of knowledge that is more indigenous and relevant to learners.

## New Venues for Action

Shaker and Kridel (1989) in "The Return to Experience: A Reconceptualist Call" invite avant-garde educators to find "new venues for action" (p. 7). Fresh possibilities are the fount of postmodern literacy as democratic classrooms practice new knowledge and power relations.

Overcoming ethnocentrism on several levels is important to the postmodern literate teacher. More reliance on theories from abroad—Europe, Australia, South America—has become helpful to self-examine educational practices in the United States (Grumet, 1989; Britzman, 1986; Kincheloe, 1993; Green, 1993; Freire, 1970). The curriculum reconceptualists recommend looking to European theories to understand the formations of what we do in education, as well as what we can do, to make education more democratic. Enhanced by foreign theories, feminist and critical literacy reveal contradictions between the rhetoric of democracy and the reality of a democracy yet to be achieved, often referred to as democratization. As the realities of the oppressed are exposed, we can better read and interpret social and political policies, history, and accepted knowledge as racist, ethnocentric, sexist, discriminatory, or classist. Through feminist and critical literacy, the contradictions between the rhetoric of democracy and the realities of the students' experiences can be illuminated. If students are inspired or angered at their discoveries, they can be inspired to take action. Those with raised consciousnesses can be empowered at least to articulate social, cultural, economic, and political inconsistencies that they see and experience. They practice "reading the world" as inspired by Freire.

The language of empowering individuals has been appropriated by several educational reform discourses—conservative, liberal, and radical—thus it is difficult to distinguish differences among them sometimes. Radical empowerment means movement beyond traditional power and knowledge relations as they have existed under patriarchal Anglo-Eurocentric domination. This concept is associated with discourses of social transformation. Emancipation, from a radical perspective, attempts to change social institutions that have historically and traditionally exploited women, minorities, and the lower classes through the knowledge and power relations that have prevailed within the Western canon, Anglo-Eurocentric patriarchy, and cultural literacy as developed by E. D. Hirsch (1987) or Alan Bloom (1987).

On the other hand, empowerment in the contexts of *A Nation at Risk* and *To Reclaim a Legacy* (Bennett, 1984) attempts to recapture the idyllic, liberal, democratic framework of ancient Greece and the modern nation-states of Europe and the United States—an ideal that is ideal for a few elites. References to such traditional foundations of democracy in social policies formulated under the leadership of William Bennett (1984), or with the widely disseminated books he has written (1992a,b), and the framework of postmodern democracy are contradictory. Understanding the contradiction between the rhetoric of democracy and realities of democracy helps us to understand how much more work needs to be done to attain democracy in this country and its institutions (Tozer et al., 1998).

As pre-service teachers confront power and knowledge formations to better understand their own personal relations to forms of oppressive knowledge, postmodern literacy results. Confronting the discourses of traditional history, literature, psychology, and political science, one finds male domination of educational institutions (Martin, 1994; Stone, 1994). Keen attention to patriarchal structures and traditions can help to disclose the relationship of knowledge to power. Such understanding requires reflection often precluded by scientific, rational approaches to education. For example, deconstructing policy texts using feminist rhetorical devices reveals inequities perpetuated in language, social and economic structures, academic knowledge, and literacy practices (Martin, 1994; Stone, 1994; Fraser, 1989). New venues for action are limitless based on students' and teachers' imaginations and their willingness to direct purposeful learning for exercising self- and social power. How power plays into personal, social, and political communication can be explored with references to students' lives, as well as through text.

**Exploring Textual Politics**

Postmodern teachers can address the politics of text with their students without excluding important literacy skills taught in classrooms. As teachers become researchers with their students, they can consider texts from several perspectives, including reader responses to race, class, and gender inclusion or exclusion in literature. With students, teachers can discuss how liberally educated forefathers' decisions about what ought to constitute knowledge help to uphold power and knowledge relations. Students can begin to probe social reproduction, questioning why we continue to practice what was decided historically. Students can question how traditions within the written and unwritten curricula keep students from various groups in their place (Davies, 1993).

Davies' work centers on ethnographic understanding of the positioning of students within "lived narratives" in classrooms as well as the location of individuals in relation to social structures (1993, pp. 229–230). From her ethnographic studies she concludes that it is particularly important for students to refuse old story lines and to have courage enough to develop, initiate, or adopt new ones. For pre-service teachers who understand and adopt the poststructural mission of rethinking the taken-for-granted curriculum, teaching and learning involve writing new curriculum story lines. Such revision of curriculum can borrow from extant material that has yet to be rewritten (Kristeva, 1980, 1988; Olson & Hirsh, 1995).

Davies' poststructural feminist scholarship in literacy emphasizes that the following processes contribute to individual understandings of the self:

> 1. Learning of the categories which include some people and exclude others (e.g. male/female, father/daughter).
> 2. Participating in the various discursive practices through which meanings are allocated to those categories. These include the story-lines through which different subject positions are elaborated.
> 3. Positioning of self in terms of categories and story-lines. This involves imaginatively positioning oneself as if one belongs in one category and not in the other (e.g. as girl and not boy, or good girl and not bad girl).
> 4. Recognition of oneself as having the characteristics that locate one as an x or not x—i.e. the development of "personal identity" or a sense of oneself as belonging in the world from the perspective of one so positioned. This recognition entails an emotional commitment to the category membership and the development of a moral system organized around the belonging. (1993, pp. 229–230)

Belonging serves a dual role in students' developing critical literacy. If they feel that they belong to a group where their identities are legitimized, students have self-knowledge and confidence to communicate within a social network. Such networks can be established in classrooms. Also, if they feel like their learning belongs to them and that they are developing something within themselves to take with them, they feel good about constructing their knowledge (Block, 1995). Unfortunately, so much of education is canned and ritual that literacy becomes repetitive skill-mastery rather than extemporaneous exercise of power through reading and writing.

The control of students exerted through literacy allows knowledge development and foreclosure in certain areas. Literacy as a mechanical recitation is also controlling. Recitation and behavior control in circle reading time is deconstructed in Luke's applications of Foucaultian analysis on a classroom reading encounter. Luke (1992) discusses how students' conduct is manipulated through tight control of a reading lesson. As the lesson dominates their thought, discussion, time, space, and habitus (way of being, way of talking, way of articulating), students learn literacy. To counteract some of the control exerted over learners in reading lessons, teachers can deconstruct the classroom discourse to reveal how well power over students is exercised. Teachers with poststructural conscientization understand that the controlling discourses of literacy also control teachers. Interrogation of classroom discourse through note taking, tape recording, or video recording can reveal local construction of power and identity within the networks of classroom communication networks (Fiske, 1993; Bourdieu, 1977; Fairclough, 1989).

By analyzing recordings of students' learning, teachers and students can become the subjects of their own learning. They can become the protagonists or antagonists of their own literature, videos, and tape recordings. Having the students analyze how they are developing literacy can bring a new dimension of literacy development into the classroom without excluding basic skills or important cultural information that teacher-directed learning might emphasize.

**Decoding Classroom Discourse**

Important findings of the Gutierrez, Rymes, and Larson (1995) study indicate that monologic control of the teacher often leads to dialogic resistance of learners. As revealed by decoded discourse analysis, conversation elicited in a current-event activity conducted by a teacher repressed student knowledge and failed to engage them in a topic that could have become an important focus of their identity formation. The teacher, after asking the students about many current events irrelevant to the students' lives, eventually refers to *Brown v. the Board of Education*,

1954. The students alluded to James Brown, Michael Jackson, and other famous names to impede serious discussion about the importance of *Brown v. Board*, thereby reproducing the social and power relationships that occur in traditional African American classrooms taught by Anglo teachers.

Gutierrez et al. illustrated how the students conversed outside of the teacher discourse, constructing their own resistant conversation to what the teacher deemed important knowledge—current events. Since the students did not read the newspaper, they did not have access to this knowledge. The main point of the study is that a dialogue, or what Gutierrez refers to as a third space, in which students and teacher construct knowledge, is important to student learning. Such a space cannot occur if teachers do not question the politics of text with their students, share in knowledge constructions with their students, or question the stance which they take toward the knowledge.

To explicate the *Brown v. Board* study (Gutierrez et al., 1995), the literacy researchers drew from Bakhtin's (1981) notion of dialogic meaning and social "heteroglossia" to define three discursive spaces in the classroom which they call script, counterscript, and a third space (where student response is possible). Their research focused on the manner in which participants complicitly constructed knowledge which impeded serious discussion, thereby constructing the social and power relationships that unfold in particular communities of practice (1995, p. 5). In a detailed structural analysis of classroom discussion about *Brown v. the Board of Education*, Gutierrez et al. (1995) emphasize how the teacher maintains power through a monologue; as the teacher stifles dialogue with, between, and among students, this manner of conducting speech acts about a topic potentially interesting to students results in curtailing the students from taking an interest, much less articulating an evaluation of the topic. Ultimately, development of a dialogue, or a third space, wherein teacher and student knowledge can be constructed in the classroom, is what was lacking in literacy development in this particular classroom. This space is possible despite traditional beliefs that pervade the curriculum determining what counts as knowledge and teachers' assumptions about what is important in everyday classroom practice.

As reflective practitioners, pre-service teachers should become acquainted with exercising reflectivity to allow the possibility of other knowledges to emerge in classrooms (Gutierrez, 1994). These other knowledges can include alternate views of reality and calling into question the authority of accepted "official" knowledge usually taught in the classroom. Such knowledge is far removed from modernist, mechanistic practice that demands keeping students on task and covering essential elements for skill mastery on future competence exams. By questioning skill mastery, students can master skills and begin to develop critical thinking as well as critical literacy.

In addition to Bakhtin's theories, other poststructural and sociocultural views of local construction of power and identity through classroom discourses illuminate classroom discourse analysis (Bourdieu, 1977; Fairclough, 1985). As McWilliam (1994) described in *In Broken Images: Feminist Tales for a Different Teacher Education*, feminist epistemology attempts to understand patriarchal inscriptions in teacher education as well as to understand how feminist ideology is also inscribed inside logocentrism. McWilliam describes a propensity of pre-service teachers' practicums to revert to total alignment with practice, rather than hinging on theoretical experimentation with knowledge formation. She discusses the contribution of several feminist theorists (Lather, 1994) and structuralist Althusser's work in relation to teacher education. She finds Althusser's structural development of ideology important to discourses of neoconservatism, postwelfarism, and determinism of postcapitalism in relation to teacher education. She looks to social theory and relates it to teacher education programs that ultimately produce teachers who help reproduce the existing status quo that is moving further to the right. The principal danger in such politics of teacher education is to blame the victims of class politics, whereby the school experiences of the bottom tier of students are abstracted from the social conditions that keep the students in their places.

As one solution, McWilliam has embraced critical and feminist pedagogies as important for pre-service teacher preparation. However, it is not without reservation that she embraces feminist pedagogy. Unconvinced that critical and feminist pedagogies are not more expert metanarratives, McWilliam says that "The role of critical pedagogy, for example, has been to deny forms of personal power that derive from the individual psychology and circumstances of human agents" (1994, p. 123). Although teaching pre-service teachers to be progressive political subjects can produce the reverse of desired effects, not teaching them to question state-mandated scientific education is more apt to incur their compliance with administrative directives from all levels. Thus, encouraging rather than mandating criticalism can promote self-agency in pre-service teachers' literacy development. As self-agents, they are better equipped to propel themselves and their students to counter-hegemonic classroom practices.

Ideally, pre-service teachers will be equipped with some knowledge of social theory, content knowledge, and recent classroom observations to inform them about classroom life. McWilliam defers to Fraser's (1989) "needs talk" (discussed in chapter 2) to allow teachers more political and politicizing language for development and transformation of their classroom situations which will change throughout their lives. The needs of students and teachers ideally comprise the literacy practices of a postmodern classroom. Such needs can no longer be assumed to be generic but rather must be related to individuals' responsibilities and future interests in the macrocosm of society. Feminist conscientization informs males and females about democratic practices of questioning the focus of traditional literature, history, and power relations of schools and classrooms, practices which heretofore have eluded literacy instruction.

**Applications for Classroom Practice**

Recent reconceptualization and rewriting of educational theory, including gender studies and reconsideration of psychology, utilize postformal considerations of academic rigor (Kincheloe & Steinberg, 1993; McWilliam, 1994). Yet, these pedagogies of dissent and transformation are hardly part of mainstream methods and theory classes within the field of education. Neither are these dissenting discourses very accessible to pre-service teachers unless criticalist or feminist literatures are emphasized as alternative ways of thinking about classroom practices. The following discussion will attempt to set forth two guidelines for teaching critical literacy as a discursive production of self: (a) how educators might reevaluate what occurs as literacy development activities in classrooms and (b) how they might rethink and reestablish the format for classroom discourse so that more critical literacy skills might be included in the reading and writing curriculum.

According to Foucault (1972) and Weedon (1987), discourses formulate our perceptions of ourselves and others. Gendered, classed, and raced concepts of reality inform politics of mainstream society, schools, and classrooms. In light of the poststructural paradigm, the ways in which individuals as subjects are constructed is being reconsidered. On this subject, Davies (1989) asserts,

> Within this model, who one is is always an open question with a shifting answer depending upon the positions made available within one's own and others' discursive practices and within those practices, the stories through which we make sense of our own and others' lives. (p. 229)

McWilliam asserts that *who pre-service teachers are* has all too often been determined or predetermined by research power relations that have univocally attempted to describe pre-service teachers' experiences (1994, pp. 46–47). Likewise, in classrooms, teachers may all too often formulate identities of girls and boys based on predetermined narratives and social relations, and then teach to reinforce those assumptions. Teachers' reflexive analysis of their own assumptions about race, class, and gender in teaching can alert them to how their own biases might perpetuate stereotypes or power relations in literacy instruction. Poststructuralists and feminists propose looking to how females, or half of the world's population, view literacy from a different perspective than that proposed by literacy policymakers.

**Feminist Conscientization**

Shakeshaft (1986) questioned President Ronald Reagan's logic of blaming educational dysfunction on recent attention given to equity through civil rights and affirmative action. An attempt to achieve equity had followed on the heels of 1960s and 1970s educational policies meant to counteract some of the educational institutions' shortcomings in dealing with female, minority, and handicapped-student issues. Yet, many of President Reagan's policies, through omission or commission, put these groups at risk (Shakeshaft, 1986; AAUW, 1995; Banks, 1994; Nieto, 1996). Through generic treatment of all students as male students, through leaving the traditional curriculum in place, and through funding of some programs for excellence, educational structures and practices continued the status quo as formulated in the 1950s, 1960s, and 1970s. Of course, some pockets of exception exist in various school districts operating in more progressive manners.

Feminist analysis as practiced by Shakeshaft promotes critical literacy necessary for rethinking the importance and positioning of marginalized people. Jean Baudrillard referred to these individuals as "the shadow of the silent majorities" (cited in Greene, 1986). These silent people are also what Foucault, feminists, and other postmodernists refer to as the "other." Understanding how literacy practices gloss over the "otherness" of students by outfitting them with few or no interpretive skills is important for all pre-service teachers. The interpretive skills that students need enable reading and writing with and against the grain of texts and allow comparisons between narratives in literature and students' lives. Interpretive skills require being able to think about the possibilities for enabling freedom to discuss given texts in comparison to real life, according to Freire's conceptualization of "reading the world and the word" (1970). Further applications of postmodern literacy are informed by Macedo's (1994a) assertions of how reading and writing can preclude the students' critical perspectives by focusing on elitist conformity and acceptable interpretations of American experiences and emulations of desired intellectual behaviors. Bringing into question the focus of the Western canon and why required American reading is requisite allows a new perspective on the interpretations of history. Greene (1986) and Martin (1994) recommend utilizing the great literary works in order to compare them to women's experiences. Greene suggests reincarnating our past to better understand what we have learned from our history. She cites Noddings' visualization critical literacy:

> I would like to think of teachers moving the young into their own interpretations of their lives and their lived worlds, opening wider and wider perspectives as they do so. I would like to see teachers ardent in their efforts to make the range of symbol systems available to the young for the ordering of experience, even as they maintain regard for their vernaculars. I would like to see teachers tapping the spectrum of intelligences, encouraging multiple readings of written texts and readings of the world. (Noddings, cited in Greene, 1986, p. 441)

By "tapping the spectrum of intelligences," teachers can begin to value the many ways in which students develop literacy based on their own life circumstances.

Having discussed human capital and the construction of literate subjects in chapters 1 through 4, we can question how postcapitalism and the international economy have driven official pedagogical discourses to form gendered, classed, and racialized literate and illiterate teachers and students in our schools. Unless educators question their own literacy, they might unintentionally continue a tradition of exerting the teacher's power in the classroom to control literacy (Gutierrez et al., 1995). Teachers as researchers who attempt analytical understanding of the discourses in their classrooms can begin to deconstruct, reconsider, and reformulate the curriculum so that vocational and college-bound students alike can become cognizant of what is entailed in being smart workers and citizens (Kincheloe, 1995). The present bureaucratic modern educational system will not bestow conscientization on students and teachers. They must claim intellectualism as a tool for practicing literacy as power (Foucault, 1980).

## Ideals and Realities

### Restructuring Reconsidered

My notions of why literacy has not been reconceptualized in spite of the rhetoric of empowering students and teachers follow. First, the national focus is on international, capitalistic competitiveness of the nation's human capital, a capital investment in its workers, rather than in citizens. Second, much of the brunt for conversion and transition as we move from industrialism to the Information Age has been put on educators and institutions of education (Berliner & Biddle, 1997). Yet, changes in education as implemented by conservative and corporate educational communities treat only the symptoms of social and economic structures and hierarchies, not the causes. Seventy million Americans (a population comparable to that of France) are struggling workers with few resources that austere social policies are diminishing (McLaren, 1998). Third, the learner is not centered in most of the reform efforts; rather the teacher, text, competency test, and curriculum guide still reign as the expert source of knowledge. Fourth, the focus of positivistic knowledge has become technological, and, instead of being questioned with respect to its ontology and epistemology, it has become scientific truth. Such knowledge is now assumed to be "critical." Fifth, critical thinking skills become associated with dealing with work problems as technical within international arenas rather than with the critical consideration of work, the environment, working conditions, social conditions, or living conditions. Technologists proclaim the importance of their "techno"-craft; critique of the craft is overpowered by the manufactured "need" to become yet more technical (Goodman, 1995a). From such an antidemocratic view it is not the task of future workers/citizens to criticize the existing political economy; it is their task to adapt to it. Human capital and cultural literacy accommodate such adaptation well; thus, they are the focus in literacy policy. Such policies do not take into account minorities, who make up a majority of Americans (Pinar, 1995).

Although the mainstream of learners is female, minority, and homosexual, as opposed to heterosexual white males, reconsideration of the curriculum has resulted in few changes in the curriculum per se (Pinar, 1995). Little attention is paid to the researchers' findings about how to improve teacher work as many policies are formulated (Smylie, 1996). For example, bilingual and foreign language research indicates that it takes about seven years to master a second language. Many bilingual education programs mainstream their students after four years. Because English as a second language students are pulled from regular classes to learn basic skills, they frequently miss what is going on in the main classroom. Few, if any, curricular links are made for these students between their school life and their home life. For the at-risk Hispanic, who according to the statistics is most likely to drop out of school, there are few connections made to community life in literacy programs. Many programs that are meant to address the needs of "illiterate" dropouts present more of the same kinds of transmission instruction that these students left when they dropped out of school (U.S. Department of Education, 1993b).

## Constructing Critical and Feminist Literacies in Classrooms

### Redefining Democracy

The best place to begin in consideration of improving knowledge and power relations through the development of literacy is with a redefinition of democracy. Moving from spectator democracy to participatory democracy is the postmodern mission for those concerned about both democracy and literacy (Slater & Boyd, 1998; Tozer et al., 1998). If students can begin to understand how democracy and representative democracy diverge, they can begin to understand the ways in which their own experiences are more and less democratic. The existence of a divergence between the real and the ideal of democracy informs us that we are living in a democracy not yet attained. Democratization is a better way to think of democracy—it is an ongoing process in which all citizens are unimpeded to exert civil rights and leadership and can accordingly expect to be included in democratized decision making.

## Making the Classroom a Model of Democratizing Practice— An Example

If students can differentiate what is optimal and what is most negative about the manner in which we practice democracy, they can be inspired to conduct their own classroom experiments in democratization. The importance of participating in rule setting can engage learners to entertain the Constitution, its amendments, and formal and informal requirements for personally and socially responsible behavior. As postliterate subjects, teachers and students will view laws and rules from different perspectives, including those of females, the poor, the culturally different, and the culturally dominant. Through analysis, analytical thinking, and writing, teachers and students can decide how to make their model systems equitable. Developing such a system, they will read, write, research, and express themselves orally. In so doing, they can meet the necessary essential elements and practice for passing exams without spending all of their learning and teaching time doing practice exam questions.

As students exert their power, they will move well beyond such basic skills to critical considerations, syntheses, and formulations of important human issues. They can also interrogate the political economy. They can study ways and means of survival within the system. Their classroom focus can also consider how the postindustrial technological society presently exists compared to how ecologically sound it needs to be to continue to support a decent quality of life. In sum, the students become agents of their own learning that is driven by their interests and needs.

## Making Human Capital Count—Developing Social Capital

As students become agents of their own literacy, they will develop social networks around which they can develop social capital. Willingness and commitment to question the popular, consumer culture's exploitation of women, minorities, and other marginalized groups should constitute a large part of literacy development within this model system. Establishing discourse communities which engage in construction and deconstruction of speech acts can result in critical literacy.

Such networks do not just happen; they are constructed through social networks. In *Educating the Poor: Literacy, Educational Leadership and Democracy*, Agnello, Slater, and Sarria (1996) argue that human capital education is inadequate to address workers' needs. Workers and the poor require developed basic skills in order to develop the kinds of communicative social networks that can advance articulations of their needs, interests, causes, and issues. Social capital more adequately describes the resources and relationships necessary to help children and adults learn, develop, and become more productive. Postmodern teachers can promote social capital development in their classrooms. They understand how becoming a citizen decision-maker enhances worker literacy. They are savvy about how adherence to literacy policy advocating human capital literacy stifles literacy development. Postmodern teachers understand how focusing on cultural and human capital literacies will exclude other discourses of literacy. Thus, postmodern literate teachers expect more analytical literacy of their students. Students and teachers together can explore how exclusion of other discourses occurs as powerful social agents act upon certain beliefs and exercise their power accordingly. As discussed in chapters 3 and 4, discerning the reasons that certain discourses are overpowered by dominant discourses is itself an exercise in critical literacy and critical policy analysis.

Reflective, critical teaching practices and teacher education research have been explored by many actors (Zeichner & Liston, 1987; Pinar, 1989; Grumet, 1989; Knoblauch & Brannon, 1993). As discussed by these scholars, the postmodern educator looks at the intersections between race, class, and gender and taken-for-granted educational practices. As postmodern research pursued by multiculturalists, feminists, and criticalists has indicated, educational research itself has presented teacher education as a metanarrative that is as oppressive as that presented by postpositivist depictions of the modern schooling bureaucracy (Grumet, 1989; Giroux, 1991; McWilliam, 1994).

As a teacher educator involved in public school classrooms, I have waded into the murky waters of theory and practice to begin to look at race, class, and gender with secondary teaching methods students. It is still too early to tell how the students are interpreting these cultural differences as they relate to secondary education methods and what difference living in a supposed democracy should make to teaching secondary students.

With this vehicle of literacy policy analysis, it is possible to research the ways that discourses of literacy evolve and how such changes impact the curriculum. Educators who can address race, class, and gender along with the politics of literacy understand the social construction of literacy and how it creates its antithesis—illiteracy. The role of teachers in forming literate subjects is one which I have never taken lightly, and now more than ever I see the complexities of the politics created by networks of literacy among the business community, politicians, and general do-gooders. What strikes me most is that teaching basic skills to any learner does not go far enough in allowing him/her to utilize the vehicle of literacy for social critique. Such critique should be the foundation of a democratizing society and educational system. As far-right policies guide decision makers in their deliberations of literacy, illiteracy, and the many problems associated with the latter, I cannot help but wonder if indeed those who resist conventional literacy are doing the most important work of a democratizing society by resisting social hegemony.

## Closing Thoughts

Postmodern literacy defies formulas yet can be guided by some specifications. Human needs and desires can be addressed and differentiated as educators question their roles in reproducing social hierarchy. Their complicity and/or resistance to cultural traditions of male domination in schools can be questioned. As teacher educators question reactionary, nostalgic, conservative, and capitalistic discourses of literacy with their students, they can better understand their self-formations as individuals and teachers.

When we understand how human capital and cultural literacy serve to mold social development of students, we can more easily interrupt such discourses. As pre-service teachers understand that literacy should pave the way for social transformation, they can better prepare themselves to meet the needs of their future students. If educators do not accept the responsibility of teaching democratization in classrooms, we should recognize ourselves as proponents of an anti-democratic society. Such totalitarian attitudes on the educators' part should not be obscured by rhetoric of freedom, equity, and democracy, but rather approached and accepted or transformed. In classrooms where disengagement and disillusionment run high, I believe that it is easier to transform the environment into a democratizing one than it is to force literary traditions and compliant worker ideologies on students. In this light, engaging students in multicultural, postmodern deconstruction of oppressive knowledge may be a route of least resistance. Teachers may not be able to deploy democratization tactics outside of their classrooms, but engaging with students in postmodern literacy practices can make a difference within classrooms.

By questioning the speech acts and texts of policy statements, we can question policies themselves. As they approach their classrooms, teachers can understand the importance of discourse communities and how power results as discourses are directed at and against individuals. The analytical power of deconstructing text and policy statements can begin with actual policy statements and can become self-reflexive applications in classroom activities. Students and teachers in postmodern classrooms can undertake to begin a democratizing enterprise to question how discourses form, control, and liberate. The hierarchical nature of social, cultural, and political formations as a result of official policy discourse becomes important for analysis. Beginning with text and moving to speech acts, the nature of power exertion to form superordinate and subordinate social relationships is suspect.

## Closing

I have attempted to underscore in this document how the analysis of literacy policy discourses relates to the formation of more and less democratic means of social control. As discussed in chapters 2, 3, and 4, the discourses of literacy policy can be deconstructed to reveal their contradictions, their undemocratic characteristics, and their propensity to promote the status quo in social and worker relations in our postcapitalistic society. As discussed in chapter 5, the discourses of teacher education promote more worker control of state educators through surveillance and accountability procedures. In chapter 6, I moved to the classroom, where I believe that changes in literacy practices can be inculcated. The democratization model that I have described is one that can be utilized in any classroom, although it might fit the rigors of a language arts or social studies classroom more appropriately than other disciplines.

The democratization model is bidirectional. The necessity to educate democracy through literacy promotes the democratization process, and the promotion of critical literacies helps to expand the reality of democratic behaviors. As literacy becomes more of an extension of student self-development and social-capital building, reading and writing become vehicles for communication rather than the reason for skill building. Moving literacy from isolated skills to personal, cultural, and sociopolitical exercises of public life, students and teachers can rewrite the discourses of literacy. Seeing and acting upon the limitations of cultural and human capital literacies promotes citizenship. Such citizenship will not deter worker proficiency but rather will enhance human experience as related to the exercise of power of individuals. Postmodern literacy will evolve as the needs for the democratization process change over time. To approach postmodern literacy practices in classrooms will not preclude skill development but rather will employ those skills in building personal and social capital, necessary for both worker and cultural competence.

Educators who study the dynamics, power, and potential of discourse can better discern the motives of authorities who are acting upon teacher work through literacy policies as well as promote more democratic discourses of literacy in their classrooms. They can discern the difference between literacy for self-control and literacy as part of self-directed development of human potential. Postmodern literate teachers understand the primary importance of developing social capital with students as future citizen-workers, as opposed to promoting limited development of culturally literate workers through cultural and human capital literacies.

# REFERENCES

Abbott, A. (1988). *The system of professions*. Chicago: University of Chicago Press.

Agnello, M. F., Sarria, M., & Slater, R. (1996, Spring/Summer). *Educating the poor: Literacy, educational leadership and democracy*. Research and Policy Report Series, 4 (2). College Station: Race and Ethnic Studies Institute, Texas A & M University.

Allen, P., Munroe, M. J., Grigg, N., & Beck, W. (1980). *Tucson desegregation model for teacher training*. (Report No. SP-017-544). Tucson: University of Arizona. (ERIC Document Reproduction Service No. ED 198 133)

Alvermann, D. E., Commeyras, M., Young, J. P., Randall, S., & Hinson, D. (1997). Interrupting gendered discursive practices in classroom talk about texts: Easy to think about, difficult to do. *Journal of Literacy Research, 29* (1), 73–104.

American Association of University Women (AAUW). (1995). *How schools shortchange girls*. New York: Marlow & Co.

Anderson, R. C., Hiebert, E. H., Scott, J. A., & Wilkinson, I. A. G. (1985). *Becoming a nation of readers: The report of the Commission on Reading*. Pittsburgh, PA: National Academy of Education.

Apple, M. (1989). *Teachers and texts: A political economy of class and gender relations in education*. New York: Routledge.

_____. (1992). The text and cultural politics. *Educational Researcher, 21* (7), 4–11.

Apple, M., & Jungck, S. (1990). You don't have to be teacher to teach this unit: Teaching, technology, and gender in the classroom. *American Educational Research Journal, 27* (2), 227–251.

Arnot, M., & Weiler, K. (1993). *Feminism and social justice in education: International perspectives*. Washington, DC: Falmer Press.

Aronowitz, S. (1988). *Science as power: Discourse and ideology in modern society*. Minneapolis: University of Minnesota Press.

Aronowitz, S., & Giroux, H. (1985). *Education under siege*. Westport, CT: Bergin & Garvey.

_____. (1993). Schooling, culture, and literacy in the age of broken dreams: A review of Bloom and Hirsch. In H. Shapiro & D. Purpel (Eds.), *Critical social issues in American education: Toward the 21st century* (pp. 305–330). New York: Longman.

Au, K. (1995). Critical issues: Multicultural perspectives on literacy research. *A Journal of Literacy, 27,* 85–100.

Bakhtin, M. M. (1981). *The dialogic imagination* (C. Emerson & M. Holquist, Trans.). Austin: The University of Texas Press.

Ball, S. (1995). In defense of realm: The departmentalization of school knowledge. *Educational Researcher, 24,* 28–29.

Ballenger, C. (1992). Teaching and practice: Because you like us: The language of control. *Harvard Educational Review, 62,* 199–208.

Banks, J. (1994). *Multiethnic education: Theory and practice*. Boston: Allyn & Bacon.

Barker, J. A. (1992). *Paradigms: The business of discovering the future*. New York: Harper Business.

Becker, G. S. (1993). *Human capital: A theoretical and empirical analysis, with special reference to education*. Chicago: University of Chicago Press.

Bennett, A. (1991). Discourses of power, the dialectics of understanding, the power of literacy. In C. Mitchell & K. Weiler (Eds.), *Rewriting literacy: Culture and the discourse of the other* (pp. 13–34). New York: Bergin & Garvey.

Bennett, W. (1984). *To reclaim a legacy: A report on the humanities in higher education.* Washington, DC: National Endowment for the Humanities.

_____. (1986a). *First lessons: A report on elementary education in America.* Washington, DC: U.S. Government Printing Office.

_____. (1986b). Foreword. In *What works: Research about teaching and learning.* Washington, DC: U.S. Department of Education.

_____. (1992a). *The index of leading cultural indicators: Facts and figures on the state of American society.* New York: Simon & Schuster.

_____. (1992b). *The devaluing of America: The fight for our culture and our children.* New York: Simon & Schuster.

Berliner, D. C., & Biddle, B. J. (1997). *The manufactured crisis: Myths, fraud, and the attack on America's public.* White Plains, NY: Longman.

Bernstein, B. (1990). *The structuring of pedagogic discourse.* New York: Routledge.

Bestor, A. (1953). *Educational wastelands.* Champaign: University of Illinois Press.

Beyer, L. E. (1989). Reconceputalizing teacher preparation: Institutions and ideologies. *Journal of Teacher Education, 40* (1), 22–26.

Block, A. (1995). *Occupied reading: Critical foundations for an ecological theory.* New York: Garland.

Bloom, A. (1987). *The closing of the American mind.* New York: Simon & Schuster.

Bloomfield, W. (1989). *Phi Delta Kappa Fastback 293: Career beginnings: Helping disadvantaged youth achieve their potential.* Bloomington, IN: Phi Delta Kappa Educational Foundation.

Bogdan, D., & Straw, S. (1990). *Beyond communication: Reading comprehension and criticism.* Portsmouth, NH: Boynton/Cook.

Borman, K., & Greenman, N. (1994). *Changing American education: Recapturing the past or inventing the future?* Albany: State University of New York Press.

Bourdieu, P. (1977). *Outline of a theory of practice* (R. Nice, Trans.). Cambridge, England: Cambridge University Press.

Bowers, C. A. (1977). Cultural literacy in developed countries. *Quarterly Review of Education, 7* (3), 323–335.

Britzman, D. (1986). Cultural myths in the making of a teacher: Biography and social structure. *Harvard Educational Review, 56,* 442–456.

Brodkey, L. (1991). Tropics of literacy. In C. Mitchell & K. Weiler (Eds.), *Rewriting literacy: Culture and the discourse of the other* (pp. 161–168). New York: Bergin & Garvey.

Burchell, G., Gordon, C., & Miller, P. (1991). *The Foucault effect: Studies in governmentality.* Chicago: University of Chicago Press.

Bush lends support to TEKS curriculum. (1997, July 1). *San Antonio Express-News,* p. A8.

Butler, J., & Scott, J. W. (Eds.). (1992). *Feminists theorize the political.* New York: Routledge.

Butler, R. (1995). Women in audiovisual education, 1920–1957: A discourse analysis. *Dissertation Abstracts International, 56,* (01), 73A. (University Microforms No. AAI95-08907)

Calderon, D., & Ramos, C. (1997, February 6). Educators eye details of Clinton's proposals. *San Antonio Express-News,* pp. A1, A13.

Carnegie Task Force on Teaching as a Profession. (1986). *A nation prepared: Teachers for the 21st century.* Washington, DC: Carnegie Forum on Education & the Economy.

Cherryholmes, C. H. (1988). *Power and criticism: Poststructural investigations in education.* New York: Teachers College Press.

Christian-Smith, L. K. (1993). *Texts of desire: Essays on fiction, femininity, and schooling.* Washington, DC: Falmer Press.

Cixous, H., & Kristeva, J. (1990). The laugh of Medusa. In P. Bizzell & B. Herzberg (Eds.), *The rhetorical tradition: Readings from classical times to the present* (pp. 1224–1266). Boston: Bedford Books of St. Martin's Press.

Clark, W. H. (1990). Literature, education, and cultural literacy. *The Journal of Aesthetic Education, 24* (1), 49–56.

Clinton lashes out at states for dragging feet on education standards. (1997, July 26). *San Antonio Express-News*, A14.

Clinton promotes testing standards. (1997, February 11). *San Antonio Express-News*, p. A6.

Clinton urges governors to back national testing. (1997, July 29). *San Antonio Express-News*, p. 8.

Cochran-Smith, M. (1991). Learning to teach against the grain. *Harvard Education Review, 61* (3), 279–309.

Cochran-Smith, M., & Lytle, S. L. (1993). *Inside outside: Teacher research and knowledge.* New York: Teachers College Press.

Coleman, J. S. (1987). Families and schools. *Educational Researcher, 16* (6), 32–38.

Collins, J. (1991). Hegemonic practice: Literacy and standard language in public education. In C. Mitchell & K. Weiler (Eds.), *Rewriting literacy: Culture and the discourse of the other* (pp. 229–254). New York: Bergin & Garvey.

Collins, P. H. (1991). *Black feminist thought: Knowledge, consciousness, and the politics of empowerment*. New York: Routledge.

Conant, J. (1963). *The education of American teachers*. New York: McGraw-Hill.

Cook-Gumperz, J. (1986). *The social construction of literacy*. New York: Cambridge University Press.

Corcoran, B. (1989, April). *Reading, re-reading, and resistance: Beyond reader response*. Paper presented at the International Conference on Reading and Response, University of East Anglia, Norwich, England.

Cremin, L. (1964). *The transformation of the school*. New York: Vintage Books.

Crook, S., Pakulski, J., & Waters, M. (1992). *Postmodernization: Change in advanced society*. Newbury Park, CA: Sage.

Crowell, S. (1989). A new way of thinking: The challenge of the future. *Educational Leadership, 47,* 60–63.

Cuban, J. (1990). Reforming again, again, and again. *Educational Researcher, 19,* 39–49.

Darder, A. (1995). Buscando America: The contributions of critical Latino educators to the academic development and empowerment of Latino students in the U.S. In C. Sleeter & P. McLaren (Eds.), *Multicultural education, critical pedagogy, and the politics of difference* (pp. 319–348). Albany: State University of New York Press.

Darling-Hammond, L. (1990). Teacher evaluation in transition: Emerging roles and evolving methods. In J. Millman & L. Darling-Hammond (Eds.), *The new handbook of teacher evaluation: Assessing elementary and secondary school teachers* (pp. 17–32). Newbury Park, CA: Sage.

Darling-Hammond, L., & Wise, A. E. (1991). From bureaucratic control to building human capital: The importance of teacher learning in education reform. *Educational Researcher, 25* (9), 9–11.

Davies, B. (1989). The discursive production of the male/female dualism in school settings. *Oxford Review of Education, 15* (3), 229–241.

_____. (1993). *Shards of glass: Children reading and writing beyond gendered identities.* Cresskill, NJ: Hampton Press.

Davis, H. E. (1996a). The phenomenology of a feminist reader: Toward the recuperation of pleasure. *Educational Theory, 46* (4), 473–499.

_____. (1996b). Docile bodies and disembodied minds. *Educational Theory, 46* (4), 525–543.

de Beauvoir, S. (1993). Woman as other. In C. Lemert (Ed.), *Social theory: The classic and multicultural readings* (pp. 367–370). Boulder, CO: Westview Press. (Original work published in 1949)

Denton, T. (1997, May 19). "Mushy" TEKS needs rethinking. *San Antonio Express-News,* p. A1.

Denzin, N., & Lincoln, Y. (Eds.). (1994). *Handbook of qualitative research.* Thousand Oaks, CA: Sage Publications.

Derrida, J. (1976). *Of grammatology* (G. C. Spivak, Trans.). Baltimore, MD: Johns Hopkins University Press.

Dewey, J. (1916). *Democracy and education.* Englewood Cliffs, NJ: Prentice Hall.

Donald, J. (1983). How illiteracy became a problem (and literacy stopped being one). *Journal of Education, 165,* 33–52.

Doyle, D. P. (1991, November). America 2000. *Phi Delta Kappan, 73,* 185–191.

Dreyfus, H. L., Rabinow, R., & Foucault, M. (1982). *Michel Foucault: Beyond structuralism and hermeneutics*. Chicago: University of Chicago Press.

D'Souza, S. (1991). *Illiberal education: The politics of race and sex on campus*. New York: Free Press.

Eagleton, T. (1983). *Literary theory: An introduction*. Minneapolis: University of Minnesota Press.

_____. (1986). *Against the grain: Essays 1975–1985*. London: Verso.

Edelsky, C. (1991a). *With literacy and justice for all: Rethinking the social in language and education*. New York: Falmer Press.

_____. (1991b). Education for democracy. *Language Arts*, *71*, 252–258.

Eder, D. (1986). Organizational constraints on reading group mobility. In J. Cook-Gumperz (Ed.), *The social construction of literacy* (pp. 138–155). New York: Cambridge University of Press.

Egea-Kuehne, D. (1995). Deconstruction revisited and Derrida's call for academic responsibility. *Educational Theory*, *45*, 293–309.

Eisenstein, Z. (1981). *The radical future of liberal feminism*. New York: Longman.

Ellsworth, N., Hedley, C., & Baratta, A. (1994). *Literacy: A redefinition*. Mahwah, NJ: Lawrence Erlbaum Associates.

Escobar, M., Fernandez, A. L., Guevara-Niebla, G., & Freire, P. (1994). *Paulo Freire on higher education: A dialogue at the National University of Mexico*. Albany: State University of New York Press.

Etzioni, A. (Ed.). (1969). *The semi-professions and their organization: Teachers, nurses, social workers*. New York: Free Press.

Fairclough, N. L. (1985). Critical and descriptive goals in discourse analysis. *Journal of Pragmatics, 9* (6), 739–763.

_____. (1989). *Language and power.* London: Longman.

Federal Advisory Committee Act, 5 U.S.C.A. § 1 *et seq.* (West 2000).

Fernandez-Balboa, J. M. (1993). Critical pedagogy: Making critical thinking really critical. *Analytic Teaching, 13,* 61–72.

Fine, M. (1991). *Framing dropouts: Notes on the politics of an urban public high school.* Albany: State University of New York Press.

Fiske, J. (1993). *Power plays, power works.* New York: Verso.

Foucault, M. (1965). *Madness and civilization: A history of insanity in the age of reason* (R. Howard, Trans.). New York: Pantheon Books.

_____. (1972). *The archaeology of knowledge* and *The discourse on language* (A. M. Sheridan Smith, Trans.). New York: Pantheon Books.

_____. (1977). *Discipline and punish: The birth of the prison* (A. Sheridan, Trans.). New York: Pantheon Books.

_____. (1978). *The history of sexuality* (R. Hurley, Trans.). New York: Pantheon Books.

_____. (1980). *Power/knowledge: Selected interviews and other writings* (C. Gordon, Ed.; C. Gordon, L. Marshall, J. Mepham, & K. Soper, Trans.). New York: Pantheon Books.

_____. (1984). *The Foucault reader* (P. Rabinow, Ed.). New York: Pantheon Books.

_____. (1985). *The history of sexuality: Vol. 2. The use of pleasure* (R. Hurley, Trans.). New York: Pantheon Books.

_____. (1990). *The history of sexuality: Vol. 1. An introduction* (R. Hurley, Trans.). New York: Vintage Books.

_____. (1993). Discourse on the West. In C. Lemert (Ed.), *Social theory: The multicultural and classical readings* (pp. 451–454). Boulder, CO: Westview Press. (Original work published in 1971)

Fraser, N. (1989). *Unruly practices: Power, discourse and gender in contemporary social theory*. Cambridge, MA: Polity Press.

Frazer, E. (1989). Feminist talk and talking about feminism: Teenage girls' discourses of gender. *Oxford Review of Education, 15* (3), 281–290.

Freire, P. (1970). *Pedagogy of the oppressed*. New York: Seabury Press.

_____. (1973). *Education for critical consciousness*. New York: Seabury Press.

Freire, P., & Faundez, A. (1989). *Learning to question: A pedagogy of liberation*. New York: Continuum.

Freire, P., & Macedo, D. (1995). A dialogue: Culture, language, and race. *Harvard Educational Review, 63* (3), 377–402.

Fullan, M. G. (1990). Staff development, innovation, and institutional development. In B. Joyce (Ed.), *Changing school culture through staff development* (pp. 3–25). Alexandria, VA: Association for Supervision and Curriculum Development.

Gadotti, M. (1994). *Reading Paulo Freire: His life and his work* (J. Milton, Trans.). Albany: State University of New York Press.

Gatens, M. (1991). *Feminism and philosophy: Perspectives on difference and equality*. Indianapolis: Indiana University Press.

Gee, J. P. (1991a). What is literacy? In C. Mitchell & K. Weiler (Eds.), *Rewriting literacy: Culture and the discourse of the other* (pp. 3–11). New York: Bergin & Garvey.

_____. (1991b). The narrativization of experience in the oral style. In C. Mitchell & K. Weiler (Eds.), *Rewriting literacy: Culture and the discourse of the other* (pp. 77–101). New York: Bergin & Garvey.

_____. (1991c). Discourse systems and aspirin bottles: On literacy. In C. Mitchell & K. Weiler (Eds.), *Rewriting literacy: Culture and the discourse of the other* (pp. 123–135). New York: Bergin & Garvey.

General Education Provisions Act, 20 U.S.C.A. § 1233 *et seq.* (West 2000).

Gibboney, R.A. (1991, May). The killing field of reform. *Phi Delta Kappan, 72,* 682–688.

Gilligan, C., Ward, J. V., Taylor, J. M., & Bardige, B. (Eds.). (1988). *Mapping the moral domain: A contribution of women's thinking to psychological theory and education.* Cambridge, MA: Harvard University Press.

Giroux, H. (1981). *Ideology, culture, and the process of schooling.* Philadelphia: Temple University Press.

_____. (1983). *Theory and resistance in education.* Westport, CT: Bergin & Garvey.

_____. (1988a). *Schooling and the struggle for public life.* Minneapolis: University of Minnesota Press.

_____. (1988b). *Teachers as intellectuals: Toward a critical pedagogy of learning.* Westport, CT: Bergin & Garvey.

_____ (Ed.). (1991). *Postmodernism, feminism, and cultural politics.* Albany: State University of New York Press.

_____. (1993). *Living dangerously: Multiculturalism and the politics of difference.* New York: Peter Lang.

Giroux, H., & McLaren, P. (1987). Teacher education as a counter public sphere: Notes towards a redefinition. In T. Popkewitz (Ed.), *Critical studies in teacher education* (pp. 266–297). Philadelphia: Falmer Press.

_____. (1988). Teacher education and the politics of democratic reform. In H. Giroux (Ed.), *Teachers as intellectuals: Toward a critical pedagogy of learning* (pp. xxix–xxxvi). Westport, CT: Bergin & Garvey.

_____. (1989). Introduction: Schooling, cultural politics, and the struggle for democracy. In H. Giroux & P. McLaren, *Critical pedagogy, the state, and cultural struggle*. Albany: State University of New York Press.

_____. (1994). *Between borders: Pedagogy and the politics of cultural studies*. New York: Routledge.

Goins, K. (1997, July 16). Literacy efforts need volunteers. *San Antonio Express-News*, p. S8.

Goodlad, J. I. (1983). *A place called school: Prospects for the future*. New York: McGraw-Hill.

_____. (1990). Teachers for our nation's schools. San Francisco: Jossey-Bass.

Goodlad, J. I., Soder, R., & Sirotnik, K. A. (Eds.). (1990). *Places where teachers are taught*. San Francisco: Jossey-Bass.

Goodman, J. (1995a). Change without difference: School restructuring in historical perspective. *Harvard Educational Review, 65*, 1–29.

_____. (1995b). Issues of misrepresentation in scholarly discourse: A meta-analysis of educational criticism. *Harvard Educational Review, 65*, 651–667.

Goodman, K., Shannon, P., Freeman, M., & Murphy, S. (1988). *Report card on basal readers*. Katonah, NY: Richard C. Owen.

Gordon, C. (1991). Governmental rationality: An introduction. In G. Burchell, C. Gordon, & P. Miller (Eds.), *The Foucault effect: Studies in governmentality* (pp. 1–51). Chicago: University of Chicago Press.

Gore, J. M. (1993). *The struggle for pedagogies: Critical and feminist discourses as regimes of truth*. New York: Routledge.

Grant, R. D. (1994). The politics of cultural literacy. *The International Journal of Social Education, 9* (1), 1–14.

Green, B. (Ed.). (1993). *The insistence of the letter: Literacy studies and curriculum theorizing*. Pittsburgh: University of Pittsburgh Press.

Greene, M. (1986). In search of a critical pedagogy. *Harvard Educational Review, 56,* 427–441.

_____. (1993a). Education, art, and mastery: Toward the spheres of freedom. In S. Shapiro & D. Purpel (Eds.), *Critical social issues in American education: Toward the 21st century* (pp. 330–344). New York: Longman.

_____. (1993b). The passions of pluralism: Multiculturalism and the expanding community. *Educational Researcher, 22* (1), 13–18.

Greenman, N. (1998). Western societal views. In *Education in American society: EDU 3103: Readings* (p. 35). San Antonio: University of Texas at San Antonio Barnes & Noble Bookstore.

Griffiths, M., & Whitford, M. (Eds.). (1988). *Feminist perspectives in philosophy*. Indianapolis: Indiana University Press.

Grubb, W. N., & Lazerson, M. (1975). Rally round the workplace: Continuities and fallacies in career education. *Harvard Educational Review, 45,* 451–474.

Grumet, M. (1988). *Bitter milk: Women and teaching*. Amherst: University of Massachusetts Press.

_____. (1989). Generations: Reconceptualist curriculum theory and teacher education. *Journal of Teacher Education, 40* (1), 13–17.

_____. (1995). The curriculum: What are the basics and are we teaching them? In J. Kincheloe & S. Steinberg (Eds.), *Thirteen questions: Reframing education's conversation* (pp. 15–21). New York: Peter Lang.

Gubrium, J. F., & Silverman, D. (1989). *The politics of field research: Sociology beyond enlightenment.* Newbury Park, CA: Sage.

Gutierrez, K. D. (1994). How talk, context, and script shape contexts for learning. A cross-case comparison of journal sharing. *Linguistics and Education, 5,* 335–365.

Gutierrez, K., & Garcia, E. (1989). Academic literacy in linguistic minority children: The connections between language, cognition and culture. *Early Child Development and Care, 51,* 109–126.

Gutierrez, K., Rymes, B., & Larson, J. (1995). Script, counterscript, and underlife in the classroom: James Brown versus *Brown v. Board of Education. Harvard Educational Review, 65,* 445–471.

Habermas, J. (1984). *Theory of communicative action* (Vol. 1). (T. McCarthy, Trans.). London: Heinemann.

Haney, W. (1990). Licensure and certification of teachers: An appraisal. In J. Millman & L. Darling-Hammond (Eds.), *The new handbook of teacher evaluation: Assessing elementary and secondary school teachers* (pp. 46–61). Newbury Park, CA: Corwin Press.

_____. (1993). Testing and minorities. In M. Fine & L. Weis (Eds.), *Beyond silenced voices: Class, race, and gender in United States schools* (pp. 45–73). New York: State University of New York Press.

Harper, H. (1990). Theory into practice: Literacy and the state: A comparison of Hirsch, Rosenblatt, and Giroux. *English Quarterly, 22* (3–4), 169–175.

Heath, S. B. (1983). *Ways with words*. New York: McGraw-Hill.

Hiebert, E. H. (1991). *Literacy for a diverse society: Perspective, practices and policies*. New York: Teachers College Press.

Hillman, C. (1989). *Creating a learning climate for the early childhood years*. Bloomington, IN: Phi Delta Kappa Educational Foundation.

Hirsch, E. D. (1987). *Cultural literacy: What every American needs to know*. Boston: Houghton Mifflin.

_____. (1990). Reflections on cultural literacy and arts education. *The Journal of Aesthetic Education, 24* (1), 1–6.

Hoeveler, J. D. (1996). *The postmodernist turn: American thought and culture in the 1970s*. New York: Twayne.

Hoholik, S. (1997, April 22). Volunteers vital to Clinton reading plan. *San Antonio Express-News,* pp. B4–B5.

Holmes Group. (1986). *Tomorrow's teachers*. East Lansing, MI: Author.

_____. (1990). *Tomorrow's schools: Principles for the design of professional development schools*. East Lansing, MI: Author.

_____. (1995a). *Tomorrow's schools of education*. East Lansing, MI: Author.

_____. (1995b). *Tomorrow's schools: Professional development schools*. East Lansing, MI: Author.

hooks, b. (1992). *Black looks: Race and representation*. Boston: South End Press.

_____. (1994). *Teaching to transgress: Education as the practice of freedom*. New York: Routledge.

Hudson, R. (1980). *Sociolinguistics*. New York: Cambridge University Press.

Hughes, K. P. (1995). Feminist pedagogy and feminist epistemology: An overview. *International Journal of Lifelong Education, 14* (3), 214–230.

Jackson, J. E. (1994). *Foucault and education policy analysis: Head Start and the special case of African Americans.* Unpublished doctoral dissertation, University of Missouri, St. Louis.

Jones, M. G. (1989). Gender issues in teacher education. *Journal of Teacher Education, 40* (1), 33–38.

Joseph, E. A. (1989). The perfectibility of means and the disregard of ends. *Journal of Teacher Education, 40* (1), 18–21.

Kaestle, C. (1983). *Pillars of the republic: Common schools and American society, 1780–1860.* New York: Hill & Wang.

_____. (1991). The history of readers. In C. Kaestle, H. Damon-Moore, L. Stedman, K. Tinsley, & W. Trollinger (Eds.), *Literacy in the United States: Readers and reading since 1880* (pp. 33–72). New Haven, CT: Yale University Press.

Kahne, J. (1996). *Reframing educational policy: Democracy, community, and the individual.* New York: Teachers College Press.

Karier, C. J. (1972). Testing for order and control in the corporate state. *Educational Theory, 22,* 159–180.

Kelly, D., & Hall, M. (1997, February 11). Poll shows Americans favor testing. *San Antonio Express-News*, p. B5.

Kincheloe, J. L. (1991). *Teachers as researchers: Qualitative inquiry as a path to empowerment.* New York: Falmer Press.

_____. (1993). *Toward a critical politics of teacher thinking: Mapping the postmodern.* Westport, CT: Bergin & Garvey.

_____. (1995). *Toil and trouble: Good work, smart workers, and the integration of academic and vocational education*. New York: Peter Lang.

Kincheloe, J., & McLaren, P. (1994). Rethinking critical theory and qualitative research. In N. Denzin & Y. Lincoln (Eds.), *The qualitative research handbook* (pp. 138–157). Thousand Oaks, CA: Sage.

Kincheloe, J., & Steinberg, S. (1993). A tentative description of post-formal thinking: The critical confrontation with cognitive theory. *Harvard Educational Review, 63,* 296–320.

_____. (1995). *Thirteen questions: Reframing education's conversation*. New York: Peter Lang.

Kliebard, H. (1995). *The struggle for the American curriculum, 1893–1958* (2nd ed.). New York: Routledge.

Knoblauch, C. H., & Brannon, L. (1993). *Critical teaching and the idea of literacy*. Portsmouth, NH: Boynton/Cook.

Koerner, J. (1963). *The miseducation of American teachers*. Boston: Houghton Mifflin.

Kozol, J. (1991). *Savage inequalities: Children in America's schools*. New York: Harper Perennial.

Kress, G., & Hodge, R. (1979). *Language as ideology*. New York: Routledge.

Kristeva, J. (1980). *Desire in language: A semiotic approach to literature and art*. New York: Columbia University Press.

_____. (1988). *The Kristeva reader* (T. Moi, Ed.). New York: Columbia University Press.

Kuhn, T. S. (1970). *The structure of scientific revolutions*. Chicago: University of Chicago Press.

Kunen, J. (1997, June 16). The test of their lives. *Time, 149,* 62–63.

Labaree, D. F. (1992). Power, knowledge, and the rationalization of teaching: A genealogy of the movement to professionalize teaching, *Harvard Educational Review, 62* (2), 123–154.

_____. (1995). A disabling vision: Rhetoric and reality in *Tomorrow's Schools of Education. Teachers College Record, 97* (2), 166–205.

Labaree, D. F., & Pallas, A. (1996). The Holmes Group's mystifying response. *Educational Researcher, 25* (5), 31–32, 47.

Lamb, L. (1993, March/April). Lifestyles of the poor and working. *Utne Reader, 56,* 19–21.

Lankshear, C., & McLaren, P. (1993). *Critical literacy: Politics, praxis, and the postmodern.* Albany: State University of New York Press.

Larrabee, M. J. (1993). *An ethic of care: Feminist and interdisciplinary perspectives.* New York: Routledge.

Lash, S. (1990). *Sociology of postmodernism.* New York: Routledge.

Lather, P. (1994). The absent presence: Patriarchy, capitalism, and the nature of teacher work. In L. Stone (Ed.), *The education feminism reader* (pp. 242–251). New York: Routledge.

Lemert, C. (1993). *Social theory: The multicultural and classic readings.* Boulder, CO: Westview Press.

Levin, H. (1981). Back-to-basics and the economy. *Radical Teacher, 20,* 8–10.

_____. (1985). Solving the shortage of mathematics and science teachers. *Education Evaluation and Policy Analysis, 7,* 371–382.

Levin, H., & Rumberger, R. (1983). *The educational implications of high technology.* Palo Alto, CA: Institute for Research on Educational Finance and Governance, Stanford University.

Lifelong certification of teachers questioned. (1997, July 1). *San Antonio Express-News*, p. 3A.

Livdahl, B. S., Smart, K., Wallman, J., Herbert, T. K., Geiger, D. K., & Anderson, J. L. (1995). *Stories from response-centered classrooms: Speaking, questioning, and theorizing from the center of the action.* New York: Teachers College Press.

Luke, A. (1992). The body literate: Discourse and inscription in early literacy training. *Linguistics and Education, 4* (1), 107–129.

_____. (1995). When basic skills and information processing just aren't enough: Rethinking reading in new times. *Teachers College Record, 97* (1), 95–115.

Luke, C. (Ed.). (1996). *Feminisms and pedagogies of everyday life.* Albany: State University of New York Press.

Luke, C., & Gore, J. (1992). *Feminisms and critical pedagogy.* New York: Routledge.

Lyotard, J.-F. (1993). The postmodern condition. In C. Lemert (Ed.), *Social theory: The classic and multicultural readings* (pp. 510–513). Boulder, CO: Westview Press. (Original work published 1979)

Macedo, D. (1991). *The politics of an emancipatory literacy in Cape Verde.* In C. Mitchell & K. Weiler (Eds.), *Rewriting literacy: Culture and the discourse of the other* (pp. 147–159). New York: Bergin & Garvey.

_____. (1994a). *Literacies of power: What Americans are not allowed to know.* Boulder, CO: Westview Press.

_____. (1994b). Preface. In P. McLaren & C. Lankshear (Eds.), *Politics of liberation: Paths from Freire* (pp. xiii–xviii). New York: Routledge.

Maher, F., & Tetreault, M. K. T. (1994). *The feminist classroom*. New York: Basic Books.

Manning, P. K. (1989). Studying policies in the field. In J. F. Gubrium & D. Silverman (Eds.), *The politics of field research* (pp. 213–235). Newbury Park, CA: Sage.

Martin, J. R. (1994). *Changing the educational landscape: Philosophy, women, and curriculum*. New York: Routledge.

Marx, K. (1993). Estranged labour. In C. Lemert (Ed.), *Social theory: The classic and multicultural readings* (pp. 36–42). Boulder, CO: Westview Press. (Original work published 1844)

Marx, K., & Engels, F. (1993). Class struggle. In C. Lemert (Ed.), *Social theory: The classic and multicultural readings* (pp. 43–48). Boulder, CO: Westview Press. (Original work published 1848)

May, T. (1993). *Between genealogy and epistemology: Psychology, politics, and knowledge in the thought of Michel Foucault*. University Park: Pennsylvania State University Press.

Maynes, M. J. (1985). *Schooling in Western Europe: A social history*. Albany: State University of New York Press.

McEwan, H., & Bull, B. (1991). The pedagogic nature of subject matter knowledge. *American Educational Research Journal, 28* (2), 316–334.

McFarland, K. P. (1992). *The use of the dialogue journal in multicultural education*. Unpublished doctoral dissertation, Texas A & M University, College Station.

McKay, S. L., & Hornberger, N. H. (Eds.). (1995). *Sociolinguistics and language teaching*. New York: Cambridge University Press.

McLaren, P. (1998). *Life in schools: An introduction to critical pedagogy in the foundations of education*. New York: Longman.

McLaren, P., & Gutierrez, K. (1994). Pedagogies of dissent and transformation: A dialogue about post modernity, social context, and the politics of literacy. *International Journal of Educational Reform, 3* (3), 327–337.

McLaren, P., & Lankshear, C. (Eds.). (1994). *Politics of liberation: Paths from Freire.* New York: Routledge.

McWilliam, E. (1994). *In broken images: Feminist tales for a different teacher education.* New York: Teachers College Press.

Millman, J., & Darling-Hammond, L. (1990). *The new handbook of teacher evaluation: Assessing elementary and secondary school teachers.* Newbury Park, CA: Corwin Press.

Mitchell, C., & Weiler, K. (Eds.). (1991). *Rewriting literacy: Culture and the discourse of the other.* New York: Bergin & Garvey.

Murray, F. B., & Fallon, D. (1989). *The reform of teacher education for the 21st century: Project 30 year one report.* Newark: University of Delaware.

National Commission on Excellence in Teacher Education. (1985). *A call for change in teacher education.* Washington, DC: Author.

National Education Defense Act of 1958, 20 U.S.C.A. §§ 15aaa *et seq.* (West 2000).

National Education Goals Panel. (1995a). *Data volume for the national education goals report* (Vol. 1). Washington, DC: Author.

_____. (1995b). *The national education goals executive summary.* Washington, DC: Author.

National Literacy Act of 1991, 20 U.S.C.A. § 1201 *et seq.* (West 2000).

New nation test shows students fall short in scientific thinking. (1997, May 3). *San Antonio Express-News*, p. B12.

Nieto, S. (1996). *Affirming diversity: The sociopolitical context of multicultural education* (2nd ed.). New York: Longman.

Noddings, N. (1984). *Caring: A feminine approach to ethics and moral education.* Berkeley: University of California Press.

Norris, C. (1983). *The deconstructive turn: Essays in the rhetoric of philosophy.* New York: Methuen.

_____. (1992). *Deconstruction: Theory and practice.* New York: Methuen.

Oakes, J. (1995). *Keeping track: How schools structure inequality.* New Haven, CT: Yale University Press.

Ogbu, J. (1978). *Minority education and caste: The American system in cross-cultural perspective.* New York: Academic Press.

Olson, G. A., & Hirsh, E. (Eds.). (1995). *Women writing culture.* Albany: State University of New York Press.

Patterson, L., Stansell, J., & Lee, S. C. (1990). *Teacher research: From promise to power.* Katonah, NY: Richard C. Owen.

Phillips, D. C. (1995). The good, the bad, and the ugly: The many faces of constructivism. *Educational Researcher, 24* (7), 5–12.

Pinar, W. F. (1989). A reconceptualization of teacher education. *Journal of Teacher Education, 40* (1), 9–12.

_____. (1995). The curriculum: What are the basics and are we teaching them? In J. Kincheloe & S. Steinberg (Eds.), *Thirteen questions: Reframing education's conversation* (pp. 15–30). New York: Peter Lang.

Popkewitz, T. (1991). *A political sociology of educational reform: Power/knowledge in teaching, teacher education, and research.* New York: Teachers College Press.

Popkewitz, T., & Brennan, M. (1994). Certification to credentialing: Reconstituting control mechanisms in teacher education. In K. M. Borman & N. P. Greenman (Eds.), *Changing American education: Recapturing the past or inventing the future* (pp. 57–69). Albany: State University of New York Press.

Prestine, N. (1991). Political system theory as an explanatory paradigm for teacher education reform. *American Educational Research Journal, 28* (2), 237–274.

Putnam, R. (1995). Bowling alone. *Journal of Democracy, 6,* 665–678.

Ramazanoglu, C. (Ed.). (1993). *Up against Foucault: Explorations of some tensions between Foucault and feminism.* London: Routledge.

Ramos, C. (1997, April 14). Ex-first lady links reading, righting society. *San Antonio Express-News*, pp. A7–A8.

_____. (1997, April 22). Teens and elders trade places for Internet training. *San Antonio Express-News,* p. B5.

_____. (1997, June 10). Curriculum rewrite reaches final stage. *San Antonio Express-News*, pp. B1, B6.

_____. (1997, June 13). Disputes mark curriculum hearing. *San Antonio Express-News*, p. B3.

_____. (1997, July 11). Education board OKs controversial curriculum. *San Antonio Express-News*, pp. A1, A6.

_____. (1997, July 12). Divided board OKs curriculum: Conservative members vow injunction. *San Antonio Express-News*, p. A8.

Resnick, D. P., & Resnick, L. (1977). The nature of literacy: An historical exploration. *Harvard Educational Review, 47* (3), 370–410.

Ricoeur, P. (1974). Metaphor and the main problem of hermeneutics. *New Literary History, 6* (1), 95–110.

Sanchez, R. (1997, February 11). Educational agenda. *San Antonio Express-News*, p. B4.

Sawicki, J. (1991). *Disciplining Foucault: Feminism, power, and the body*. New York: Routledge.

Scheurich, J. J. (1994). Policy archaeology: A new policy studies methodology. *Journal of Educational Policy, 9* (40), 297–316.

Schon, D. (1983). *The reflective practitioner: How professionals think in action*. New York: Basic Books.

Schubert, W. H. (1989). Reconceptualizing and the matter of paradigms. *Journal of Teacher Education, 40* (1), 27–32.

Shaker, P., & Kridel, C. (1989). The return to experience: A reconceptualist call. *Journal of Teacher Education, 40* (1), 2–8.

Shakeshaft, C. (1986, March). A gender at risk. *Phi Delta Kappan, 67,* 499–503.

Shannon, P. (1989). *Broken promises: Reading instruction in twentieth-century America*. Westport, CT: Bergin & Garvey.

_____ (Ed.). (1990a). *Becoming political: Readings and writings in the politics of literacy education*. Portsmouth, NH: Heinemann.

_____ (Ed.). (1990b). *The struggle to continue: Progressive reading instruction in the United States*. Portsmouth, NH: Heinemann.

Shannon, P., & Goodman, K. (1994). *Basal readers: A second look*. Katonah, NY: Richard C. Owen.

Shapiro, H. S., & Purpel, D. (Eds.). (1993). *Critical social issues in American education: Toward the 21st century*. New York: Longman.

Shor, I. (1986a). Equality is excellence: Transforming teacher education and the learning process. *Harvard Educational Review, 56,* 406–426.

_____. (1986b). *Culture wars: School and society in the conservative restoration 1969–1984.* Boston, MA: Routledge.

Shutkin, D. (1994). *The deployment of information technology and the child as subject: A discourse analysis of school restructuring initiatives, psychological research, and educational policy.* Unpublished doctoral dissertation, University of Wisconsin-Madison.

Slater, R. O., & Boyd, W. L. (1998, April). *Schools as polities.* Paper presented at the American Educational Research Association Annual Convention, San Diego, CA.

Slattery, P. (1995). A postmodern vision of time and learning: A response to the National Education Commission Report "Prisoners of Time." *Harvard Educational Review, 65,* 612–633.

Sleeter, C. E., & McLaren, P. (Eds.). (1995). *Multicultural education, critical pedagogy, and the politics of difference.* Albany: State University of New York Press.

Smart, B. (1993). *Postmodernity.* New York: Routledge.

Smith, M. L. (1991). Put to the test: The effects of external testing on teachers. *Educational Researcher, 20* (5), 8–11.

Smith, O. (1980). *A design for a school of pedagogy.* Washington, DC: U.S. Government Printing Office.

Smylie, M. A. (1996). From bureaucratic control to building human capital: The importance of teacher learning in education reform. *Educational Researcher, 25* (9), 9–11.

Sontag, S. (1982). *A Barthes reader.* New York: Hill & Wang.

214

Sowell, E. (1996). *Curriculum: An integrative introduction*. Columbus, OH: Merrill.

Spring, J. (1972). *Education and the rise of the corporate state*. Boston: Beacon Press.

_____. (1980). *Educating the worker-citizen: The social, economic, and political foundations of education*. New York: Longman.

_____. (1993). *Conflict of interests: The politics of American education*. New York: Longman.

_____. (1996). *American education*. New York: McGraw-Hill.

_____. (1997). *Deculturalization and the struggle for equality: A brief history of the education of dominated cultures in the United States*. New York: McGraw-Hill.

Stearns, P. N., & Hinshaw, J. H. (1996). *The ABC-CLIO world history companion to the Industrial Revolution*. Santa Barbara, CA: ABC-CLIO.

Stone, L. (Ed.). (1994). *The education feminism reader*. New York: Routledge.

Stringer, E., Agnello, M. F., Conant Baldwin, S., McFayden Christensen, L., Philbrook Henry, D., Henry, K., Payne Katt, T., Gathman Nason, P., Newman, V., Petty, R., & Tinsley-Batson, P. (1997). *Community-based ethnography: Breaking traditional boundaries of research, teaching, and learning*. Mahwah, NJ: Lawrence Erlbaum.

Survey finds high school students want an easy challenge. (1997, February 11). *San Antonio Express-News*, p. A6.

Sweetland, S. (1996). Human capital theory: Foundations of a field of inquiry. *Review of Educational Research, 66* (3), 341–360.

Teacher prep programs to be put to the test. (1997, October 3). *San Antonio Express-News*, p. A26.

Teachers are stung by recertification plan. (1997, September 14). *San Antonio Express-News,* p. F26.

Texas Education Agency. (1994). *Learner-centered schools for Texas: A vision of Texas educators.* Austin: Author.

Thurow, R. (1995, November 19). Why their world might crumble. *New York Times Magazine,* 78–79.

Tozer, S., Violas, P., & Senese, G. (1998). *School and society: Historical and contemporary perspectives.* New York: McGraw-Hill.

Tyack, D. (1966). Forming the national character: Paradox in the educational thought of the revolutionary generation. *Harvard Educational Review, 36* (1), 29–41.

U.S. Department of Education, National Commission on Excellence in Education. (1983). *A nation at risk: The imperative for educational reform.* Washington, DC: U.S. Government Printing Office.

U.S. Department of Education. (1984a). *Alliance for excellence: Librarians respond to A Nation at Risk.* Washington, DC: U.S. Government Printing Office.

_____. (1984b). *The nation responds: Recent efforts to improve education.* Washington, DC: U.S. Government Printing Office.

_____, Office of Educational Research and Improvement. (1986). *What works: Research about teaching and learning.* Washington, DC: U.S. Department of Education.

U.S. Department of Education. (1991). *America 2000: An education strategy.* Washington, DC: U.S. Government Printing Office.

_____, Office of Educational Research and Improvement, Goal 5 Work Group. (1993a). *Reaching the goals: Goal 5: Adult literacy and lifelong learning.* Washington, DC: U.S. Government Printing Office.

_____, Office of Educational Research and Improvement, Goal 2 Work Group. (1993b). *Reaching the goal: Goal 2: High school completion*. Washington, DC: U.S. Government Printing Office.

U.S. Department of Labor. (1987). *Workforce 2000: Work and workers for the 21st century*. Washington, DC: U.S. Government Printing Office.

University of Arizona, College of Education, Multicultural Education Center. (1973). *The Cultural Literacy Laboratory: A new dimension in multicultural teacher education*. (Report No. SP-007-529). Tucson: University of Arizona. (ERIC Document Reproduction Service No. ED 087 698)

Vygotsky, L. S. (1962). *Thought and language* (E. Hanfmann & G. Vakar, Trans.). Cambridge: Massachusetts Institute of Technology Press.

Wallis, C. (1989, December 4). Onward women! *Time, 134,* 80–89.

Weber, M. (1947). *The theory of social and economic organizations* (A. M. Henderson & T. Parsons, Trans.). New York: Oxford University Press.

Weedon, C. (1987). *Feminist practice and poststructural theory*. New York: Basil Blackwell.

Weiner, G. (1993). Shell-shock or sisterhood: English school history and feminist practice. In M. Arnot & K. Weiler (Eds.), *Feminism and social justice in education: International perspectives* (pp. 79–100). Washington, DC: Falmer Press.

Weisburd, C. (1994). *Representing democracy: Discourse of civic space and citizenship in English as a second language texts*. Unpublished doctoral dissertation, Cornell University.

Wells, M. C. (1996). *Literacies lost: When students move from a progressive middle school to a traditional high school*. New York: Teachers College Press.

Wexler, P. (1992). *Becoming somebody: Toward a social psychology of school.* Washington, DC: Falmer Press.

White, H. (1978). *Tropics of discourse: Essays in cultural criticsm.* Baltimore, MD: Johns Hopkins University Press.

_____. (1987). *The content of the form: Narrative discourse and historical representation.* Baltimore, MD: Johns Hopkins University Press.

Willinsky, J. (1990). *The new literacy: Redefining reading and writing in the schools.* New York: Routledge.

Wolcott, H. F. (1977). *Teachers versus technocrats: An educational innovation in anthropological perspective.* Eugene: University of Oregon Press.

Wollstonecraft, M. (1992). *A vindication of the rights of woman.* London: Penguin Books. (Original work published in 1792)

Young, R. (1990). *A critical theory of education: Habermas and our children's future.* New York: Teachers College Press.

Zeichner, K. (1996a). Teachers as reflective practitioners and the democratization of school reform. In K. Zeichner, S. Melnick, & M. L. Gomez (Eds.), *Currents of reform in preservice teacher education* (pp. 199–214). New York: Teachers College Press.

_____. (1996b). Designing educative practicum experiences for prospective teachers. In K. Zeichner, S. Melnick, & M. L. Gomez (Eds.), *Currents of reform in preservice teacher education* (pp. 215–234). New York: Teachers College Press.

Zeichner, K., & Liston, D. (1987). Teaching student teachers to reflect. *Harvard Educational Review, 57,* 23–48.

Zeichner, K., Melnick, S., & Gomez, M. L. (1996). *Currents of reform in preservice teacher education.* New York: Teachers College Press.

# AUTHOR INDEX

# SUBJECT INDEX

230